Student Research Workshop

(RANLPStud 2013)

Associated with the 9th International Conference on Recent Advances in Natural Language Processing (RANLP 2013)

Hissar, Bulgaria
9 – 11 September 2013

ISBN: 978-1-62993-556-0

Printed from e-media with permission by:

Curran Associates, Inc.
57 Morehouse Lane
Red Hook, NY 12571

Some format issues inherent in the e-media version may also appear in this print version.

Printed by Curran Associates, Inc. (2014)

For permission requests, please contact the Association for Computational Linguistics at the address below.

Association for Computational Linguistics
209 N. Eighth Street
Stroudsburg, Pennsylvania 18360

Phone: 1-570-476-8006
Fax: 1-570-476-0860

acl@aclweb.org

Additional copies of this publication are available from:

Curran Associates, Inc.
57 Morehouse Lane
Red Hook, NY 12571 USA
Phone: 845-758-0400
Fax: 845-758-2634
Email: curran@proceedings.com
Web: www.proceedings.com

Preface

The Recent Advances in Natural Language Processing (RANLP) conference, which is ranked among the most influential NLP conferences, has always been a meeting venue for scientists coming from all over the world. Since 2009, we decided to give arena to the younger and less experienced members of the NLP community to share their results with an international audience. For this reason, further to the first and second successful and highly competitive Student Research Workshops associated with the conference RANLP 2009 and RANLP 2011, we are pleased to announce the third edition of the workshop which is held during the main RANLP 2013 conference days, 9–11 September 2013.

The aim of the workshop is to provide an excellent opportunity for students at all levels (Bachelor, Masters, and Ph.D.) to present their work in progress or completed projects to an international research audience and receive feedback from senior researchers. We received 36 high quality submissions, among which 4 papers have been accepted for oral presentation, and 18 as posters. Each submission has been reviewed by at least 2 reviewers, who are experts in their field, in order to supply detailed and helpful comments. The papers' topics cover a broad selection of research areas, such as:

- application-orientated papers related to NLP;
- computer-aided language learning;
- dialogue systems;
- discourse;
- electronic dictionaries;
- evaluation;
- information extraction, event extraction, term extraction;
- information retrieval;
- knowledge acquisition;
- language resources, corpora, terminologies;
- lexicon;
- machine translation;
- morphology, syntax, parsing, POS tagging;
- multilingual NLP;
- NLP for biomedical texts;
- NLP for the Semantic web;
- ontologies;
- opinion mining;
- question answering;
- semantic role labelling;
- semantics;
- speech recognition;
- temporality processing;
- text categorisation;
- text generation;
- text simplification and readability estimation;
- text summarisation;
- textual entailment;
- theoretical papers related to NLP;
- word-sense disambiguation;

We are also glad to admit that our authors comprise a very international group with students coming from: Belgium, China, Croatia, France, Germany, India, Italy, Luxembourg, Russian Federation, Spain, Sweden, Tunisia and the United Kingdom.

We would like to thank the authors for submitting their articles to the Student Workshop, the members of the Programme Committee for their efforts to provide exhaustive reviews, and the mentors who agreed to have a deeper look at the students' work. We hope that all the participants will receive invaluable feedback about their research.

Irina Temnikova, Ivelina Nikolova and Natalia Konstantinova
Organisers of the Student Workshop, held in conjunction with
The International Conference RANLP-13

Organizers:

Irina Temnikova (Bulgarian Academy of Sciences, Bulgaria)
Ivelina Nikolova (Bulgarian Academy of Sciences, Bulgaria)
Natalia Konstantinova (University of Wolverhampton, UK)

Program Committee:

Chris Biemann (Technical University Darmstadt, Germany)
Kevin Bretonnel Cohen (University of Colorado School of Medicine, USA)
Iustin Dornescu (University of Wolverhampton, UK)
Laura Hasler (University of Wolverhapton, UK)
Diana Inkpen (University of Ottawa, Canada)
Natalia Konstantinova (University of Wolverhampton, UK)
Sebastian Krause (DFKI, Germany)
Sandra Kübler (University of Indiana, USA)
Lori Lamel (CNRS/LIMSI, France)
Annie Louis (University of Edinburgh, UK)
Preslav Nakov (QCRI, Qatar)
Ivelina Nikolova (Bulgarian Academy of Sciences, Bulgaria)
Constantin Orasan (University of Wolverhampton, UK)
Petya Osenova (Sofia University and IICT-BAS, Bulgaria)
Ivandre Paraboni (University of Sao Paulo, Brazil)
Michael Poprat (Averbis GmbH, Freiburg)
Rashmi Prasad (University of Wisconsin-Milwaukee, USA)
Raphael Rubino (Dublin City University and Symantec, Ireland)
Doaa Samy (Autonoma University of Madrid, Spain)
Thamar Solorio (University of Alabama at Birmingham, USA)
Stan Szpakowicz (University of Ottawa, Canada)
Irina Temnikova (Bulgarian Academy of Sciences, Bulgaria)
Eva Maria Vecchi (University of Trento, Italy)
Cristina Vertan (University of Hamburg, Germany)
Feiyu Xu (DFKI, Germany)
Torsten Zesch (Technical University Darmstadt, Germany)

Table of Contents

Perceptual Feedback in Computer Assisted Pronunciation Training: A Survey
Renlong Ai 1

A Dataset for Arabic Textual Entailment
Maytham Alabbas 7

Answering Questions from Multiple Documents – the Role of Multi-Document Summarization
Pinaki Bhaskar 14

Multi-Document Summarization using Automatic Key-Phrase Extraction
Pinaki Bhaskar 22

Automatic Evaluation of Summary Using Textual Entailment
Pinaki Bhaskar and Partha Pakray 30

Towards a Discourse Model for Knowledge Elicitation
Eugeniu Costetchi 38

Detecting Negated and Uncertain Information in Biomedical and Review Texts
Noa Cruz 45

Cross-Language Plagiarism Detection Methods
Vera Danilova 51

Rule-based Named Entity Extraction for Ontology Population
Aurore De Amaral 58

Towards Definition Extraction Using Conditional Random Fields
Luis Espinosa Anke 63

Event-Centered Simplification of News Stories
Goran Glavaš and Sanja Štajner 71

Random Projection and Geometrization of String Distance Metrics
Daniel Hromada 79

Improving Language Model Adaptation using Automatic Data Selection and Neural Network
Shahab Jalalvand 86

Unsupervised Learning of A-Morphous Inflection with Graph Clustering
Maciej Janicki 93

Statistical-based System for Morphological Annotation of Arabic Texts
Nabil Khoufi and Manel Boudokhane 100

A System for Generating Cloze Test Items from Russian-Language Text
Andrey Kurtasov 107

Korean Word-Sense Disambiguation Using Parallel Corpus as Additional Resource
Chungen Li 113

Towards Basque Oral Poetry Analysis: A Machine Learning Approach
Mikel Osinalde, Aitzol Astigarraga, Igor Rodriguez and Manex Agirrezabal 119

GF Modern Greek Resource Grammar
Ioanna Papadopoulou 126

Collection, Annotation and Analysis of Gold Standard Corpora for Knowledge-Rich Context Extraction in Russian and German
Anne-Kathrin Schumann 134

Named Entity Recognition in Broadcast News Using Similar Written Texts
Niraj Shrestha and Ivan Vulić 142

Reporting Preliminary Automatic Comparable Corpora Compilation Results
Ekaterina Stambolieva 149

Workshop Programme

Monday September 9, 2013 (16:30 - 18:30)

Methods, Resources and Language Processing Tasks (Posters Session 1)

A Dataset for Arabic Textual Entailment
Maytham Alabbas

Automatic Evaluation of Summary Using Textual Entailment
Pinaki Bhaskar and Partha Pakray

Detecting Negated and Uncertain Information in Biomedical and Review Texts
Noa Cruz

Cross-Language Plagiarism Detection Methods
Vera Danilova

Random Projection and Geometrization of String Distance Metrics
Daniel Hromada

Improving Language Model Adaptation using Automatic Data Selection and Neural Network
Shahab Jalalvand

Towards Basque Oral Poetry Analysis: A Machine Learning Approach
Mikel Osinalde, Aitzol Astigarraga, Igor Rodriguez and Manex Agirrezabal

Reporting Preliminary Automatic Comparable Corpora Compilation Results
Ekaterina Stambolieva

Tuesday September 10, 2013 (11:30 - 12:50)

Oral Presentations

Event-Centered Simplification of News Stories
Goran Glavaš and Sanja Štajner

Named Entity Recognition in Broadcast News Using Similar Written Texts
Niraj Shrestha and Ivan Vulić

Collection, Annotation and Analysis of Gold Standard Corpora for Knowledge-Rich Context Extraction in Russian and German
Anne-Kathrin Schumann

Unsupervised Learning of A-Morphous Inflection with Graph Clustering
Maciej Janicki

Wednesday September 11, 2013 (15:30 - 17:30)

Applications (Poster Session 2)

Perceptual Feedback in Computer Assisted Pronunciation Training: A Survey
Renlong Ai

Answering Questions from Multiple Documents – the Role of Multi-Document Summarization
Pinaki Bhaskar

Multi-Document Summarization using Automatic Key-Phrase Extraction
Pinaki Bhaskar

Towards a Discourse Model for Knowledge Elicitation
Eugeniu Costetchi

Rule-based Named Entity Extraction for Ontology Population
Aurore De Amaral

Towards Definition Extraction Using Conditional Random Fields
Luis Espinosa Anke

Statistical-based System for Morphological Annotation of Arabic Texts
Nabil Khoufi and Manel Boudokhane

A System for Generating Cloze Test Items from Russian-Language Text
Andrey Kurtasov

GF Modern Greek Resource Grammar
Ioanna Papadopoulou

Korean Word-Sense Disambiguation Using Parallel Corpus as Additional Resource
Chungen Li

Perceptual Feedback In Computer Assisted Pronunciation Training: A Survey

Renlong Ai
Language Technology Laboratory, DFKI GmbH
Alt-Moabit 91c, Berlin, Germany
renlong.ai@dfki.de

Abstract

This survey examines the feedback in current Computer Assisted Pronunciation Training (CAPT) systems and focus on perceptual feedback. The advantages of perceptual feedback are presented, while on the other hand, the reasons why it has not been integrated into commercial CAPT systems are also discussed. This is followed by a suggestion of possible directions of future work.

1 Introduction

In the last decades, CAPT has proved its potential in digital software market. Modern CAPT software aims no longer at simply assisting human teachers by providing various attractive teaching materials, but rather at replacing them by providing the learners with a private learning environment, self-paced practises, and especially instant feedback. Different types of feedback have always been highlighted in CAPT systems. However, it remains to be seen whether these types of feedback are really helpful to the learners, or are rather a demonstration of what modern technology can achieve. Considering whether a feedback is effective and necessary in CAPT systems, Hansen (2006) described four criteria in his work, namely:

- *Comprehensive*: if the feedback is easy to understand.
- *Qualitative*: if the feedback can decide whether a correct phoneme was used.
- *Quantitative*: if the feedback can decide whether a phoneme of correct length was used.
- *Corrective*: if the feedback provides information for improvement.

Ways of providing feedback grow as far as technology enables, but the four points above should be considered seriously while designing a practical and user-friendly feedback.

In Section 2 the existing feedback in available CAPT systems is examined. In Section 3 recent works on perceptual feedback are reviewed, which is still not quite common in commercial CAPT systems. In Section 4, some suggestions on integrating perceptual feedback into current CAPT systems in a more reliable way are sketched. Finally, conclusions are presented in Section 5.

2 Feedback In CAPT Systems

Feedback nowadays has been playing a much more significant role than simply telling the learner "You have done right!" or "This doesn't sound good enough". Thanks to the newer technologies in signal processing, it can pinpoint specific errors and even provide corrective information (Crompton and Rodrigues, 2001). One of the earliest type of feedback, which is still used in modern CAPT systems like TELLMEMORE (2013), is to show the waveform of both the L1 (the teacher's or native's) speech and the L2 learner's one. Although the difference of the two curves can be perceived via comparison, the learner is still left with the question why they are different and what he should do to make his own curve similar to the native one. He might then try many times randomly to produce the right pronunciation, which may lead to reinforcing bad habits and result in fossilisation (Eskenazi, 1999). To solve this, forced alignment was introduced. It allowed to pinpoint the wrong phoneme, and give suggestion to increase or decrease the pitch or energy, like in EyeSpeak (2013), or mark the wrong pronounced phoneme to notify the learner, like in FonixTalk SDK (2013).

Another common type of feedback among CAPT systems is to provide a score. A score of the overall comprehensibility of learner's utterance is usually acquired via Automatic Speech Recognition (ASR), like in SpeechRater Engine (Zechner et al., 2007), which is part of TOFEL (Test of English as a Foreign Language) since 2006. Many CAPT systems also provide word-level or even phoneme-level scoring, like in speexx (2013). Although scoring is appreciated among language students due to the immediate information on the quality it provides (Atwell et al., 1999) , it is regarded merely as an overall feedback, because if no detail follows, the number itself will not show any information for the learner to improve his speech.

To provide more pedagogical and intuitive feedback, the situation of classroom teaching is considered. Imaging a student makes a wrong pronunciation, the teacher would then show him how exactly the phoneme is pronounced, maybe by slowing down the action of mouth while pronouncing or pointing out how the tongue should be placed (Morley, 1991). After investigating such behaviours, Engwall et. al. (2006) presented different levels of feedback implemented in the ARTUR (the ARticulaton TUtoR) pronunciation training system. With the help of a camera and knowledge of the relation between facial and vocal tract movements, the system can provide feedback on which part of the human vocal system did not move in the right way to produce the correct sound, the tongue, the teeth or the palate, and show in 3D animations how to pronounce the right way.

These types of feedback are known as visual feedback and automatic diagnoses (Bonneau and Colotte, 2011) that show information with graphic user interface. Besides these, perceptual feedback, which is provided via speech and/or speech manipulations, is also used more and more common in modern CAPT systems.

3 Types Of Perceptual Feedback

Simple playback of the native and learner's speech and leaving the work of comparing them to the learners will not help them to perceive difference between the sound they produced and the correct targets sound because of their L1 influence (Flege, 1995), hence, the importance of producing perceivable feedback has been increasingly realised by CAPT system vendors and many ways of enhancing learns' perception have been tried.

3.1 Speech Synthesis For Corrective Feedback

Meng et. al. (2010) implemented a perturbation model that resynthesise the speech to convey focus. They modified the energy, max and min f0 and the duration of the focused speech, and then use STRAIGHT (Kawahara, 2006), a speech signal process tool, for the resynthesising. This perturbation model was extended later to provide emphasis (Meng et al., 2012). A two-pass decision tree was constructed to cluster acoustic variations between emphatic and neutral speech. The questions for decision tree construction were designed according to word, syllable and phone layers. Finally, Support vector machines (SVMs) were used to predict acoustic variations for all the leaves of main tree (at word and syllable layers) and subtrees (at phone layer). In such way, learner's attention can be drawn onto the emphasised segments so that they can perceive the feedback in the right way.

In the study of De La Rosa et. al. (2010), it was shown that students of English Language benefit from spoken language input, which they are encourage to listen; in particular this study shows that English text-to-speech may be good enough for that purpose. A similar study for French Language was presented in (Handley, 2009), where four French TTS systems are evaluated to be used within CALL applications. In these last two cases speech synthesis is used more as a complement to reinforce the learning process, that is, in most of the cases as a way of listen and repeat, without further emphasis.

3.2 Emphasis And Exaggeration

Yoram and Hirose (1996) presented a feedback in their system which produces exaggerated speech to emphasis the problematic part in the learner's utterance, as a trial to imitate human teachers, e.g. if the learner placed a stress on the wrong syllable in a word, the teacher would use a more extreme pitch value, higher energy and slower speech rate at the right and wrong stressing points to demonstrate the difference. As feedback, the system plays a modified version of the learner's speech with exaggerated stress to notify him where his problem is. A Klatt formant synthesiser was used to modify the f0, rate and intensity of the speech.

Lu et. al. (2012) looked into the idea of exaggeration further by investigating methods that modified different parameters. They evaluated duration-based, pitch-based and intensity-based stress exaggeration, and in the end combined these three to perform the final automatic stress exaggeration, which, according to their experiment, raised the perception accuracy from 0.6229 to 0.7832.

3.3 Prosody Transplantation Or Voice Conversion

In the previous sections we have seen that speech synthesis techniques can be used to provide feedback to the learner by modifying some prosody parameters of the learner's speech in order to focus on particular problems or to exaggerate them. Other forms of feedback intend to modify the learner's voice by replacing or "transplanting" properties of the teacher's voice. The objective is then that the learner can hear the correct prosody in his/her own voice. This idea has been motivated by studies that indicate that learners benefit more from audio feedback when they can listen to a voice very similar to their own (Eskenazi, 2009) or when they can hear their own voice modified with correct prosody (Bissiri et al., 2006) (Felps et al., 2009).

Prosody transplantation tries to adjust the prosody of the learner to the native's, so that the learner can perceive the right prosody in his own voice. According to the research of Nagano and Ozawa (1990), learners' speech sounds more like native after they tried to mimic their own voice with modified prosody than to mimic the original native voice. The effect is more remarkable if the L1 language is non-tonal, e.g. English and the target language is tonal, e.g. Mandarin (Peabody and Seneff, 2006). Pitch synchronous overlap and add (PSOLA) (Moulines and Charpentier, 1990) has been widely used in handling pitch modifications. Many different approaches, namely time-domain (TD) PSOLA, linear prediction (LP) PSOLA and Fourier-domain (FD) PSOLA, have been applied to generate effective and robust prosody transplantation.

Felps et. al. (2009) provided prosodically corrected versions of the learners' utterances as feedback by performing time and pitch scale before applying FD PSOLA to the user and target speech. Latsch and Netto (2011) presented in their PS-DTW-OLA algorithm a computationally efficient method that maximises the spectral similarity between the target and reference speech. They performed dynamic time warping (DTW) algorithm to the target and reference speech signals so that their time-warping become compatible to what the TD PSOLA algorithm requires. By combining the two algorithms, pitch-mark interpolations was avoided and the target was transplanted with high frame similarity. Cabral and Oliveira (2005) modified the standard LP-PSOLA algorithm, in which they used smaller period instead of twice of the original period for the weighting window length to prevent the overlapping factor to increase above 50%. They also developed a pitch synchronous time-scaling (PSTS) algorithm, which gives a better representation of the residual after prosodic modification and overcomes the problem of energy fluctuation when the pitch modification factor is large.

Vocoding, which was originally used in radio communication, can be also utilised in performing prosody transplantation and/or voice conversion. By passing the f0, bandpass voicing and Fourier magnitude of the target speech and the Mel-frequency cepstral coefficients (MFCCs) of the learner's speech, the vocoder is able to generate utterance with L2 learner's voice and the pitch contours of the native voice. Recently, vocoder techniques have been also used in flattening the spectrum for further processing, as shown in the work of Felps et. al. (2009).

An overview of the different types of perceptual feedback, the acoustic parameters they changed and the techniques they used, is summarised in Table 1.

4 Perceptual Feedback: Pros, Cons And Challenges

Compared to other feedback, the most obvious advantage of perceptual feedback is that the corrective information is provided in a most comprehensive way: via the language itself. To overcome the problem that it is hard for L2 learners to perceive the information in a utterance read by a native speaker, methods can be applied to their own voice so that it is easier for them to tell the difference. However, the most directly way to tell the learners where the error is located is still to show them via graphic or text. Hence, the ideal feedback that a CAPT system should provide is a combination of visual and perceptual feedback in the way that automatic diagnoses identify the errors and show them, while perceptual feedback

Perceptual Feedback	Ref	Modify/replaced parameters	Method or technique
Speech synthesis	(Meng et al., 2010)	F0, duration	STRAIGHT
	(Meng et al., 2012)	F0, duration	decision tree, support vector machines
Emphasis and exaggeration	(Yoram and Hirose, 1996)	F0, rate and intensity	Klatt formant synthesiser
	(Lu et al., 2012)	F0, duration and intensity	PSOLA
Voice conversion or prosody transplantation	(Felps et al., 2009)	duration, pitch contour, spectrum	FD-PSOLA, spectral envelope vocoder
	(Latsch and Netto, 2011)	duration, pitch contour	TD-PSOLA, DTW
	(Cabral and Oliveira, 2005)	pitch and duration	LP-PSOLA, time-scaling

Table 1: Perceptual feedback, acoustic parameters modified or replaced and the techniques used.

helps to correct them.

One argument about perceptual feedback is: in most works, only prosodic errors like pitch and durations are taken care of, and in most experiments that prove the feasibility of perceptual feedback, the native and L2 speech that are used as input differ only prosodically. Although the results of these experiments show the advantage of perceptual feedback, e.g. the learners did improve their prosody better after hearing modified version of their own speech than simply hearing the native ones, it is not the real case in L2 language teaching, at least not for the beginners, who might usually change the margins between syllables or delete the syllables depending on their familiarity to the syllables and their sonority (Carlisle, 2001). These add difficulties to the forced alignment or dynamic time warping procedure, which is necessary before the pitch modification, and hence the outcome will also not be as expected (Brognaux et al., 2012).

Perceptual feedback has been widely discussed and researched but not yet fully deployed in commercial CAPT systems. In order to provide more reliable feedback, the following considerations should be taken into account:

- For the moment, perceptual feedback should be applied to advanced learners who focus on improving their prosody, or to the case that only prosodic errors are detected in the learner's speech, i.e. if other speech errors are found, e.g. phoneme deletion, the learner gets notified via other means and corrects it; if only a stress is misplaced by the learner, he will hear a modified version of his own speech where the stress is placed right so that he can perceive his stress error.

- More robust forced alignment tool for non-native speech has been under development for years. In the near future, it should be able to handle pronunciation errors and provide right time-alignment even if the text and audio do not 100% match. Until then, an L1 independent forced alignment tool, which is one of the bottlenecks in speech technology nowadays, will be open to researchers, so in the near future, more accurate perceptual feedback can be generated.

5 Conclusions

In this paper first, various visual and diagnostic feedback in current CAPT systems are examined. Then existing research on providing perceptual feedback via multiple means is summarised. After the literature review presented in this paper, it has been found that the perceptual feedback in CAPT systems can be classified in 3 types: via speech synthesis, providing emphasis and exaggeration, and performing prosody transplantation. The three methods modify or replace prosody parameters like F0 and durations and the most used speech signal processing technology is PSOLA. Subsequently, the pros and cons of perceptual feedback are analysed taking into consideration the difficulties of its implementation in commercial CAPT systems. Finally, a suggestion on integrating perceptual feedback in future work is made.

6 Acknowledgement

This work is supported by the project SPRINTER, funded by the German Ministry of Education and Research (BMBF) within the program KMU-innovativ under number 01IS12006A. The author would like to express his very great appreciation to Marcela Charfuelan for her valuable suggestions during the survey.

References

Eric Atwell, Dan Herron, Peter Howarth, Rachel Morton, and Hartmut Wick. 1999. Pronunciation training: Requirements and solutions. *ISLE Deliverable*, 1.

Maria Paola Bissiri, Hartmut R Pfitzinger, and Hans G Tillmann. 2006. Lexical stress training of german compounds for italian speakers by means of resynthesis and emphasis. In *Proc. of the 11th Australasian Int. Conf. on Speech Science and Technology (SST 2006). Auckland*, pages 24–29.

Anne Bonneau and Vincent Colotte. 2011. Automatic feedback for l2 prosody learning. *Speech and Language Technologies*, pages 55–70.

Sandrine Brognaux, Sophie Roekhaut, Thomas Drugman, and Richard Beaufort. 2012. Train&align: A new online tool for automatic phonetic alignment. In *Spoken Language Technology Workshop (SLT), 2012 IEEE*, pages 416–421. IEEE.

Joao P Cabral and Luıs C Oliveira. 2005. Pitch-synchronous time-scaling for prosodic and voice quality transformations. In *Proc. Interspeech*, pages 1137–1140.

Robert S Carlisle. 2001. Syllable structure universals and second language acquisition. *IJES, International Journal of English Studies*, 1(1):1–19.

P. Crompton and S. Rodrigues. 2001. The role and nature of feedback on students learning grammar: A small scale study on the use of feedback in call in language learning. In *Proceedings of the workshop on Computer Assisted Language Learning, Artificial Intelligence in Education Conference*, pages 70–82.

Kevin De-La-Rosa, Gabriel Parent, and Maxine Eskenazi. 2010. Multimodal learning of words: A study on the use of speech synthesis to reinforce written text in l2 language learning. In *Proceedings of the Second Language Studies: Acquisition, Learning, Education and Technology*, Tokyo, Japan.

Olov Engwall, Olle Bälter, Anne-Marie Öster, and Hedvig Kjellström. 2006. Feedback management in the pronunciation training system artur. In *CHI'06 extended abstracts on Human factors in computing systems*, pages 231–234. ACM.

Maxine Eskenazi. 1999. Using automatic speech processing for foreign language pronunciation tutoring: Some issues and a prototype. *Language learning & technology*, 2(2):62–76.

Maxine Eskenazi. 2009. An overview of spoken language technology for education. *Speech Communication*, 51(10):832 – 844.

EyeSpeak. 2013. Language learning software. Online: http://www.eyespeakenglish.com.

Daniel Felps, Heather Bortfeld, and Ricardo Gutierrez-Osuna. 2009. Foreign accent conversion in computer assisted pronunciation training. *Speech communication*, 51(10):920–932.

James E Flege. 1995. Second language speech learning: Theory, findings, and problems. *Speech Perception and Linguistic Experience: Theoretical and Methodological Issues*, pages 233–273.

FonixTalk SDK. 2013. Speech FX Text to Speech. Online: http://www.speechfxinc.com.

Zöe Handley. 2009. Is text-to-speech synthesis ready for use in computer-assisted language learning? *Speech Communication*, 51(10):906 – 919.

Thomas K Hansen. 2006. Computer assisted pronunciation training: the four'k's of feedback. In *4th Internat. Conf. on Multimedia and Information and Communication Technologies in Education, Seville, Spain*, pages 342–346. Citeseer.

Hideki Kawahara. 2006. STRAIGHT, exploitation of the other aspect of VOCODER: Perceptually isomorphic decomposition of speech sounds. *Acoustical Science and Technology*, 27(6):349–353.

V. L. Latsch and S. L. Netto. 2011. Pitch-synchronous time alignment of speech signals for prosody transplantation. In *IEEE International Symposium on Circuits and Systems (ISCAS)*, Rio de Janeiro, Brazil.

Jingli Lu, Ruili Wang, and LiyanageC. Silva. 2012. Automatic stress exaggeration by prosody modification to assist language learners perceive sentence stress. *International Journal of Speech Technology*, 15(2):87–98.

Fanbo Meng, Helen Meng, Zhiyong Wu, and Lianhong Cai. 2010. Synthesizing expressive speech to convey focus using a perturbation model for computer-aided pronunciation training. In *Proceedings of the Second Language Studies: Acquisition, Learning, Education and Technology*, Tokyo, Japan.

Fanbo Meng, Zhiyong Wu, Helen Meng, Jia Jia, and Lianhong Cai. 2012. Generating emphasis from neutral speech using hierarchical perturbation model by decision tree and support vector machine. In *Proceedings of International Colloquium on Automata, Languages and Programming (ICALP 2012)*, Warwik, UK.

Joan Morley. 1991. The pronunciation component in teaching english to speakers of other languages. *Tesol Quarterly*, 25(3):481–520.

Eric Moulines and Francis Charpentier. 1990. Pitch-synchronous waveform processing techniques for text-to-speech synthesis using diphones. *Speech Communication*, 9(5-6):453–467.

Keiko Nagano and Kazunori Ozawa. 1990. English speech training using voice conversion. In *First International Conference on Spoken Language Processing*.

Mitchell Peabody and Stephanie Seneff. 2006. Towards automatic tone correction in non-native mandarin. In *Chinese Spoken Language Processing*, pages 602–613. Springer.

speexx. 2013. Language learning software. Online: http://speexx.com/en/.

TELLMEMORE. 2013. Language learning software. Online: http://www.tellmemore.com.

M. Yoram and K. Hirose. 1996. Language training system utilizing speech modification. In *Spoken Language, 1996. ICSLP 96. Proceedings., Fourth International Conference on*, volume 3, pages 1449–1452 vol.3.

Klaus Zechner, Derrick Higgins, and Xiaoming Xi. 2007. Speechrater: A construct-driven approach to scoring spontaneous non-native speech. *Proc. SLaTE*.

A Dataset for Arabic Textual Entailment

Maytham Alabbas
School of Computer Science, University of Manchester, Manchester, M13 9PL, UK
alabbasm@cs.man.ac.uk
Department of Computer Science, College of Science, Basrah University, Basrah, Iraq
maytham.alabbas@gmail.com

Abstract

There are fewer resources for textual entailment (TE) for Arabic than for other languages, and the manpower for constructing such a resource is hard to come by. We describe here a semi-automatic technique for creating a first dataset for TE systems for Arabic using an extension of the 'headline-lead paragraph' technique. We also sketch the difficulties inherent in volunteer annotators-based judgment, and describe a regime to ameliorate some of these.

1 Introduction

One key task for natural language systems is to determine whether one natural language sentence entails another. One of the most popular generic tasks nowadays is called *textual entailment* (TE). Dagan and Glickman (2004) describe that *text T* textually entails *hypothesis H* if the truth of *H*, as interpreted by a typical language user, can be inferred from the meaning of *T*. For instance, (1a) entails (1b) whereas the reverse does not.

(1) a. *The couple are divorced.*
    b. *The couple were married.*

Tackling this task will open the door to applications of these ideas in many areas of natural language processing (NLP), such as question answering (QA), semantic search, information extraction (IE), and multi-document summarisation.

Our main goal is to develop a TE system for Arabic. To achieve this goal we need firstly to create an appropriate dataset because there are, to the best of our knowledge, no such datasets available.

The remainder of this paper is organised as follows. The current technique for creating a textual entailment dataset is explained in Section 2 . Section 3 describes the Arabic dataset. A spammer detection technique is described in Section 4. Section 5 presents a summary discussion.

2 Dataset Creation

In order to train and test a TE system for Arabic, we need an appropriate dataset. We did not want to produce a set of *T-H* pairs by hand–partly because doing so is a lengthy and tedious process, but more importantly because hand-coded datasets are liable to embody biases introduced by the developer. If the dataset is used for training the system, then the rules that are extracted will be little more than an unfolding of information explicitly supplied by the developers. If it is used for testing then it will only test the examples that the developers have chosen, which are likely to be biased, albeit unwittingly, towards the way they think about the problem.

Our current technique for building an Arabic dataset for the TE task consists of two tools. The first tool is responsible for automatically collecting *T-H* pairs from news websites (Section 2.1), while the second tool is an online annotation system that allows annotators to annotate our collected pairs manually (Section 2.2).

2.1 Collecting *T-H* Pairs

A number of TE datasets have been produced for different languages, such as English,[1] Greek (Marzelou et al., 2008), Italian (Bos et al., 2009), German and Hindi (Faruqui and Padó, 2011). Some of these datasets were collected by the so-called *headline-lead paragraph* technique (Bayer et al., 2005; Burger and Ferro, 2005) from newspaper corpora, pairing the first paragraph of an article, as *T*, with its headline, as *H*. This is based on the observation that a news article's headline is very often a partial paraphrase of the first para-

[1] Available at: http://www.nist.gov/tac/2011/RTE/index.html

Source	Headline (Hypothesis)	Lead paragraph (Text)	Result
CNN	Berlusconi says he will not seek another term.	Italian Prime Minister Silvio Berlusconi said Friday he will not run again when his term expires in 2013.	YES
BBC	Silvio Berlusconi vows not to run for new term in 2013.	Italian Prime Minister Silvio Berlusconi has confirmed that he will not run for office again when his current term expires in 2013.	YES
Reuters	Berlusconi says he will not seek new term.	Italian Prime Minister Silvio Berlusconi declared on Friday he would not run again when his term expires in 2013.	YES

Figure 1: Some English *T-H* pairs collected by headline-lead paragraph technique.

graph of this article, conveying thus a comparable meaning.

We are building a corpus of *T-H* pairs by using headlines that have been automatically acquired from Arabic newspapers' and TV channels' websites[2] as queries to be input to Google via the standard Google-API. Then, we select the first paragraph, which usually represents the most related sentence(s) in the article with the headline (Bayer et al., 2005; Burger and Ferro, 2005), of each of the first 10 returned pages. This technique produces a large number of *T-H* pairs without any bias in either *Ts* or *Hs*. To improve the quality of the sentence pairs that resulted from the query, we use two conditions to filter the results: (i) the length of a headline must be at least more than five words to avoid very small headlines; and (ii) the number of common words (either in surface forms or lemma forms) between both sentences must be less than 80% of the headline length to avoid having excessively similar sentences. In the current work, we apply both conditions above to 85% of the *T-H* pairs from both training and testing sets. We then apply the first condition only to the remaining 15% of *T-H* pairs in order to leave some similar pairs, especially non entailments, to foil simplistic approaches (e.g. bag-of-words).

The problem here is that the headline and the lead-paragraph are often so similar that there would be very little to learn from them if they were used in the training phase of a TE system; and they would be almost worthless as a test pair–virtually any TE system will get this pair right, so they will not serve as a discriminatory test pair. In order to overcome this problem, we matched headlines from one source with stories from another. Using a headline from one source and the first sentence from an article about the same story but from another source is likely to produce *T-H* pairs which are not unduly similar. Figure 1 shows, for instance, the results of headlines from various sites (CNN, BBC and Reuters) that mention Berlusconi in their headlines on a single day.

We can therefore match a headline of one newspaper with related sentences from another one. We have tested this technique on different languages, such as English, Spanish, German, Turkish, Bulgarian, Persian and French. We carried out a series of informal experiment with native speakers and the results were encouraging, to the point where we took this as the basic method for suggesting *T-H* pairs.

Most of the Arabic articles that are returned by this process typically contain very long sentences (100+ words), where only a small part has a direct relationship to the query. With very long sentences of this kind, it commonly happens that only the first part of *T* is relevant to *H*. This is typical of Arabic text, which is often written with very little punctuation, with elements of the text linked by conjunctions rather than being broken into implicit segments by punctuation marks such as full stops and question marks. Thus what we really want as the text is actually the first conjunct of the first sentence, rather than the whole of the first sentence.

In order to overcome this problem, we simply need to find the first conjunction that links two sentences, rather than linking two substructures (e.g. two noun phrases (NPs)). MSTParser (McDonald and Pereira, 2006) does this quite reliably, so that parsing and looking for the first conjunct is a more reliable way of segmenting long Arabic sentences than simply segmenting the text at the first conjunction. For instance, selecting the second conjunction in segment (2) will give us the complete sentence *'John and Mary go to school in the morning'*, since it links two sentences. In contrast, selecting the first conjunction in segment (2) will give us solely the proper noun *'John'*, since it links two NPs (i.e. *'John'* and *'Mary'*).

[2]We use here Al Jazeera `http://www.aljazeera.net/`, Al Arabiya `http://www.alarabiya.net/` and BBC Arabic `http://www.bbc.co.uk/arabic/` websites as resources for our headlines.

(2) *John **and** Mary go to school in the morning **and** their mother prepares the lunch.*

2.2 Annotating *T-H* Pairs

The annotation is performed by volunteers, and we have to rely on their goodwill both in terms of how many examples they are prepared to annotate and how carefully they do the job. We therefore have to make the task as easy possible, to encourage them to do large numbers of cases, and we have to manage the problems that arise from having a mixture of people, with different backgrounds, as annotators. In one way having non-experts is very positive: as noted above, TE is about the judgements that a typical speaker would make. Not the judgements that a logician would make, or the judgements that a carefully briefed annotator would make, but the judgements that a typical speaker would make. From this point of view, having a mixture of volunteers carrying out the task is a good thing: their judgements will indeed be those of a typical speaker.

At the same time, there are problems associated with this strategy. Our volunteers may just have misunderstood what we want them to do, or they may know what we want but be careless about how they carry it out. We therefore have to be able to detect annotators who, for whatever reason, have not done the job properly (Section 4).

Because our annotators are geographically distributed, we have developed an online annotation system. The system presents the annotator with sentences that they have not yet seen and that are not fully annotated (here, annotated by three annotators) and asks them to mark this pair as positive 'YES', negative 'NO' and unknown 'UN'. The system also provides other options, such as revisiting a pair that they have previously annotated, reporting sentences that have such gross misspellings or syntactic anomalies that it is impossible to classify, skipping the current pair when a user chooses not to annotate this pair, and general comments (to send any suggestion about improving the system). The final annotation of each pair is computed when it is fully annotated by three annotators–when an annotator clicks 'Next', they are given the next sentence that has not yet been fully annotated. This has the side-effect of mixing up annotators: since annotators do their work incrementally, it is very unlikely that three people will all click 'Next' in lock-step, so there will be inevitable shuffling of annotators, with each person having a range of different co-annotators. All information about articles, annotators, annotations and other information such as comments is stored in a MySQL database.

3 Arabic TE Dataset

The preliminary dataset, namely Arabic TE dataset (ArbTEDS), consists of 618 *T-H* pairs. These pairs are randomly chosen from thousands of pairs collected by using the tool explained in Section 2.1. These pairs cover a number of subjects such as politics, business, sport and general news. We used eight expert and non-expert volunteer annotators[3] to identify the different pairs as 'YES', 'NO' and 'UN' pairs. Those annotators follow nearly the same annotation guidelines as those for building the RTE task dataset (Dagan et al., 2006). They used the online system explained in Section 2.2 to annotate our collected *T-H* pairs.

Table 1 summarises these individual results: the rates on the cases where an annotator agrees with at least one co-annotator (average around 91% between annotators) are considerably higher than those in the case where the annotator agrees with both the others (average around 78% between annotators). This suggests that the annotators found this is a difficult task. This table shows that comparatively few of the disagreements involve one or more of the annotators saying 'UN'–for 600 of the 618 pairs at least two annotators both chose 'YES' or both chose 'NO' (the missing 18 pairs arise entirely from cases where two or three annotators chose 'UN' or where one said 'YES', one said 'NO' and one said 'UN'. These 18 pairs are annotated as 'UN' and they are eliminated from our dataset, leaving 600 binary annotated pairs).

Agreement	YES	NO
≥ 2 agree	478 (80%)	122 (20%)
3 agree	409 (68%)	69 (12%)

Table 1: ArbTEDS annotation rates.

As can be seen in Table 1, if we take the majority verdict of the annotators we find that 80% of the dataset are marked as entailed pairs, 20% as not entailed pairs. When we require unanimity between annotators, this becomes 68% entailed and

[3]All our annotators are Arabic native speaker PhD students, who are the author's colleagues. Some of them are linguistics students, whereas the others are working in fields related to NLP.

12% not entailed pairs. This drop in coverage, together with the fact that the ratio of entailed:not entailed moves from 100:25 to 100:17, suggests that relying on the majority verdict is unreliable, and we therefore intend to use only cases where all three annotators agree for both training and testing.

One obvious candidate is sentence length. It seems plausible that people will find long sentences harder to understand than short ones, and that there will be more disagreement about sentences that are hard to understand than about easy ones. Further statistical analysis results for the version of the dataset when there is unanimity between annotators are summarised in Table 2. We analyse the rates of this strategy that are shown in Table 1 according to the text's length, when the *H* average length is around 10 words and the average of common words between *T* and *H* is around 4 words. The average length of sentence in this dataset is 25 words per sentence, with some sentences containing 40+ words.

T's length	#pairs	#YES	#NO	At least one disagree
<20	131	97	11	23
20-29	346	233	38	75
30-39	110	69	20	21
>39	13	10	0	3
Total	**600**	**409**	**69**	**122**

Table 2: T's range annotation rates, three annotators agree.

Contrary to the expectation above, there does not seem to be any variation in agreement amongst annotators as sentence length changes. We therefore select the candidate *T-H* pairs without any restrictions on the length of the text to diversify the level of the examples' complexity, and hence to make the best use for our dataset.

3.1 Testing Dataset

It is worth noting in Table 1 that a substantial majority of pairs are marked positively–that *T* does indeed entail *H*. This is problematic, at least when we come to use the dataset for testing. For testing we need a balanced set: if we use a test set where 80% of cases are positive then a system which simply marks every pair positively will score 80%. It is hard, however, to get pairs where *T* and *H* are related but *T* does not entail *H* automatically. To solve this problem, we select the paragraph (other than the lead paragraph) in the article that shares the highest number of words with the headline for the first 10 returned pages. We called this technique *headline keywords-rest paragraph*. It produces a large number of potential texts, which are related to the main keywords of the headlines, without any bias.

In the case of testing set, we need a balanced 'YES' and 'NO' pairs (i.e. 50% pairs for each group). For this reason, we are currently following two stages to create our testset: (i) we apply our updated headline-lead paragraph technique for collecting positive pairs, since such technique is promising in this regard (see Table 1); and (ii) apply the strategy *headline keywords-rest paragraph* for collecting negative pairs and we will ask our annotators to select a potential text for each headline that it does not entail. Again we avoid asking the annotators to generate texts, in order to avoid introducing any unconscious bias. All the texts and hypotheses in our dataset were obtained from the news sources–the annotators' sole task is to judge entailment relations.

The preliminary results for collecting such dataset are promising. For instance, (3) shows example of positive pair where the annotators all agree for illustration.

(3) Positive pair

a. وزارة الدفاع الأمريكية البنتاغون تعد استراتيجية جديدة تضع الهجمات الألكترونية في مصاف الأعمال الحربية حسبما ذكرت صحف أمريكية
wzArħ Al+dfAς Al+Âmrykyħ Al+bntAγwn tςd AstrAtyjyħ jdydħ tDς Al+hjmAt Al+Âlktrwnyħ fy mSAf Al+ÂςmAl Al+Hrbyħ HsbmA ðkrt SHf Âmrykyħ
"The US Department of Defense, the Pentagon, draw up a new strategy that categorises cyber-attacks as acts of war, according to US newspapers"

b. البنتاغون يعتبر الهجمات الألكترونية أعمالا حربية
Al+bntAγwn yςtbr Al+hjmAt Al+Âlktrwnyħ ÂςmAl Hrbyħ
"The Pentagon considers cyber-attacks as acts of war"

By applying the headline keywords-rest paragraph on the entailed pair in (3), you could get not entailed pair as illustrated in (4).

(4) Negative pair for positive pair in (3)

a. صرح المتحدث باسم البنتاغون بأن: الرد على أي هجوم الكتروني تتعرض له الولايات المتحدة ليس ضروريا أن يكون بالمثل ولكن كل الخيارات مطروحة على الطاولة للرد على هذا الهجوم
SrH Al+mtHdθ bAsm Al+bntAγwn bÂn: Al+rd ςlý Ây hjwm Alktrwny ttςrD lh Al+wlAyAt Al+mtHdħ lys DrwryA Ân ykwn bAlmθl wlkn kl Al+xyarAt mTrwHħ llrd ςlý hðA Al+hjwm
"The Pentagon spokesman declared that: a response to any cyber-attacks on the US would not necessarily be a cyber-response and all options would be on the table to respond to this attack"

b. البنتاغون يعتبر الهجمات الألكترونية أعمالا حربية
Al+bntAγwn yςtbr Al+hjmAt Al+Âlktrwnyħ ÂςmAl Hrbyħ
"The Pentagon considers cyber-attacks as acts of war"

4 Spammer Checker

In order to check the reliability of our annotators, we used a statistical measure for assessing the reliability of agreement among our annotators when assigning categorical ratings to a number of annotating *T-H* pair of sentences. This measure is called *kappa*, which takes chance agreement into consideration. We use Fleiss's kappa (Fleiss, 1971), which is a generalisation of Cohen's kappa (Cohen, 1960) statistic to provide a measurement of agreement among a constant number of raters.

In our case, we need a global measure of agreement, which corresponds to the annotator reliability. We carry out the following steps:

1. The current annotator is ANT_i, $i=1$.
2. Create table for the ANT_i. This table includes all sentences annotated by ANT_i, and includes also as columns the other annotators who annotated the same sentences as ANT_i since each annotator has a range of different co-annotators. If an annotator does not annotate a sentence, then the corresponding cell should be left blank.
3. Compute the multiple-annotator version of kappa for all annotators in that table.
4. Compute another kappa for all annotators except ANT_i in that table.
5. If the kappa calculated in the step 4 exceeds that of step 3 significantly, then ANT_i is possibly a *spammer*.
6. $i=i+1$
7. If *i* exceeds 8 (i.e. number of our annotators), then stop.
8. Repeat this process from step 2 for the ANT_i.

To identify a 'spammer', you need to compare each annotator to something else (or some other group of annotators). If you take one annotator at a time, you will not be able to compute kappa, which takes chance agreement into consideration. You need two annotators or more to compute kappa.

We find out the kappa for each annotator with his/her co-annotators and another kappa for his/her co-annotators only for our eight annotators using the above steps, as shown in Table 3.

Annotator ID	Kappa for current annotator	Kappa for co-annotators
ANT_1	0.62	0.55
ANT_2	0.47	0.50
ANT_3	0.60	0.53
ANT_4	0.49	0.52
ANT_5	0.58	0.61
ANT_6	0.59	0.61
ANT_7	0.65	0.68
ANT_8	0.58	0.57
Average	**0.57**	**0.57**

Table 3: Reliability measure of our annotators.

The first thing to note about the results in Table 3 is that all kappa values between 0.4-0.79 represent a moderate to substantial level of agreement beyond chance alone according to the kappa interpretation given by Landis and Koch (1977) and Altman (1991). Also, the variation between the kappa including an annotator and the kappa of his/her co-annotators only is comparatively slight for all annotators. The average of both kappas for all annotators is equal (i.e. 0.57), which suggests that the strength of agreement among our annotators is moderate (i.e. $0.4 \leq kappa \leq 0.59$). We have solely three annotators (ANT_1, ANT_3 and ANT_8) where the kappas including them are higher than kappas for their co-annotators. The other annotators have kappas less than the kappas of their co-annotators but these differences are very slight. These findings suggest that all our annotators are reasonably reliable and we can use their annotated dataset in our work, but they also provide us with an indication of who is most reliable for tasks such as the extra annotation described in Section 3.1.

5 Summary

We have outlined an approach to the task of creating a first dataset for a TE task for working with a language where we have to rely on volunteer annotators. To achieve this goal, we tested two main tools. The first tool, which depends on the Google-API, is responsible for acquisition of *T-H* pairs based on the headline-lead paragraph technique of news articles. We have updated this idea in two ways: (i) for training dataset, we use the lead paragraph from an article with a closely linked headline. This notion is applicable to the collection of such a dataset for any language. It has two benefits. Firstly, it makes it less likely that the headline will be extracted directly from the sentence that it is being linked to, since different sources will report the same event slightly differently. Secondly, it will be more likely than the original technique to produce *T-H* pairs where *T* entails *H* with few common words between *T* and *H*; and (ii) for testing dataset, we use the same technique for training except that we take the paragraph from the rest of the article (i.e. each paragraph in the article except the lead one) that gives the highest number of common words between both headline and paragraph. This is particularly important for testing, since for testing you want a collection which is balanced between pairs where *T* does entail *H* and ones where it does not. This technique will be more likely than the original technique and the updated technique for training to produce *T-H* pairs where *T* does not entail *H* with partly higher common words between *T* and *H*, which will pose a problem to a TE system. Automatically obtaining *T-H* pairs where *T* is reasonably closely linked to *H* but does not entail it is quite tricky. If the two are clearly distinct then they will not pose a very difficult test. As shown in Table 1, by using updated headline-lead paragraph technique, we have a preponderance of positive examples, but there is a non-trivial set of negative ones, so it is at least possible to extract a balanced test set. We therefore apply the headline keywords-rest paragraph technique to construct a balanced test set from our annotated dataset.

In order to make sure that our data is reliable, we check unreliable annotator(s) using kappa coefficient based strategy, which takes chance into consideration rather than agreement between annotators only. This strategy suggests that all our annotators are reliable.

We intend to make our dataset available to the scientific community thus allowing other researchers to duplicate their methodology and confront the results obtained.

Acknowledgments

My special thanks and appreciations go to my supervisor, Professor Allan Ramsay (UK), Dr. Kilem L. Gwet (USA) and Dr. Yasser Sabtan (Egypt) for productive discussions. I also owe my deepest gratitude to Iraqi Ministry of Higher Education and Scientific Research for financial support in my PhD study.

References

Douglas G. Altman. 1991. *Practical Statistics for Medical Research.* Chapman and Hall, London, UK.

Samuel Bayer, John Burger, Lisa Ferro, John Henderson, and Alexander Yeh. 2005. MITRE's submissions to the EU PASCAL RTE Challenge. In *Proceedings of the1st PASCAL Recognising Textual Entailment Challenge*, pages 41–44, Southampton, UK.

Johan Bos, Fabio Massimo Zanzotto, and Marco Pennacchiotti. 2009. Textual entailment at EVALITA 2009. In *Proceedings of the 11th Conference of the Italian Association for Artificial Intelligence*, pages 1–7, Reggio Emilia, Italy.

John Burger and Lisa Ferro. 2005. Generating an entailment corpus from news headlines. In *Proceedings of the ACL Workshop on Empirical Modeling of Semantic Equivalence and Entailment*, pages 49–54, Ann Arbor, Michigan, USA. Association for Computational Linguistics.

Jacob Cohen. 1960. A coefficient of agreement for nominal scales. *Educational and Psychological Measurement*, 20(1):37–46.

Ido Dagan and Oren Glickman. 2004. Probabilistic textual entailment: generic applied modeling of language variability. In *PASCAL Workshop on Learning Methods for Text Understanding and Mining*, pages 26–29, Grenoble, France.

Ido Dagan, Oren Glickman and Bernardo Magnini. 2006. The PASCAL recognising textual entailment challenge. In J. Quiñonero-Candela, I. Dagan, B. Magnini, and F. d'Alché Buc, editors, *Machine Learning Challenges. Evaluating Predictive Uncertainty, Visual Object Classification, and Recognising Tectual Entailment*, volume 3944 of *Lecture Notes in Computer Science*, pages 177–190. Springer Berlin-Heidelberg.

Manaal Faruqui and Sebastian Padó. 2011. Acquiring entailment pairs across languages and domains: a data analysis. In *Proceedings of the 9th International Conference on Computational Semantics (IWCS'11)*, pages 95–104, Oxford, UK. Association for Computational Linguistics.

Joseph L. Fleiss. 1971. Measuring nominal scale agreement among many raters. *Psychological Bulletin*, 76(5):378–382.

J. Richard Landis and Gary G. Koch. 1977. The measurement of observer agreement for categorical data. *Biometrics*, 33:159–174.

Evi Marzelou, Maria Zourari, Voula Giouli, and Stelios Piperidis. 2008. Building a Greek corpus for textual entailment. In *Proceedings of the 6th International Conference on Language Resources and Evaluation (LREC'08)*, pages 1680–1686, Marrakech, Morocco. European Language Resources Association.

Ryan McDonald and Fernando Pereira. 2006. Online learning of approximate dependency parsing algorithms. In *Proceedings of the 11th Conference of the European Chapter of the Association for Computational Linguistics (EACL 2006)*, pages 81–88, Trento, Italy. Association for Computational Linguistics.

Answering Questions from Multiple Documents – the Role of Multi-Document Summarization

Pinaki Bhaskar
Department of Computer Science & Engineering,
Jadavpur University, Kolkata – 700032, India
pinaki.bhaskar@gmail.com

Abstract

Ongoing research work on Question Answering using multi-document summarization has been described. It has two main sub modules, document retrieval and Multi-document Summarization. We first preprocess the documents and then index them using Nutch with NE field. Stop words are removed and NEs are tagged from each question and all remaining question words are stemmed and then retrieve the most relevant 10 documents. Now, document graph-based query focused multi-document summarizer is used where question words are used as query. A document graph is constructed, where the nodes are sentences of the documents and edge scores reflect the correlation measure between the nodes. The system clusters similar texts from the graph using this edge score. Each cluster gets a weight and has a cluster center. Next, question dependent weights are added to the corresponding cluster score. Top two-ranked sentences of each cluster is identified in order and compressed and then fused to a single sentence. The compressed and fused sentences are included into the output summary with a limit of 500 words, which is presented as answer. The system is tested on data set of INEX QA track from 2011 to 2013 and best readability score was achieved.

1 Introduction

With the explosion of information in Internet, Natural language Question Answering (QA) is recognized as a capability with great potential. Traditionally, QA has attracted many AI researchers, but most QA systems developed are toy systems or games confined to laboratories and to a very restricted domain. Several recent conferences and workshops have focused on aspects of the QA research. Starting in 1999, the Text Retrieval Conference (TREC)[1] has sponsored a question-answering track, which evaluates systems that answer factual questions by consulting the documents of the TREC corpus. A number of systems in this evaluation have successfully combined information retrieval and natural language processing techniques. More recently, Conference and Labs of Evaluation Forums (CLEF)[2] are organizing QA lab from 2010.

INEX[3] has also started Question Answering track. INEX 2011 designed a QA track (SanJuan et al., 2011) to stimulate the research for real world application. The Question Answering (QA) task is contextualizing tweets, i.e., answering questions of the form "what is this tweet about?" INEX 2012 Tweet Contextualization (TC) track gives QA research a new direction by fusing IR and summarization with QA. The first task is to identify the most relevant document, for this a focused IR is needed. And the second task is to extract most relevant passages from the most relevant retrieved documents. So an automatic summarizer is needed. The general purpose of the task involves tweet analysis, passage and/or XML elements retrieval and construction of the answer, more specifically, the summarization of the tweet topic.

Automatic text summarization (Jezek and Steinberger, 2008) has become an important and timely tool for assisting and interpreting text information in today's fast-growing information age. An Abstractive Summarization ((Hahn and Romacker, 2001) and (Erkan and Radev, 2004)) attempts to develop an understanding of the main concepts in a document and then expresses those concepts in clear natural language. Extractive Summaries (Kyoomarsi et al., 2008) are formu-

[1] http://trec.nist.gov/
[2] http://www.clef-initiative.eu//
[3] https://inex.mmci.uni-saarland.de/

lated by extracting key text segments (sentences or passages) from the text, based on statistical analysis of individual or mixed surface level features such as word/phrase frequency, location or cue words to locate the sentences to be extracted. Our approach is based on Extractive Summarization.

In this paper, we describe a hybrid Question Answering system of document retrieval and multi-document summarization. The document retrieval is based on Nutch[4] architecture and the multi-document summarization system is based graph, cluster, sentence compression & fusion and sentence ordering. The same sentence scoring and ranking approach of Bhaskar and Bandyopadhyay (2010a and 2010b) has been followed. The proposed system was run on the data set of three years of INEX QA track from 2011 to 2013.

2 Related Work

Recent trend shows hybrid approach of question answering (QA) using Information Retrieval (IR) can improve the performance of the QA system. Schiffman et al. (2007) successfully used methods of IR into QA system. Rodrigo et al. (2010) removed incorrect answers of QA system using an IR engine. Pakray et al. (2010) used the IR system into QA and Pakray et al. (2011) proposed an efficient hybrid QA system using IR.

Tombros and Sanderson (1998) presents an investigation into the utility of document summarization in the context of IR, more specifically in the application of so-called query-biased summaries: summaries customized to reflect the information need expressed in a query. Employed in the retrieved document list displayed after retrieval took place, the summaries' utility was evaluated in a task-based environment by measuring users' speed and accuracy in identifying relevant documents.

A lot of research work has been done in the domain of both query dependent and independent summarization. MEAD (Radev et al., 2004) is a centroid based multi document summarizer, which generates summaries using cluster centroids produced by topic detection and tracking system. NeATS (Lin and Hovy, 2002) selects important content using sentence position, term frequency, topic signature and term clustering. XDoX (Hardy et al., 2002) identifies the most salient themes within the document set by passage clustering and then composes an extraction summary, which reflects these main themes. Graph-based methods have been also proposed for generating summaries. A document graph-based query focused multi-document summarization system has been described by Paladhi et al. (2008) and Bhaskar and Bandyopadhyay (2010a and 2010b).

In the present work, we have used the IR system as described by Pakray et al. (2010 and 2011) and Bhaskar et al. (2011) and the automatic summarization system as discussed by Bhaskar and Bandyopadhyay (2010a and 2010b) and Bhaskar et al. (2011).

3 System Architecture

In this section the overview of the system framework of the current INEX system has been shown. The current INEX system has two major sub-systems; one is the Focused IR system and the other one is the Automatic Summarization system. The Focused IR system has been developed on the basic architecture of Nutch, which use the architecture of Lucene[5]. Nutch is an open source search engine, which supports only the monolingual Information Retrieval in English, etc. The Higher-level system architecture of the combined Tweet Contextualization system of Focused IR and Automatic Summarization is shown in the Figure 1.

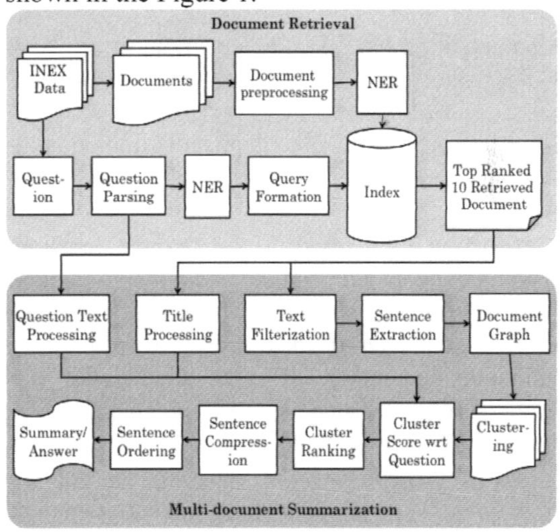

Figure 1. Higher-level system architecture

4 Document Retrieval

4.1 Document Parsing and Indexing

The web documents are full of noises mixed with the original content. In that case it is very diffi-

[4] http://nutch.apache.org/

[5] http://lucene.apache.org/

cult to identify and separate the noises from the actual content. INEX 2012 corpus had some noise in the documents and the documents are in XML tagged format. So, first of all, the documents had to be preprocessed. The document structure is checked and reformatted according to the system requirements.

XML Parser: The corpus was in XML format. All the XML test data has been parsed before indexing using our XML Parser. The XML Parser extracts the Title of the document along with the paragraphs.

Noise Removal: The corpus has some noise as well as some special symbols that are not necessary for our system. The list of noise symbols and the special symbols like """, "&", """", multiple spaces etc. is initially developed manually by looking at a number of documents and then the list is used to automatically remove such symbols from the documents.

Named Entity Recognizer (NER): After cleaning the corpus, the named entity recognizer identifies all the named entities (NE) in the documents and tags them according to their types, which are indexed during the document indexing.

Document Indexing: After parsing the documents, they are indexed using Lucene, an open source indexer.

4.2 Question Parsing

After indexing has been done, the questions had to be processed to retrieve relevant documents. Each question / topic was processed to identify the question words for submission to Lucene. The questions processing steps are described below:

Stop Word Removal: In this step the question words are identified from the questions. The stop words[6] and question words (what, when, where, which etc.) are removed from each question and the words remaining in the questions after the removal of such words are identified as the question tokens.

Named Entity Recognizer (NER): After removing the stop words, the named entity recognizer identifies all the named entities (NE) in the question and tags them according to their types, which are used during the scoring of the sentences of the retrieved document.

Stemming: Question tokens may appear in inflected forms in the questions. For English, standard Porter Stemming algorithm[7] has been used to stem the question tokens. After stemming all the question tokens, queries are formed with the stemmed question tokens.

4.3 Document Retrieval

After searching each query into the Lucene index, a set of retrieved documents in ranked order for each question is received.

First of all, all queries were fired with AND operator. If at least ten documents are retrieved using the query with AND operator then the query is removed from the query list and need not be searched again. If not then the query is fired again with OR operator. OR searching retrieves at least ten documents for each query. We always ranked the retrieved document using AND operator higher than the same using OR operator. Now, the top ranked ten relevant documents for each question is considered for milti-document summarization. Document retrieval is the most crucial part of this system. We take only the top ranked ten relevant documents assuming that these are the most relevant documents for the question from which the query had been generated.

5 Multi-Document Summarization

5.1 Graph-Based Clustered Model

The proposed graph-based multi-document summarization method consists of following steps:

(1) The document set $D = \{d_1, d_2, \ldots d_{10}\}$ is processed to extract text fragments, which are sentences in this system as it has been discussed earlier. Let for a document d_i, the sentences are $\{s_{i1}, s_{i2}, \ldots s_{im}\}$. Each text fragment becomes a node of the graph.

(2) Next, edges are created between nodes across the documents where edge score represents the degree of correlation between inter-documents nodes.

(3) Seed nodes are extracted which identify the relevant sentences within D and a search graph is built to reflect the semantic relationship between the nodes.

(4) Now, each node is assigned a question dependent score and the search graph is expanded.

(5) A question dependent multi-document summary is generated from the search graph.

Each sentence is represented as a node in the graph. The text in each document is split into

[6] http://members.unine.ch/jacques.savoy/clef/

[7] http://tartarus.org/~martin/PorterStemmer/java.txt

sentences and each sentence is represented with a vector of constituent words. If pair of related document is considered, then the inter document graph can be represented as a set of nodes in the form of bipartite graph. The edges connect two nodes corresponding to sentences from different documents.

Construct the Edge and Calculate Edge Score: The similarity between two nodes is expressed as the edge weight of the bipartite graph. Two nodes are related if they share common words (except stop words) and the degree of relationship can be measured by equation 1 adapting some traditional IR formula (Varadarajan and Hristidis, 2006).

$$\text{Edge\_Score} = \frac{\sum_{w \in (t(u) \cap t(v))} ((tf(t(u), w) + tf(t(v), w)) \times idf(w))}{size(t(u)) + size(t(v))} \quad (1)$$

where, $tf(d, w)$ is number of occurrence of w in d, $idf(w)$ is the inverse of the number of documents containing w, and $size(d)$ is the size of the documents in words. Actually for a particular node, total edge score is defined as the sum of scores of all out going edges from that node. The nodes with higher total edge scores than some predefined threshold are included as seed nodes.

But the challenge for multi-document summarization is that the information stored in different documents inevitably overlap with each other. So, before inclusion of a particular node (sentence), it has to be checked whether it is being repeated or not. Two sentences are said to be similar if they share for example, 70% words in common.

Construction of Search Graph: After identification of seed/topic nodes a search graph is constructed. For nodes, pertaining to different documents, edge scores are already calculated, but for intra document nodes, edge scores are calculated in the similar fashion as said earlier. Since, highly dense graph leads to higher search / execution time, only the edges having edge scores well above the threshold value might be considered.

5.2 Identification of Sub-topics through Markov Clustering

In this section, we will discuss the process to identify shared subtopics from related multi source documents. We already discussed that the subtopics shared by different news articles on same event form natural (separate) clusters of sentences when they are represented using document graph. We use Markov principle of graph clustering to identify those clusters from the document graph as described by Bhaskar and Bandyopadhyay (2010b).

The construction of question independent part of the Markov clusters completes the document-based processing phase of the system.

5.3 Key Term Extraction

Key Term Extraction module has two sub modules, i.e., question term extraction and Title words extraction.

Question Term Extraction: First the question is parsed using the Question Parsing module. In this Question Parsing module, the Named Entities (NE) are identified and tagged in the given question using the Stanford NER[8] engine. The remaining words after stop words removal are stemmed using Porter Stemmer.

Title Word Extraction: The titles of each retrieved documents are extracted and forwarded as input given to the Title Word Extraction module. After removing all the stop words from the titles, the remaining tile words are extracted and used as the keywords in this system.

5.4 Question Dependent Process

The nodes of the already constructed search graph are given a question dependent score. Using the combined scores of question independent score and question dependent score, clusters are reordered and relevant sentences are collected from each cluster in order. Then each collected sentence has processed and compressed removing the unimportant phrases. After that the compressed sentences are used to construct the summary.

Recalculate the Cluster Score: There are three basic components in the sentence weight like question terms, title words and synonyms of question terms dependent scores, which are calculated using equation 2.

$$w = \sum_{t=1}^{n_t} (n_t - t + 1) \left(\sum_p \left(1 - \frac{f_p^t - 1}{N_i} \right) \right) \times b \quad (2)$$

where, w is the term dependent score of the sentence i, t is the no. of the term, n_t is the total no. of term, f_p^t is the possession of the word which was matched with the term t in the sentence i, N_i is the total no. of words in sentence i and b is boost factor of the term, which is 3, 2 or 1 for question terms, title words and synonyms respectively. These three components are added to get the final weight of a sentence.

Recalculate the Cluster Ranking: We start by defining a function that attributes values to

[8] http://www-nlp.stanford.edu/ner/

the sentences as well as to the clusters. We refer to sentences indexed by i and question terms indexed by j. We want to maximize the number of question term covered by selection of sentences:

$$maximize \sum_j w_j^q q_j \quad (3)$$

where, w_j^q is the weight of question term j in the sentence i and q_j is a binary variable indicating the presence of that question term in the cluster. We also take the selection over title words and synonyms of the question terms. We collect the list of synonyms of the each word in the questions from the WordNet 3.0[9]. The general sets of tile words and synonyms are indexed by k and l respectively. So we also want to maximize the number of title words and synonyms covered by a selection of sentences using similar calculation like question terms using equation 3.

So, the question dependent score of a cluster is the weighted sum of the question terms it contains. If clusters are indexed by x, the question dependent score of the cluster x is:

$$c_x^q = \sum_{i=1}^{n} \sum_{j} w_j^q q_j + \sum_{i=1}^{n} \sum_{k} w_k^t t_k + \sum_{i=1}^{n} \sum_{l} w_l^s s_l \quad (4)$$

where, c_x^q is the question dependent score of the cluster x, n is the total no. of sentences in cluster x. Now, the new recalculated combined score of cluster x is:

$$c_x = c_x^g + c_x^q \quad (5)$$

where, c_x is the new score of the cluster x and c_x^g is the question independent cluster score in the graph of cluster x. Now, all the clusters are ranked with their new score c_x.

5.5 Retrieve Sentences for Summary

Get the highest weighted two sentences of each cluster, by the following equation:

$$\max\left(\sum_j w_j^q q_j + \sum_k w_k^t t_k + \sum_l w_l^s s_l\right) \forall i \quad (6)$$

where, i is the sentence index of a cluster. The original sentences in the documents are generally very lengthy to place in the summary. So, we are actually interested in a selection over phrases of sentence. After getting the top two sentences of a cluster, they are split into multiple phrases. The Stanford Parser[10] is used to parse the sentences and get the phrases of the sentence.

5.6 Sentence Compression

All the phrases which are in one of those 34 relations in the training file, whose probability to drop was 100% and also do not contain any question term, are removed from the selected summary sentence as described by Bhaskar and Bandyopadhyay (2010a). Now the remaining phrases are identified from the parser output of the sentence and search phrases that contain at least one question term then those phrases are selected. The selected phrases are combined together with the necessary phrases of the sentence to construct a new compressed sentence for the summary. The necessary phrases are identified from the parse tree of the sentence. The phrases with `nsubj` and the `VP` phrase related with the `nsubj` are some example of necessary phrases.

5.7 Sentence Selection for Summary

The compressed sentences for summary have been taken until the length restriction of the summary is reached, i.e. until the following condition holds:

$$\sum_i l_i S_i < L \quad (7)$$

where, l_i is the length (in no. of words) of compressed sentence i, S_i is a binary variable representing the selection of sentence i for the summary and L (=100 words) is the maximum summary length. After taking the top two sentences from all the clusters, if the length restriction L is not reached, then the second iteration is started similar to the first iteration and the next top most weighted sentence of each cluster are taken in order of the clusters and compressed. If after the completion of the second iteration same thing happens, then the next iteration will start in the same way and so on until the length restriction has been reached.

5.8 Sentence Ordering and Coherency

In this paper, we will propose a scheme of ordering; in that, it only takes into consideration the semantic closeness of information pieces (sentences) in deciding the ordering among them. First, the starting sentence is identified which is the sentence with lowest positional ranking among selected ones over the document set. Next for any source node (sentence) we find the summary node that is not already selected and have (correlation value) with the source node. This node will be selected as next source node in ordering. This ordering process will continue until the nodes are totally ordered. The above ordering scheme will order the nodes independent of the

[9] http://wordnet.princeton.edu/
[10] http://nlp.stanford.edu/software/lex-parser.shtml

actual ordering of nodes in the original document, thus eliminating the source bias due to individual writing style of human authors. Moreover, the scheme is logical because we select a sentence for position p at output summary, based on how coherent it is with the $(p-1)^{th}$ sentence. The main sentence's number has been taken as the sentence number of the fused sentence.

Now the generated multi-document summary is presented as the answer of the corresponding question.

6 Experiment Result

The proposed system has been tested on the data set of INEX QA track from 2011 to 2013.

6.1 Informative Content Evaluation

The Informative Content evaluation (SanJuan et al., 2011) by selecting relevant passages using simple log difference of equation 8 was used:

$$\sum \log\left(\frac{\max\left(P(t/reference),P(t/summary)\right)}{\min\left(P(t/reference),P(t/summary)\right)}\right) \quad (8)$$

The year wise evaluation scores of informativeness of all topics are shown in the figure 2.

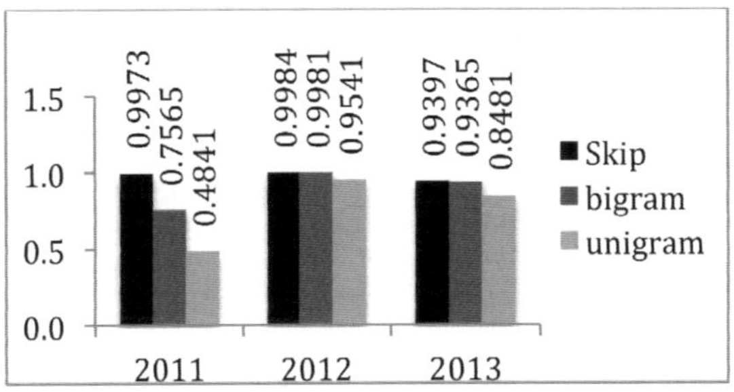

Figure 2. The evaluation scores of Informativeness by organizers of all topics

6.2 Readability Evaluation

For Readability evaluation (SanJuan et al., 2011) all passages in a summary have been evaluated according to Syntax (S), Soundness/Anaphora (A), Redundancy (R) and Relevancy/Trash (T). If a passage contains a syntactic problem (bad segmentation for example) then it has been marked as Syntax (S) error. If a passage contains an unsolved anaphora then it has been marked as Anaphora (A) error. If a passage contains any redundant information, i.e., an information that have already been given in a previous passage then it has been marked as Redundancy (R) error. If a passage does not make any sense in its context (i.e., after reading the previous passages) then these passages must be considered as trashed, and readability of following passages must be assessed as if these passages were not present, so they were marked as Trash (T). The readability evaluation scores are shown in the figure 3. Our relaxed metric i.e relevancy (T) score is the best score and strict metric i.e average of non redundancy (R), soundness (A) and syntax (S) score is the 4th best score among all the runs from all the participants of INEX 2011.

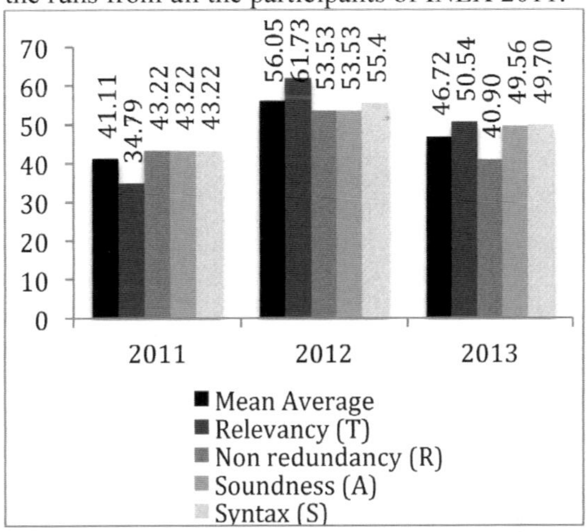

Figure 3. The evaluation scores of Readability Evaluation

7 Discussion

The tweet question answering system has been developed and tested on the data set of the Question Answering (QA) / Tweet Contextualization (TC) track of the INEX evaluation campaign from 2011 to 2013. The overall system has been evaluated using the evaluation metrics provided as part of the QA/TC track of INEX. Considering that the system is completely automatic and rule based and run on web documents, the evaluation results are satisfactory as readability scores are very high and in the relaxed metric we got the highest score of 43.22% in 2011, which will really encourage us to continue work on it in future.

Future works will be motivated towards improving the performance of the system by concentrating on co-reference and anaphora resolution, multi-word identification, para-phrasing, feature selection etc. In future, we will also try to use semantic similarity, which will increase our relevance score.

Acknowledgments

We acknowledge the support of the DeitY, MCIT, Govt. of India funded project "Development of Cross Lingual Information Access (CLIA) System Phase II".

References

Álvaro Rodrigo, Joaquın Pérez-Iglesias, Anselmo Peñas, Guillermo Garrido, and Lourdes Araujo. 2010. *A Question Answering System based on Information Retrieval and Validation*, In: CLEF 2010 Workshop on Multiple Language Question Answering (MLQA 2010), Padua, Italy.

Anastasios Tombros, and Mark Sanderson. 1998. *Advantages of Query Biased Summaries in Information Retrieval*. In: the 21st annual international ACM SIGIR conference on Research and development in information retrieval, pp. 2-10, ISBN:1-58113-015-5, ACM New York, USA.

Barry Schiffman, Kathleen McKeown, Ralph Grishman, and James Allan. 2007. *Question Answering using Integrated Information Retrieval and Information Extraction*. In: HLT/NAACL 07, pp. 532-539, Rochester, NY, USA.

Bidhan Chandra Pal, Pinaki Bhaskar, and Sivaji Bandyopadhyay. 2011. *A Rule Base Approach for Analysis of Comparative and Evaluative Question in Tourism Domain*. In: 6th Workshop on Knowledge and Reasoning for Answering Questions (KRAQ'11) in IJCNLP 2011, pp 29-37, Thailand.

Chin-Yew Lin, and Eduard Hovy. 2002. *From Single to Multidocument Summarization: A Prototype System and its Evaluation*. In: ACL, pp. 457-464.

Dragomir R. Radev, Hongyan Jing, Małgorzata Stys, Daniel Tam. 2004. *Centroid- based summarization of multiple documents*. In: Information Processing and Management. 40, pp. 919–938.

Eric SanJuan, V´eronique Moriceau, Xavier Tannier, Patrice Bellot, and Josiane Mothe. 2011. *Overview of the INEX 2011 Question Answering Track (QA@INEX)*. In: Focused Retrieval of Content and Structure, 10th International Workshop of the Initiative for the Evaluation of XML Retrieval (INEX), Geva, S., Kamps, J., Schenkel, R. (Eds.). Lecture Notes in Computer Sc., Springer.

Farshad Kyoomarsi, Hamid Khosravi, Esfandiar Eslami, and Pooya Khosravyan Dehkordy. 2008. *Optimizing Text Summarization Based on Fuzzy Logic*. In: Seventh IEEE/ACIS International Conference on Computer and Information Science, pp. 347--352. IEEE, University of Shahid Bahonar Kerman, UK.

Gu¨ne¸s Erkan, and Dragomir R. Radev. 2004. *LexRank: Graph-based Centrality as Salience in Text Summarization*. In: Journal of Artificial Intelligence Research, vol. 22, pp. 457-479.

Hilda Hardy, Nobuyuki Shimizu, Tomek Strzalkowski, Liu Ting, G. Bowden Wise, and Xinyang Zhang. 2002. *Cross-document summarization by concept classification*. In: the 25th annual international ACM SIGIR conference on Research and development in information retrieval, pp. 121-128, ISBN: 1-58113-561-0, ACM New York, NY, USA.

Karel Jezek, and Josef Steinberger. 2008. *Automatic Text summarization*. In: Snasel, V. (ed.) Znalosti 2008. ISBN 978-80-227-2827-0, pp.1--12. FIIT STU Brarislava, Ustav Informatiky a softveroveho inzinierstva.

Partha Pakray, Pinaki Bhaskar, Santanu Pal, Dipankar Das, Sivaji Bandyopadhyay, and Alexander Gelbukh. 2010. *JU_CSE_TE: System Description QA@CLEF 2010 – ResPubliQA*. In: CLEF 2010 Workshop on Multiple Language Question Answering (MLQA 2010), Padua, Italy.

Partha Pakray, Pinaki Bhaskar, Somnath Banerjee, Bidhan Chandra Pal, Alexander Gelbukh, and Sivaji Bandyopadhyay. 2011. *A Hybrid Question Answering System based on Information Retrieval and Answer Validation*. In: Question Answering for Machine Reading Evaluation (QA4MRE) at CLEF 2011, Amsterdam.

Pinaki Bhaskar, and Sivaji Bandyopadhyay. 2010a. *A Query Focused Multi Document Automatic Summarization*. In: the 24th Pacific Asia Conference on Language, Information and Computation (PACLIC 24), pp 545-554, Tohoku University, Sendai, Japan.

Pinaki Bhaskar, and Sivaji Bandyopadhyay. 2010b. *A Query Focused Automatic Multi Document Summarizer*. In: the International Conference on Natural Language Processing (ICON), pp. 241--250. IIT, Kharagpur, India.

Pinaki Bhaskar, Amitava Das, Partha Pakray, and Sivaji Bandyopadhyay. 2010c. *Theme Based English and Bengali Ad-hoc Monolingual Information Retrieval in FIRE 2010*. In: the Forum for Information Retrieval Evaluation (FIRE) – 2010, Gandhinagar, India.

Pinaki Bhaskar, Somnath Banerjee, Snehasis Neogi, and Sivaji Bandyopadhyay. 2012a. *A Hybrid QA System with Focused IR and Automatic Summarization for INEX 2011*. In: Geva, S., Kamps, J., Schenkel, R.(eds.): Focused Retrieval of Content and Structure: 10th International Workshop of the Initiative for the Evaluation of XML Retrieval, INEX 2011. Lecture Notes in Computer Science, vol. 7424. Springer Verlag, Berlin, Heidelberg.

Pinaki Bhaskar, and Sivaji Bandyopadhyay. 2012b. *Answer Extraction of Comparative and Evaluative Question in Tourism Domain*. In: International Journal of Computer Science and Information Technologies (IJCSIT), ISSN: 0975-9646, Vol. 3, Issue 4, pp. 4610 – 4616.

Pinaki Bhaskar, and Sivaji Bandyopadhyay. 2012c. *Cross Lingual Query Dependent Snippet Genera-*

tion. In: International Journal of Computer Science and Information Technologies (IJCSIT), ISSN: 0975-9646, Vol. 3, Issue 4, pp. 4603 – 4609.

Pinaki Bhaskar, and Sivaji Bandyopadhyay. 2012d. *Language Independent Query Focused Snippet Generation*. In: T. Catarci et al. (Eds.): Information Access Evaluation. Multilinguality, Multimodality, and Visual Analytics: Third International Conference of the CLEF Initiative, CLEF 2012, Rome, Italy, Proceedings, Lecture Notes in Computer Science Volume 7488, pp 138-140, DOI 10.1007/978-3-642-33247-0_16, ISBN 978-3-642-33246-3, ISSN 0302-9743, Springer Verlag, Berlin, Heidelberg, Germany.

Pinaki Bhaskar, Somnath Banerjee, and Sivaji Bandyopadhyay. 2012e. *A Hybrid Tweet Contextualization System using IR and Summarization*. In: the Initiative for the Evaluation of XML Retrieval, INEX 2012 at Conference and Labs of the Evaluation Forum (CLEF) 2012, Pamela Forner, Jussi Karlgren, Christa Womser-Hacker (Eds.): CLEF 2012 Evaluation Labs and Workshop, pp. 164-175, ISBN 978-88-904810-3-1, ISSN 2038-4963, Rome, Italy.

Pinaki Bhaskar, Partha Pakray, Somnath Banerjee, Samadrita Banerjee, Sivaji Bandyopadhyay, and Alexander Gelbukh. 2012f. *Question Answering System for QA4MRE@CLEF 2012*. In: Question Answering for Machine Reading Evaluation (QA4MRE) at Conference and Labs of the Evaluation Forum (CLEF) 2012, Rome, Italy.

Pinaki Bhaskar, Bidhan Chandra Pal, and Sivaji Bandyopadhyay. 2012g. *Comparative & Evaluative QA System in Tourism Domain*. In: Meghanathan, N., Wozniak, M.(eds.): Computational Science, Engineering and Information Technology: the Second International Conference on Computational Science, Engineering and Informationa Technology (CCSEIT-2012), ACM International Conference Proceeding Series. ICPS, pp. 454-460, Coimbatore, India.

Pinaki Bhaskar, Kishorjit Nongmeikapam, and Sivaji Bandyopadhyay. 2012h. *Keyphrase Extraction in Scientific Articles: A Supervised Approach*. In: 24th International Conference on Computational Linguistics (Coling 2012), pp. 17-24, IIT, Bombay, Mumbai, India.

Pinaki Bhaskar 2013a. *A Query Focused Language Independent Multi-document Summarization*. Jian, A. (Eds.), ISBN 978-3-8484-0089-8, LAMBERT Academic Publishing, Saarbrücken, Germany.

Pinaki Bhaskar 2013b. *Multi-document Summarization using Automatic Key-phrase Extraction*. In: Student Research Workshop in the Recent Advances in Natural Language Processing (RANLP), Hissar, Bulgaria.

Pinaki Bhaskar, Somnath Banerjee, and Sivaji Bandyopadhyay. 2013c. *Tweet Contextualization (Answering Tweet Question) – the Role of Multi-document Summarization*. In: the Initiative for the Evaluation of XML Retrieval, INEX 2013 at CLEF 2013 Conference and Labs of the Evaluation Forum, Valencia, Spain.

Pinaki Bhaskar, Somnath Banerjee, Partha Pakray, Samadrita Banerjee, Sivaji Bandyopadhyay, and Alexander Gelbukh. 2013d. *A Hybrid Question Answering System for Multiple Choice Question (MCQ)*. In: Question Answering for Machine Reading Evaluation (QA4MRE) at CLEF 2013 Conference and Labs of the Evaluation Forum, Valencia, Spain.

Sibabrata Paladhi, and Sivaji Bandyopadhyay. 2008. *A Document Graph Based Query Focused Multi-Document Summarizer*. In: the 2nd International Workshop on Cross Lingual Information Access (CLIA), pp. 55-62.

Sivaji Bandyopadhyay, Amitava Das, and Pinaki Bhaskar. 2008. *English Bengali Ad-hoc Monolingual Information Retrieval Task Result at FIRE 2008*. In: the Forum for Information Retrieval Evaluation (FIRE) - 2008, Kolkata, India.

Somnath Banerjee, Partha Pakray, Pinaki Bhaskar, and Sivaji Bandyopadhyay, Alexander Gelbukh. 2013. *Multiple Choice Question (MCQ) Answering System for Entrance Examination*. In: Question Answering for Machine Reading Evaluation (QA4MRE) at CLEF 2013 Conference and Labs of the Evaluation Forum, Valencia, Spain.

Udo Hahn, and Martin Romacker. 2001. *The SYNDIKATE text Knowledge base generator*. In: the first International conference on Human language technology research, Association for Computational Linguistics , ACM, Morristown, NJ, USA.

Utsab Barman, Pintu Lohar, Pinaki Bhaskar, and Sivaji Bandyopadhyay. 2012. *Ad-hoc Information Retrieval focused on Wikipedia based Query Expansion and Entropy Based Ranking*. In: the Forum for Information Retrieval Evaluation (FIRE) – 2012, Kolkata, India.

Multi-Document Summarization using Automatic Key-Phrase Extraction

Pinaki Bhaskar
Department of Computer Science & Engineering,
Jadavpur University, Kolkata – 700032, India
pinaki.bhaskar@gmail.com

Abstract

The development of a multi-document summarizer using automatic key-phrase extraction has been described. This summarizer has two main parts; first part is automatic extraction of Key-phrases from the documents and second part is automatic generation of a multi-document summary based on the extracted key-phrases. The CRF based Automatic Key-phrase extraction system has been used here. A document graph-based topic/query focused automatic multi-document summarizer is used for summarization where extracted key-phrases are used as topic. The summarizer has been tested on the standard TAC 2008 test data sets of the Update Summarization Track. Evaluation using the ROUGE-1.5.5 tool has resulted in ROUGE-2 and ROUGE–SU-4 scores of 0.10548 and 0.13582 respectively.

1 Introduction

Text Summarization, as the process of identifying the most salient information in a document or set of documents (for multi document summarization) and conveying it in less space, became an active field of research in both Information Retrieval (IR) and Natural Language Processing (NLP) communities. Summarization shares some basic techniques with indexing as both are concerned with identification of the essence of a document. Also, high quality summarization requires sophisticated NLP techniques in order to deal with various Parts Of Speech (POS) taxonomy and inherent subjectivity. Typically, one may distinguish various types of summarizers.

Multi document summarization requires creating a short summary from a set of documents, which concentrate on the same topic. Sometimes an additional query is also given to specify the information need of the summary. Generally, an effective summary should be relevant, concise and fluent. It means that the summary should cover the most important concepts in the original document set, contains less redundant information and should be well organized.

In this paper, we proposes a multi-document summarizer, based on key-phrase extraction, clustering technique and sentence fusion. Unlike traditional extraction based summarizers, which do not take into consideration the inherent structure of the document, our system will add structure to documents in the form of graph. During initial preprocessing, text fragments are identified from the documents, which constitute the nodes of the graph. Edges are defined as the correlation measure between nodes of the graph. We define our text fragments as sentence.

First, during preprocessing stage it performs some document-based tasks like identifying seed summary nodes and constructing graph over them. Then key-phrase extraction module extracts the key-phrases form the documents and it performs key-phrase search over the cluster to find a sentence identifying relevant phrases. With the relevant phrases, the new compressed sentence has been constructed and then fused for summary. The performance of the system depends much on the identification of relevant phrases and compression of the sentences where the previous one again highly depends on the key-phrase extraction module.

Although, we have presented all the examples in the current discussion for English language only, we argue that our system can be adapted to work on other language (i.e. Hindi, Bengali etc.) with some minor addition in the system like incorporating language dependent stop word list, the stemmer and the parser for the language.

2 Related Work

Currently, most successful multi-document summarization systems follow the extractive summarization framework. These systems first rank all the sentences in the original document set and then select the most salient sentences to compose summaries for a good coverage of the concepts. For the purpose of creating more concise and fluent summaries, some intensive post-processing approaches are also appended on the extracted sentences. For example, redundancy removal (Carbonell and Goldstein, 1998) and sentence compression (Knight and Marcu, 2000) approaches are used to make the summary more concise. Sentence re-ordering approaches (Barzilay et al., 2002) are used to make the summary more fluent. In most systems, these approaches are treated as independent steps. A sequential process is usually adopted in their implementation, applying the various approaches one after another.

A lot of research work has been done in the domain of multi-document summarization (both query dependent and independent). MEAD (Radev et al., 2004) is a centroid based multi document summarizer, which generates summaries using cluster centroids produced by topic detection and tracking system. NeATS (Lin and Hovy, 2002) selects important content using sentence position, term frequency, topic signature and term clustering. XDoX (Hardy et al., 2002) identifies the most salient themes within the document set by passage clustering and then composes an extraction summary, which reflects these main themes.

Graph-based methods have been proposed for generating query independent summaries. Websumm (Mani and Bloedorn, 2000) uses a graph-connectivity model to identify salient information. Zhang et al. (2004) proposed the methodology of correlated summarization for multiple news articles. In the domain of single document summarization a system for query-specific document summarization has been proposed (Varadarajan and Hristidis, 2006) based on the concept of document graph. A document graph-based query focused multi-document summarization system is described by Bhaskar and Bandyopadhyay, (2010a and 2010b). In the present work, the same summarization approach has been followed. As this summarizer is query independent, it extract the key-phrases and then the extracted key-phrases are used as query or keywords.

Works on identification of key-phrase using noun phrase are reported in (Barker and Cornacchia, 2000). Noun phrases are extracted from a text using a base noun phrase skimmer and an off-the-shelf online dictionary. Key-phrase Extraction Algorithm (KEA) was proposed in order to automatically extract key-phrase (Witten et al., 1999). The supervised learning methodologies have also been reported (Frank et al, 1999). Some works have been done for automatic keywords extraction using CRF technique. A comparative study on the performance of the six keyword extraction models, i.e., CRF, SVM, MLR, Logit, BaseLine1 and BaseLine2 has been reported in (Chengzhi et al., 2008). The study shows that CRF based system outperforms SVM based system. Bhaskar and Bandyopadhyay (2012) have developed a supervised system for automatic extraction of Key-phrases using Conditional Random Fields (CRF).

First a key-phrase extraction system has been developed based on the Bhaskar and Bandyopadhyay's (2012) method. Then a graph-based summarization system has been developed, where the key-phrase extraction system has been integrated for extraction key-phrases from document, which are serves as query or topic during summary generation.

3 Document-Based Process

3.1 Graph-Based Clustered Model

The proposed graph-based multi-document summarization method consists of following steps:

(1) The document set $D = \{d_1, d_2, \ldots d_n\}$ is processed to extract text fragments, which are sentences in this system as it has been discussed earlier. Let for a document d_i, the sentences are $\{s_{i1}, s_{i2}, \ldots s_{im}\}$. Each text fragment becomes a node of the graph.

(2) Next, edges are created between nodes across the documents where edge score represents the degree of correlation between inter-documents nodes.

(3) Seed nodes are extracted which identify the relevant sentences within D and a search graph is built to reflect the semantic relationship between the nodes.

(4) At query time, each node is assigned a key-phrase dependent score and the search graph is expanded.

(5) A key-phrase dependent multi-document summary is generated from the search graph.

Each sentence is represented as a node in the graph. The text in each document is split into sentences and each sentence is represented with a vector of constituent words. If pair of related document is considered, then the inter document graph can be represented as a set of nodes in the form of bipartite graph. The edges connect two nodes corresponding to sentences from different documents.

3.2 Construct the Edge and Calculate Edge Score

The similarity between two nodes is expressed as the edge weight of the bipartite graph. Two nodes are related if they share common words (except stop words) and the degree of relationship can be measured by equation 1 adapting some traditional IR formula (Varadarajan and Hristidis, 2006).

$$\text{Edge\_Score} = \frac{\sum_{w \in (t(u) \cap t(v))} ((tf(t(u), w) + tf(t(v), w)) \times idf(w))}{size(t(u)) + size(t(v))} \quad (1)$$

where, $tf(d, w)$ is number of occurrence of w in d, $idf(w)$ is the inverse of the number of documents containing w, and $size(d)$ is the size of the documents in words. Actually for a particular node, total edge score is defined as the sum of scores of all out going edges from that node. The nodes with higher total edge scores than some predefined threshold are included as seed nodes.

But the challenge for multi-document summarization is that the information stored in different documents inevitably overlap with each other. So, before inclusion of a particular node (sentence), it has to be checked whether it is being repeated or not. Two sentences are said to be similar if they share for example, 70% words in common.

Construction of Search Graph: After identification of seed/topic nodes a search graph is constructed. For nodes, pertaining to different documents, edge scores are already calculated, but for intra document nodes, edge scores are calculated in the similar fashion as said earlier. Since, highly dense graph leads to higher search / execution time, only the edges having edge scores well above the threshold value might be considered.

3.3 Identification of Sub-topics through Markov Clustering

In this section, we will discuss the process to identify shared subtopics from related multi source documents. We already discussed that the subtopics shared by different news articles on same event form natural (separate) clusters of sentences when they are represented using document graph. We use Markov principle of graph clustering to identify those clusters from the document graph as described by Bhaskar and Bandyopadhyay (2010b).

The construction of query independent part of the Markov clusters completes the document-based processing phase of the system.

4 Key-Phrase Extraction

A CRF based key-phrase extraction system as described by Bhaskar et al. (2012) is used to extract key-phrases from the documents.

4.1 Features Identification for the System

Selection of features is important in CRF. Features used in the system are,

F = {Dependency, POS tag(s), Chunk, NE, TF, Title, Body, Stem of word, $W_{i-m}, \ldots, W_{i-1}, W_i, W_{i+1}, \ldots, W_{i-n}$ ***}.***

The features are detailed as follows:

i) **Dependency parsing:** Some of the key-phrases are multiword. So relationship of verb with subject or object is to be identified through dependency parsing and thus used as a feature.

ii) **POS feature:** The Part of Speech (POS) tags of the preceding word, the current word and the following word are used as a feature in order to know the POS combination of a key-phrase.

iii) **Chunking:** Chunking is done to mark the Noun phrases and the Verb phrases since much of the key-phrases are noun phrases.

iv) **Named Entity (NE):** The Named Entity (NE) tag of the preceding word, the current word and the following word are used as a feature in order to know the named entity combination of a key-phrase.

v) **Term frequency (TF) range:** The maximum value of the term frequency (max_TF) is divided into five equal sizes *(size_of_range)* and each of the term frequency values is mapped to the appropriate range (0 to 4). The term frequency range value is used as a feature. i.e.

$$size\_of\_range = \frac{\max\_TF}{5} \quad (2)$$

Thus Table 1 shows the range representation. This is done to have uniform values for the term frequency feature instead of random and scattered values.

Class	Range
0 to size_of_range	*0*
*size_of_range + 1 to 2*size_of_range*	*1*
*2*size_of_range + 1 to 3*size_of_range*	*2*
*3*size_of_range + 1 to 4*size_of_range*	*3*
*4*size_of_range + 1 to 5*size_of_range*	*4*

Table 1: Term frequency (TF) range

vi) **Word in Title:** Every word is marked with T if found in the title else O to mark other. The title word feature is useful because the words in title have a high chance to be a key-phrase.

vii) **Word in Body:** Every word is marked with B if found in the body of the text else O to mark other. It is a useful feature because words present in the body of the text are distinguished from other words in the document.

viii) **Stemming:** The Porter Stemmer algorithm is used to stem every word and the output stem for each word is used as a feature. This is because words in key-phrases can appear in different inflected forms.

ix) **Context word feature:** The preceding and the following word of the current word are considered as context feature since key-phrases can be a group of words.

4.2 Generating Feature File for CRF

The features used in the key-phrase extraction system are identified in the following ways.

Step 1: The dependency parsing is done by the Stanford Parser[1]. The output of the parser is modified by making the word and the associated tags for every word appearing in a line.

Step 2: The same output is used for chunking and for every word it identifies whether the word is a part of a noun phrase or a verb phrase.

Step 3: The Stanford POS Tagger[2] is used for POS tagging of the documents.

Step 4: The term frequency (*TF*) range is identified as defined before.

Step 5: Using the algorithms described by Bhaskar et al. (2012), every word is marked as *T* or *O* for the title word feature and marked as *B* or *O* for the body word feature.

Step 6: The Porter Stemming Algorithm[3] is used to identify the stem of every word that is used as another feature.

Step 7: In the training data with the combined key-phrases, the words that begin a key-phrase are marked with *B-KP* and words that are present intermediate in a key-phrase are marked as *I-KP*. All other words are marked as *O*. But for test data only *O* is marked in this column.

4.3 Training the CRF and Extracting Key-Phrases

A template file was created in order to train the system using the feature file generated. After training the C++ based CRF++ 0.53 package[4], a model file is produced. The model file is required to run the system. The feature file is again created from the document set. After running this files into the system, the system produce the output file with the key-phrases marked with *B-KP* and *I-KP*. All the Key-phrases are extracted from the output file and stemmed using Porter Stemmer. Now, these extracted key-phrases are used as query or topic to generate the summary.

5 Key-Phrase Dependent Process

After key-phrase extraction, first the nodes of the already constructed search graph are given a key-phrase dependent score. With the combined scores of key-phrase independent score and key-phrase dependent score, clusters are reordered and relevant sentences are collected from each cluster in order. Then each collected sentence has processed and compressed removing the unimportant phrases. After that the compressed sentences are used to construct the summary.

5.1 Recalculate the Cluster Score

There are two basic components in the sentence weight like key-phrases dependent scores and synonyms of key-phrases dependent scores. We collect the list of synonyms of the each word in the key-phrases from the WordNet 3.0[5]. The term dependent score (both for key-phrases and synonyms) are calculated using equation 2.

$$w = \sum_{t=1}^{n_t}(n_t - t + 1)\left(\sum_p \left(1 - \frac{f_p^{t}-1}{N_i}\right)\right) \times b \quad (3)$$

where, w is the term dependent score of the sentence i, t is the no. of the term, n_t is the total

[1] http://nlp.stanford.edu/software/lex-parser.shtml
[2] http://nlp.stanford.edu/software/tagger.shtml

[3] http://tartarus.org/~martin/PorterStemmer/
[4] http://crfpp.sourceforge.net/
[5] http://wordnet.princeton.edu/

no. of term, f_p^t is the possession of the word which was matched with the term t in the sentence i, N_s is the total no. of words in sentence i and b is boost factor of the term, which is 2 or 1 for key-phrases and synonyms respectively. These two components are added to get the final weight of a sentence.

5.2 Recalculate the Cluster Ranking

We start by defining a function that attributes values to the sentences as well as to the clusters. We refer to sentences indexed by i and key-phrases indexed by l. We want to maximize the number of key-phrase covered by a selection of sentences:

$$maximize \sum_l w_l^k k_l \qquad (4)$$

where, w_l^k is the weight of key-phrase l in the sentence i and k_l is a binary variable indicating the presence of that key-phrase in the cluster.

We also take the selection over the synonyms of the key-phrases. The general sets of synonyms are indexed by s. So we also want to maximize the number of synonyms covered by a selection of sentences using similar calculation like for key-phrase using equation 2.

So, the key-phrase dependent score of a cluster is the weighted sum of the key-phrases it contains. If clusters are indexed by x, the key-phrase dependent score of the cluster x is:

$$c_x^k = \sum_{i=x_1}^{x_n} \sum_l w_l^k k_l + \sum_{i=x_1}^{x_n} \sum_s w_s^s k_s \qquad (5)$$

where, c_x^k is the key-phrase dependent score of the cluster x, x_1 is the starting sentence number and x_n is the ending sentence number of the cluster x. Now, the new recalculated combined score of cluster x is:

$$c_x = c_x^g + c_x^k \qquad (6)$$

where, c_x is the new score of the cluster x and c_x^g is the key-phrase independent cluster score in the graph of cluster x. Now, all the clusters are ranked with their new score c_x.

5.3 Retrieve Sentences for Summary

Get the highest weighted two sentences of each cluster, by the following equation:

$$\max\left(\sum_l w_l^k k_l + \sum_s w_s^s k_s\right) \forall i, x_1 \le i \le x_n \qquad (7)$$

where, x_1 is the first sentence and x_n is the nth i.e. last sentence of a cluster.

The highest weighted two sentences are taken from each cluster in order one by one. The original sentences in the documents are generally very lengthy to place in the summary. So, we are actually interested in a selection over phrases of sentence. After getting the top two sentences of a cluster, they are split into multiple phrases. The Stanford Parser[6] is used to parse the sentences and get the phrases of the sentence.

5.4 Sentence Compression

All the phrases which are in one of those 34 relations in the training file, whose probability to drop was 100% and also do not contain any key-phrase, are removed from the selected summary sentence as described by Bhaskar and Bandyopadhyay (2010a). Now the remaining phrases are identified from the parser output of the sentence and search phrases that contain at least one key-phrase then those phrases are selected. The selected phrases are combined together with the necessary phrases of the sentence to construct a new compressed sentence for the summary. The necessary phrases are identified from the parse tree of the sentence. The phrases with `nsubj` and the `VP` phrase related with the `nsubj` are some example of necessary phrases.

5.5 Sentence Selection for Summary

The compressed sentences for summary have been taken until the length restriction of the summary is reached, i.e. until the following condition holds:

$$\sum_i l_i S_i < L \qquad (8)$$

where, l_i is the length (in no. of words) of compressed sentence i, S_i is a binary variable representing the selection of sentence i for the summary and L (=100 words) is the maximum summary length. After taking the top two sentences from all the clusters, if the length restriction L is not reached, then the second iteration is started similar to the first iteration and the next top most weighted sentence of each cluster are taken in order of the clusters and compressed. If after the completion of the second iteration same thing happens, then the next iteration will start in the same way and so on until the length restriction has been reached.

6 Sentence Ordering and Coherency

In this paper, we will propose a scheme of ordering which is different from the above two approaches in that, it only takes into consideration the semantic closeness of information pieces (sentences) in deciding the ordering among them. First, the starting sentence is identified which is the sentence with lowest positional ranking among selected ones over the document set. Next for any source node (sentence) we find the sum-

[6] http://nlp.stanford.edu/software/lex-parser.shtml

mary node that is not already selected and have (correlation value) with the source node. This node will be selected as next source node in ordering. This ordering process will continue until the nodes are totally ordered. The above ordering scheme will order the nodes independent of the actual ordering of nodes in the original document, thus eliminating the source bias due to individual writing style of human authors. Moreover, the scheme is logical because we select a sentence for position p at output summary, based on how coherent it is with the $(p\text{-}1)^{th}$ sentence.

7 Evaluation

We evaluate our summaries by ROUGE[7], an automatic evaluation tool. We have run our system on Text Analysis Conference (TAC, formerly DUC, conducted by NIST) 2008 Update Summarization track's data sets[8]. This data set contains 48 sets and each set has two subsets of 10 documents, i.e. there are 960 documents. The evaluation data set has 4 model summaries for each document set, i.e. 8 model summaries for each set. We have evaluated our output summaries on those model summaries using ROUGE-1.5.5. The baseline scores provided by the organizer were 0.058 and 0.093 of ROUGE-2 and ROUGE-SU4 respectively. The system's score is 0.10548 and 0.13582 respectively. All the results are shown in table 2. The comparison of ROUGE-2 and ROUGE-SU4 among the proposed system, the system developed by Bhaskar and Bandyopadhyay (2010b), the best system of TAC 2008 Update Summarization track and the baseline system of TAC 2008 Update Summarization track are also shown in table 2.

8 Conclusion and Future Work

In this work we present a graph-based approach for multi document summarization system using automatic key-phrase extraction. The experimental results suggest that our algorithm is effective. It can be used in web based system like search engine or QA system, where offline summary of multiple document on same topic can be pre-generated and will be used during online phase, which will reduce many burden on online modules. The proposed algorithm can be improved to handle more noisy WEB articles or work on other domain too.

As the topic or query are given to the system along with the document sets, it's has been extracted automatically as key-phrases. The key-phrase extraction module is not 100% accurate and sometimes extracts some extra or noisy phrases as key-phrase. Hence the performance of the summarizer slightly decreases. But it is very useful where the topic or query is not available and we still need the summary from documents.

The important aspect is that our system can be tuned to generate summary with custom size specified by users. Lastly, it is shown that our system can generate summary for other non-English documents also if some simple resources of the language like stemmer and parser are available.

Acknowledgments

We acknowledge the support of the DeitY, MCIT, Govt. of India funded project "Development of Cross Lingual Information Access (CLIA) System Phase II".

ROUGE Evaluation	**Average_R**				Average_P		Average_F	
	Proposed System	Bhaskar et al. (2010b)'s System	Top score of TAC 2008	Baseline of TAC 2008	**Proposed System**	Bhaskar et al. (2010b)'s System	**Proposed System**	Bhaskar et al. (2010b)'s System
ROUGE-1	0.50626	0.53291	-	-	0.48655	0.51216	0.49512	0.52118
ROUGE-2	**0.10548**	**0.11103**	**0.111**	**0.058**	**0.09248**	**0.09735**	**0.09491**	**0.09991**
ROUGE-3	0.03301	0.03475	-	-	0.03061	0.03223	0.03169	0.03336
ROUGE-4	0.01524	0.01604	-	-	0.01397	0.01471	0.01454	0.01530
ROUGE-L	0.37204	0.39162	-	-	0.35727	0.37607	0.36368	0.38282
ROUGE-W-1.2	0.12407	0.13060	-	-	0.21860	0.23011	0.16027	0.16870
ROUGE- SU4	**0.13582**	**0.14297**	**0.143**	**0.093**	**0.12693**	**0.13361**	**0.12954**	**0.13636**

Table 2: Evaluation scores of ROUGE

[7] http://berouge.com/default.aspx

[8] http://www.nist.gov/tac/data/index.html

References

Chengzhi ZHANG, Huilin WANG, Yao LIU, Dan WU, Yi LIAO, and Bo WANG. 2008. *Automatic keyword Extraction from Documents Using Conditional Random Fields*. Journal of Computational Information Systems, 4:3, pp. 1169-1180.

Chin-Yew Lin, and Eduard Hovy. 2002. *From Single to Multidocument Summarization: A Prototype System and its Evaluation*. ACL, pp. 457-464.

Dragomir R. Radev, Hongyan Jing, Małgorzata Stys, Daniel Tam. 2004. *Centroid- based summarization of multiple documents*. J. Information Processing and Management. 40, 919–938

Ernesto D'Avanzo, and Bernardo Magnini. 2005. *A Keyphrase-Based Approach to Summarization:the LAKE System at DUC-2005*. In: Proc. of Document Understanding Conferences.

Eibe Frank, Gordon Paynter, Ian Witten, Carl Gutwin, and Craig Nevill-Manning. 1999. *Domain-specific keyphrase extraction*. In: the Sixteenth International Joint Conference on Artificial Intelligence (IJCAI-99), pp. 668-673, California.

Hilda Hardy, Nobuyuki Shimizu, Tomek Strzalkowski, Liu Ting, G. Bowden Wise, and Xinyang Zhang. 2002. *Cross-document summarization by concept classification*. In: the 25th annual international ACM SIGIR conference on Research and development in information retrieval, pp. 121-128, ISBN: 1-58113-561-0, ACM New York, NY, USA.

Ian H. Witten, Gordon W. Paynter, Eibe Frank, Carl Gutwin, and Craig G. Nevill-Manning. 1999. *KEA:Practical Automtic Key phrase Extraction*. In: the fourth ACM conference on Digital libraries, pp. 254-256, ISBN:1-58113-145-3, ACM New York, NY, USA.

Inderjeet Mani, and Eric Bloedorn. 1999. *Summarizing Similarities and Differences Among Related Documents*. In: Information Retrieval, Volume 1, Issue 1-2, pp. 35-67, Kluwer Academic Publishers Hingham, MA, USA.

Jaime Carbonell, and Jade Goldstein. 1998. *The Use of MMR, Diversity-based Reranking for Reordering Documents and Producing Summaries*. In: the 21st annual international ACM SIGIR conference on Research and development in information retrieval, ISBN:1-58113-015-5, pp. 335-336, NY, USA.

John D. Lafferty, Andrew McCallum, and Fernando C. N. Pereira. 2001. *Conditional Random Fields: Probabilistic Models for Segmenting and Labeling Sequence Data*. In: Proc. of the 18th International Conference on Machine Learning (ICML01), pp. 282-289, ISBN: 1-55860-778-1, Williamstown, MA, USA.

Ken Barker, and Nadia Cornacchia. 2000. *Using noun phrase heads to extract document keyphrases*. In: Proc. of the 13th Biennial Conference of the Canadian Society on Computational Studies of Intelligence: Advances in Artificial Intelligence. Canada. pp. 40-52.

Kevin Knight, and Daniel Marcu. 2000. *Statistics-based summarization --- step one: Sentence compression*. In: the American Association for Artificial Intelligence Conference (AAAI-2000), pp. 703--710.

Martin Porter. 1980. *An algorithm for suffix stripping*. Program, 14(3), 130–137.

Peter Turney. 1999. *Learning to Extract Keyphrases from Text*. National Research Council, Institute for Information Technology, Technical Report ERB-1057. (NRC \#41622).

Pinaki Bhaskar, and Sivaji Bandyopadhyay. 2010a. *A Query Focused Multi Document Automatic Summarization*. In: the 24th Pacific Asia Conference on Language, Information and Computation (PACLIC 24), pp 545-554, Tohoku University, Sendai, Japan.

Pinaki Bhaskar, and Sivaji Bandyopadhyay. 2010b. *A Query Focused Automatic Multi Document Summarizer*. In: the International Conference on Natural Language Processing (ICON), pp. 241--250. IIT, Kharagpur, India.

Pinaki Bhaskar, Somnath Banerjee, Snehasis Neogi, and Sivaji Bandyopadhyay. 2012a. *A Hybrid QA System with Focused IR and Automatic Summarization for INEX 2011*. In: Geva, S., Kamps, J., Schenkel, R.(eds.): Focused Retrieval of Content and Structure: 10th International Workshop of the Initiative for the Evaluation of XML Retrieval, INEX 2011. Lecture Notes in Computer Science, vol. 7424. Springer Verlag, Berlin, Heidelberg.

Pinaki Bhaskar, and Sivaji Bandyopadhyay. 2012b. *Cross Lingual Query Dependent Snippet Generation*. In: International Journal of Computer Science and Information Technologies (IJCSIT), ISSN: 0975-9646, Vol. 3, Issue 4, pp. 4603 – 4609.

Pinaki Bhaskar, and Sivaji Bandyopadhyay. 2012c. *Language Independent Query Focused Snippet Generation*. In: T. Catarci et al. (Eds.): Information Access Evaluation. Multilinguality, Multimodality, and Visual Analytics: Third International Conference of the CLEF Initiative, CLEF 2012, Rome, Italy, Proceedings, Lecture Notes in Computer Science Volume 7488, pp 138-140, DOI 10.1007/978-3-642-33247-0_16, ISBN 978-3-642-33246-3, ISSN 0302-9743, Springer Verlag, Berlin, Heidelberg, Germany.

Pinaki Bhaskar, Somnath Banerjee, and Sivaji Bandyopadhyay. 2012d. *A Hybrid Tweet Contextualization System using IR and Summarization*. In: the

Initiative for the Evaluation of XML Retrieval, INEX 2012 at Conference and Labs of the Evaluation Forum (CLEF) 2012, Pamela Forner, Jussi Karlgren, Christa Womser-Hacker (Eds.): CLEF 2012 Evaluation Labs and Workshop, pp. 164-175, ISBN 978-88-904810-3-1, ISSN 2038-4963, Rome, Italy.

Pinaki Bhaskar, Kishorjit Nongmeikapam, and Sivaji Bandyopadhyay. 2012e. *Keyphrase Extraction in Scientific Articles: A Supervised Approach*. In: the proceedings of 24th International Conference on Computational Linguastics (Coling 2012), pp. 17-24, India.

Pinaki Bhaskar. 2013a. *A Query Focused Language Independent Multi-document Summarization*. Jian, A. (Eds.), ISBN 978-3-8484-0089-8, LAMBERT Academic Publishing, Saarbrücken, Germany.

Pinaki Bhaskar. 2013b. *Answering Questions from Multiple Documents – the Role of Multi-document Summarization*. In: Student Research Workshop in the Recent Advances in Natural Language Processing (RANLP), Hissar, Bulgaria.

Pinaki Bhaskar, Somnath Banerjee, and Sivaji Bandyopadhyay. 2013c. *Tweet Contextualization (Answering Tweet Question) – the Role of Multi-document Summarization*. In: the Initiative for the Evaluation of XML Retrieval, INEX 2013 at CLEF 2013 Conference and Labs of the Evaluation Forum, Valencia, Spain.

Ramakrishna Varadarajan, and Vagelis Hristidis. 2006. *A system for query specific document summarization*. In: the 15th ACM international conference on Information and knowledge management, pp. 622-631, ISBN: 1-59593-433-2, ACM New York, NY, USA.

Regina Barzilay, Noemie Elhadad, and Kathleen R. McKeown. 2002. *Inferring strategies for sentence ordering in multidocument news summarization*, In: Artificial Intelligence Research. 17, pp. 35—55

Sibabrata Paladhi, and Sivaji Bandyopadhyay. 2008. *A Document Graph Based Query Focused Multi-Document Summarizer*. In: the 2nd International Workshop on Cross Lingual Information Access (CLIA), pp. 55-62

Stijn Van Dongen. 2000a. *A stochastic uncoupling process for graphs*. Report No. INS- R0011, Centre for Mathematics and Computer Science(CWI), Amsterdam.

Stijn Van Dongen. 2000b. *Graph clustering by flow simulation*. PhD Thesis, University of Utrecht, The Netherlands.

Su Nam Kim and Min-Yen Kan. 2009. *Re-examining Automatic Keyphrase Extraction Approaches in Scientific Articles*. In: Proc. of the 2009 Workshop on multiword Expressions, ACL-IJCNLP 2009. Suntec, Singapore. pp. 9-16.

Ya Zhang, Chao-Hsien Chu, Xiang Ji, and Hongyuan Zha. 2004. *Correlating Summarization of Multi-Source News with K-Way Graph Biclustering*. In: SIGKDD Explorations. 6(2), Association for Computing Machinery. Volume 6 Issue 2, pp. 34-42, ACM New York, NY, USA.

Automatic Evaluation of Summary Using Textual Entailment

Pinaki Bhaskar
Department of Computer Science & Engineering, Jadavpur University,
Kolkata – 700032, India
pinaki.bhaskar@gmail.com

Partha Pakray
Department of Computer Science & Engineering, Jadavpur University,
Kolkata – 700032, India
parthapakray@gmail.com

Abstract

This paper describes about an automatic technique of evaluating summary. The standard and popular summary evaluation techniques or tools are not fully automatic; they all need some manual process. Using textual entailment (TE) the generated summary can be evaluated automatically without any manual evaluation/process. The TE system is the composition of lexical entailment module, lexical distance module, Chunk module, Named Entity module and syntactic text entailment (TE) module. The syntactic TE system is based on the Support Vector Machine (SVM) that uses twenty five features for lexical similarity, the output tag from a rule based syntactic two-way TE system as a feature and the outputs from a rule based Chunk Module and Named Entity Module as the other features. The documents are used as text (T) and summary of these documents are taken as hypothesis (H). So, if the information of documents is entailed into the summary then it will be a very good summary. After comparing with the ROUGE 1.5.5 evaluation scores, the proposed evaluation technique achieved a high accuracy of 98.25% w.r.t ROUGE-2 and 95.65% w.r.t ROUGE-SU4.

1 Introduction

Automatic summaries are usually evaluated using human generated reference summaries or some manual efforts. The summary, which has been generated automatically from the documents, is difficult to evaluated using completely automatic evaluation process or tool. The most popular and standard summary evaluation tool is ROUGE and Pyramid. ROUGE evaluates the automated summary by comparing it with the set of human generated reference summary. Where as Pyramid method needs to identify the nuggets manually. Both the processes are very hectic and time consuming. So, automatic evaluation of summary is very much needed when a large number of summaries have to be evaluated, specially for multi-document summaries. For summary evaluation we have developed an automated evaluation technique based on textual entailment.

Recognizing Textual Entailment (RTE) is one of the recent research areas of Natural Language Processing (NLP). Textual Entailment is defined as a directional relationship between pairs of text expressions, denoted by the entailing "Text" (T) and the entailed "Hypothesis" (H). T entails H if the meaning of H can be inferred from the meaning of T. Textual Entailment has many applications in NLP tasks, such as Summarization, Information Extraction, Question Answering, Information Retrieval.

2 Related Work

Most of the approaches in textual entailment domain take Bag-of-words representation as one option, at least as a baseline system. The system (Herrera et al., 2005) obtains lexical entailment relations from WordNet[1]. The lexical unit T entails the lexical unit H if they are synonyms, Hyponyms, Multiwords, Negations and Antonyms according to WordNet or if there is a relation of similarity between them. The system accuracy was 55.8% on RTE-1 test dataset.

Based on the idea that meaning is determined by context, (Clarke, 2006) proposed a formal definition of entailment between two sentences in the form of a conditional probability on a measure space. The system submitted in RTE-4 provided three practical implementations of this formalism: a bag of words comparison as a baseline and two methods based on analyzing subsequences of the sentences possibly with intervening symbols. The system accuracy was 53% on RTE-2 test dataset.

[1] http://wordnet.princeton.edu/

Adams et al. (2007) has used linguistic features as training data for a decision tree classifier. These features are derived from the text–hypothesis pairs under examination. The system mainly used ROUGE (Recall–Oriented Understudy for Gisting Evaluation), NGram overlap metrics, Cosine Similarity metric and WordNet based measure as features. The system accuracy was 52% on RTE-2 test dataset.

Montalvo-Huhn et al. (2008) guessed at entailment based on word similarity between the hypotheses and the text. Three kinds of comparisons were attempted: original words (with normalized dates and numbers), synonyms and antonyms. Each of the three comparisons contributes a different weight to the entailment decision. The two-way accuracy of the system was 52.6% on RTE-4 test dataset.

Litkowski's (2009) system consists solely of routines to examine the overlap of discourse entities between the texts and hypotheses. The two-way accuracy of the system was 53% on RTE-5 Main task test dataset.

Majumdar and Bhattacharyya (2010) describe a simple lexical based system, which detects entailment based on word overlap between the Text and Hypothesis. The system is mainly designed to incorporate various kinds of co-referencing that occur within a document and take an active part in the event of Text Entailment. The accuracy of the system was 47.56% on RTE-6 Main Task test dataset.

The MENT (Microsoft ENTailment) (Vanderwende et al., 2006) system predicts entailment using syntactic features and a general purpose thesaurus, in addition to an overall alignment score. MENT is based on the premise that it is easier for a syntactic system to predict false entailments. The system accuracy was 60.25% on RTE-2 test set.

Wang and Neumannm (2007) present a novel approach to RTE that exploits a structure-oriented sentence representation followed by a similarity function. The structural features are automatically acquired from tree skeletons that are extracted and generalized from dependency trees. The method makes use of a limited size of training data without any external knowledge bases (e.g., WordNet) or handcrafted inference rules. They achieved an accuracy of 66.9% on the RTE-3 test data.

The major idea of Varma et al. (2009) is to find linguistic structures, termed templates that share the same anchors. Anchors are lexical elements describing the context of a sentence. Templates that are extracted from different sentences (text and hypothesis) and connect the same anchors in these sentences are assumed to entail each other. The system accuracy was 46.8% on RTE-5 test set.

Tsuchida and Ishikawa (2011) combine the entailment score calculated by lexical-level matching with the machine-learning based filtering mechanism using various features obtained from lexical-level, chunk-level and predicate argument structure-level information. In the filtering mechanism, the false positive T-H pairs that have high entailment score but do not represent entailment are discarded. The system accuracy was 48% on RTE-7 test set.

Lin and Hovy (2003) developed an automatic summary evaluation system using n-gram co-occurrence statistics. Following the recent adoption by the machine translation community of automatic evaluation using the BLEU/NIST scoring process, they conduct an in-depth study of a similar idea for evaluating summaries. They showed that automatic evaluation using unigram co-occurrences between summary pairs correlates surprising well with human evaluations, based on various statistical metrics; while direct application of the BLEU evaluation procedure does not always give good results.

Harnly et al. (2005) also proposed an automatic summary evaluation technique by the Pyramid method. They presented an experimental system for testing automated evaluation of summaries, pre-annotated for shared information. They reduced the problem to a combination of similarity measure computation and clustering. They achieved best results with a unigram overlap similarity measure and single link clustering, which yields high correlation to manual pyramid scores (r=0.942, p=0.01), and shows better correlation than the n-gram overlap automatic approaches of the ROUGE system.

3 Textual Entailment System

A two-way hybrid textual entailment (TE) recognition system that uses lexical and syntactic features has been described in this section. The system architecture has been shown in Figure 1. The hybrid TE system as (Pakray et al., 2011b) has used the Support Vector Machine Learning technique that uses thirty four features for training. Five features from Lexical TE, seventeen features from Lexical distance measure and eleven features from the rule based syntactic two-way TE system have been selected.

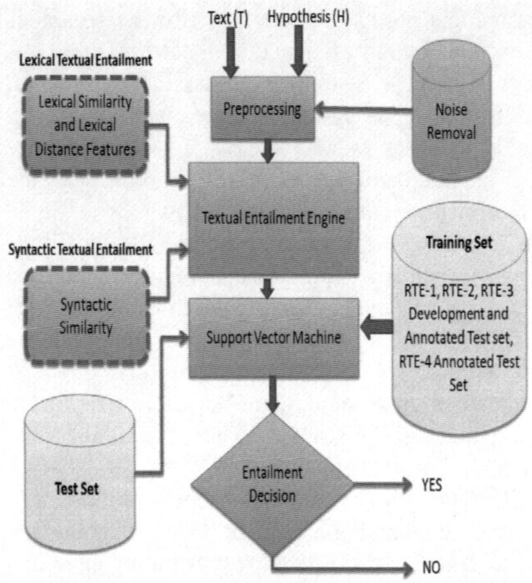

Figure 1. Hybrid Textual Entailment System

3.1 Lexical Similarity

In this section the various lexical features (Pakray et al., 2011b) for textual entailment are described in detail.

i. WordNet based Unigram Match. In this method, the various unigrams in the hypothesis for each text-hypothesis pair are checked for their presence in text. WordNet synset are identified for each of the unmatched unigrams in the hypothesis. If any synset for the hypothesis unigram matches with any synset of a word in the text then the hypothesis unigram is considered as a WordNet based unigram match.

ii. Bigram Match. Each bigram in the hypothesis is searched for a match in the corresponding text part. The measure Bigram_Match is calculated as the fraction of the hypothesis bigrams that match in the corresponding text, i.e., Bigram_Match = (Total number of matched bigrams in a text-hypothesis pair /Number of hypothesis bigrams).

iii. Longest Common Subsequence (LCS). The Longest Common Subsequence of a text-hypothesis pair is the longest sequence of words, which is common to both the text and the hypothesis. LCS(T,H) estimates the similarity between text T and hypothesis H, as LCS_Match=LCS(T,H)/length of H.

iv. Skip-grams. A skip-gram is any combination of n words in the order as they appear in a sentence, allowing arbitrary gaps. In the present work, only 1-skip-bigrams are considered where 1-skip-bigrams are bigrams with one word gap between two words in order in a sentence. The measure 1-skip_bigram_Match is defined as

$$\text{1\_skip\_bigram\_Match} = \frac{\text{skip\_gram(T,H)}}{n} \quad (1)$$

where, skip_gram(T,H) refers to the number of common 1-skip-bigrams (pair of words in sentence order with one word gap) found in T and H and n is the number of 1-skip-bigrams in the hypothesis H.

v. Stemming. Stemming is the process of reducing terms to their root forms. For example, the plural forms of a noun such as 'boxes' are stemmed into 'box', and inflectional endings with 'ing', 'es', 's' and 'ed' are removed from verbs. Each word in the text and hypothesis pair is stemmed using the stemming function provided along with the WordNet 2.0.

If s1= number of common stemmed unigrams between text and hypothesis and s2= number of stemmed unigrams in Hypothesis, then the measure Stemming_match is defined as Stemming_Match=s1/s2

WordNet is one of most important resource for lexical analysis. The WordNet 2.0 has been used for WordNet based unigram match and stemming step. API for WordNet Searching[2] (JAWS) is an API that provides Java applications with the ability to retrieve data from the WordNet database.

3.2 Syntactic Similarity

In this section the various syntactic similarity features (Pakray et al., 2011b) for textual entailment are described in detail. This module is based on the Stanford Dependency Parser[3], which normalizes data from the corpus of text and hypothesis pairs, accomplishes the dependency analysis and creates appropriate structures Our Entailment system uses the following features.

a. Subject. The dependency parser generates nsubj (nominal subject) and nsubjpass (passive nominal subject) tags for the subject feature. Our entailment system uses these tags.

b. Object. The dependency parser generates dobj (direct object) as object tags.

c. Verb. Verbs are wrapped with either the subject or the object.

d. Noun. The dependency parser generates nn (noun compound modifier) as noun tags.

e. Preposition. Different types of prepositional tags are prep_in, prep_to, prep_with etc. For example, in the sentence "A plane crashes in Ita-

[2] http://wordnetweb.princeton.edu/perl/webwn

[3] http://www-nlp.stanford.edu/software/lex-parser.shtml

ly." the prepositional tag is identified as prep_in(in, Italy).

f. Determiner. Determiner denotes a relation with a noun phase. The dependency parser generates det as determiner tags. For example, the parsing of the sentence "A journalist reports on his own murders." generates the determiner relation as det(journalist,A).

g. Number. The numeric modifier of a noun phrase is any number phrase. The dependency parser generates num (numeric modifier). For example, the parsing of the sentence "Nigeria seizes 80 tonnes of drugs." generates the relation num (tonnes, 80).

Matching Module: After dependency relations are identified for both the text and the hypothesis in each pair, the hypothesis relations are compared with the text relations. The different features that are compared are noted below. In all the comparisons, a matching score of 1 is considered when the complete dependency relation along with all of its arguments matches in both the text and the hypothesis. In case of a partial match for a dependency relation, a matching score of 0.5 is assumed.

i. Subject-Verb Comparison. The system compares hypothesis subject and verb with text subject and verb that are identified thROUGE the nsubj and nsubjpass dependency relations. A matching score of 1 is assigned in case of a complete match. Otherwise, the system considers the following matching process.

ii. WordNet Based Subject-Verb Comparison. If the corresponding hypothesis and text subjects do match in the subject-verb comparison, but the verbs do not match, then the WordNet distance between the hypothesis and the text is compared. If the value of the WordNet distance is less than 0.5, indicating a closeness of the corresponding verbs, then a match is considered and a matching score of 0.5 is assigned. Otherwise, the subject-subject comparison process is applied.

iii. Subject-Subject Comparison. The system compares hypothesis subject with text subject. If a match is found, a score of 0.5 is assigned to the match.

iv. Object-Verb Comparison. The system compares hypothesis object and verb with text object and verb that are identified through dobj dependency relation. In case of a match, a matching score of 0.5 is assigned.

v. WordNet Based Object-Verb Comparison. The system compares hypothesis object with text object. If a match is found then the verb associated with the hypothesis object is compared with the verb associated with the with text object. If the two verbs do not match then the WordNet distance between the two verbs is calculated. If the value of WordNet distance is below 0.50 then a matching score of 0.5 is assigned.

vi. Cross Subject-Object Comparison. The system compares hypothesis subject and verb with text object and verb or hypothesis object and verb with text subject and verb. In case of a match, a matching score of 0.5 is assigned.

vii. Number Comparison. The system compares numbers along with units in the hypothesis with similar numbers along with units in the text. Units are first compared and if they match then the corresponding numbers are compared. In case of a match, a matching score of 1 is assigned.

viii. Noun Comparison. The system compares hypothesis noun words with text noun words that are identified through nn dependency relation. In case of a match, a matching score of 1 is assigned.

ix. Prepositional Phrase Comparison. The system compares the prepositional dependency relations in the hypothesis with the corresponding relations in the text and then checks for the noun words that are arguments of the relation. In case of a match, a matching score of 1 is assigned.

x. Determiner Comparison. The system compares the determiners in the hypothesis and in the text that are identified through det relation. In case of a match, a matching score of 1 is assigned.

xi. Other relation Comparison. Besides the above relations that are compared, all other remaining relations are compared verbatim in the hypothesis and in the text. In case of a match, a matching score of 1 is assigned.

3.3 Part-of-Speech (POS) Matching

This module basically matches common POS tags between the text and the hypothesis pairs. Stanford POS tagger[4] is used to tag the part of speech in both text and hypothesis. System matches the verb and noun POS words in the hypothesis with those in the text. A score POS_match is defined in equation 2.

$$\text{POS\_Match} = \frac{\text{Number of Verb and Noun Match in Text and Hypothesis}}{\text{Total number of Verb and Noun in Hypothesis}} \quad (2)$$

[4] http://nlp.stanford.edu/software/tagger.shtml

3.4 Lexical Distance

The important lexical distance measures that are used in the present system include Vector Space Measures (Euclidean distance, Manhattan distance, Minkowsky distance, Cosine similarity, Matching coefficient), Set-based Similarities (Dice, Jaccard, Overlap, Cosine, Harmonic), Soft-Cardinality, Q-Grams Distance, Edit Distance Measures (Levenshtein distance, Smith-Waterman Distance, Jaro). These lexical distance features have been used as described in detail by Pakray et al. (2011b).

3.5 Chunk Similarity

The part of speech (POS) tags of the hypothesis and text are identified using the Stanford POS tagger. After getting the POS information, the system extracts the chunk output using the CRF Chunker[5]. Chunk boundary detector detects each individual chunk such as noun chunk, verb chunk etc. Thus, all the chunks for each sentence in the hypothesis are identified. Each chunk of the hypothesis is now searched in the text side and the sentences that contain the key chunk words are extracted. If chunks match then the system assigns scores for each individual chunk corresponding to the hypothesis. The scoring values are changed according to the matching of chunk and word containing the chunk. The entire scoring calculation is given in equations 3 and 4 below:

$$\text{Match score } (M[i]) = \frac{W_m[i]}{W_c[i]} \tag{3}$$

where, $W_m[i]$ = Number of words that match in the ith chunk and $W_c[i]$ = Total number of words containing the ith chunk.

$$\text{Overall score } (S) = \sum_{i=1}^{N} \frac{M[i]}{N} \tag{4}$$

where, N = Total number of chunks in the hypothesis.

3.6 Support Vector Machines (SVM)

In machine learning, support vector machines (SVMs)[6] are supervised learning models used for classification and regression analysis. Associated learning algorithms analyze data and recognize patterns. The basic SVM takes a set of input data and predicts, for each given input, which of two possible classes form the output, making it a non-probabilistic binary linear classifier. Given a set of training examples, each marked as belonging to one of two categories; an SVM training algorithm builds a model that assigns new examples into one category or the other. An SVM model is a representation of the examples as points in space, mapped so that the examples of the separate categories are divided by a clear gap as wide as possible. New examples are then mapped into that same space and predicted to belong to a category based on which side of the gap they fall on.

The system has used LIBSVM[7] for building the model file. The TE system has used the following data sets: RTE-1 development and test set, RTE-2 development and annotated test set, RTE-3 development and annotated test set and RTE-4 annotated test set to deal with the two-way classification task for training purpose to build the model file. The LIBSVM tool is used by the SVM classifier to learn from this data set. For training purpose, 3967 text-hypothesis pairs have been used. It has been tested on the RTE test dataset and we have got 60% to 70% accuracy on RTE datasets. We have applied this textual entailment system on summarize data sets and system gives the entailment score with entailment decisions (i.e., “YES” / “NO”). We have tested in both directions.

4 Automatic Evaluation of Summary

Ideally summary of some documents should contain all the necessary information contained in the documents. So the quality of a summary should be judged on how much information of the documents it contains. If the summary contains all the necessary information from the documents, then it will be a perfect summary. But manual comparison is the best way to judge that how much information it contains from the document. But manual evaluation is a very hectic process, specially when the summary generated from multiple documents. When a large number of multi-document summaries have to be evaluated, then an automatic evaluation method needs to evaluate the summaries. Here we propose textual entailment (TE) based automatic evaluation technique for summary.

4.1 Textual Entailment (TE) Based Summary Evaluation

Textual Entailment is defined as a directional relationship between pairs of text expressions,

[5] http://crfchunker.sourceforge.net/

[6] http://en.wikipedia.org/wiki/Support_vector_machine

[7] http://www.csie.ntu.edu.tw/~cjlin/libsvm/

denoted by the entailing "Text" (T) and the entailed "Hypothesis" (H). Text (T) entails hypothesis (H) if the information of text (T) is inferred into the hypothesis (H). Here the documents are used as text (T) and summary of these documents are taken as hypothesis (H). So, if the information of documents is entailed into the summary then it will be a very good summary, which should get a good evaluation score.

As our textual entailment system works on sentence level each sentence of documents are taken as text (T) and calculate the entailment score comparing with each sentence of the summary assuming them as hypothesis (H). For example, if T_i is the ith sentence of documents, then it will compared with each sentence of the summary, i.e. H_j, where, $j = 1$ to n; and n is the total number of sentences in the summary. Now if T_i is validated with any one of the summary sentences using our textual entailment system, then it will be marked as validated. After get the entailment result of all the sentences of documents, the percentage or ratio of the marked/validated sentences w.r.t unmarked/rejected sentences will be the evaluation score of the summary.

5 Data Collection

We have collected Text Analysis Conference (TAC, formerly DUC, conducted by NIST) 2008 Update Summarization track's data sets[8] for this experiment. This data set contains 48 topics and each topic has two sets of 10 documents, i.e. there are 960 documents. The evaluation data set has 4 model summaries for each document set, i.e. 8 model summaries for each topic. In 2008, there are 72 participants and we also take the summaries of all the participants of this year.

6 Comparison of Automatic v/s Manual Evaluation

We have the evaluation scores of all the 72 participants of TAC 2008 using ROUGE 1.5.5. We have calculated the evaluation scores of the same summaries of 72 participants using the proposed automated evaluation technique and compared it with ROUGE scores. The comparison of both the evaluation scores of top five participants is shown in the table 1.

For measuring the accuracy of this proposed method, we take the ROUGE 1.5.5 evaluation score as the gold standard score and then calculate the accuracy using equation 5.

[8] http://www.nist.gov/tac/data/index.html

Summaries	ROUGE-2 Average_R	ROUGE-SU4 Average_R	Proposed method
Top ranked participant (id:43)	0.111	0.143	0.7063
2nd ranked participant (id:13)	0.110	0.140	0.7015
3rd ranked participant (id:60)	0.104	0.142	0.6750
4th ranked participant (id:37)	0.103	0.143	0.6810
5th ranked participant (id:6)	0.101	0.140	0.6325

Table 1. Comparison of Summary Evaluation Score

$$Accuracy = 1 - \frac{\sum_{i=1}^{n} |(r_i - r_i^R)|}{n^2} \quad (5)$$

where, r_i = the rank of ith summary after evaluated by the proposed method

r_i^R = the rank of ith summary after evaluated by ROUGE 1.5.5

and n = total number of multi-document summaries.

After evaluating 48 (only set A) multi-document summaries of 72 participants, i.e total 3456 multi-document summaries using the evaluation method, ROUGE 1.5.5 and the proposed method, the accuracy of this proposed method calculated using equation 4 comparing with the ROUGE's evaluation scores. The accuracy figures are **0.9825** w.r.t ROUGE-2 and **0.9565** w.r.t ROUGE-SU4.

7 Conclusion

From the comparison of evaluation score of the proposed method and ROUGE 1.5.5, it is clear that it can be easily judged that which summary is better like evaluation done by ROUGE. But if evaluation is done using ROUGE then evaluator has to make reference summaries manually, which is a very hectic task as well as time consuming task and can not be generated any automated process. Hence if we have to evaluate multiple summaries of same set of documents, then this proposed automated evaluation process could be very useful method.

Acknowledgments

We acknowledge the supports of the DST India-CONACYT Mexico project "Answer Validation thROUGE Textual Entailment" funded by DST, Govt. of India and the DeitY, MCIT, Govt. of India funded project "Development of Cross Lingual Information Access (CLIA) System Phase II".

References

Aaron Harnly, Ani Nenkova, Rebecca Passonneau, and Owen Rambow. 2005. *Automation of summary evaluation by the pyramid method.* In: Recent Advances in Natural Language Processing (RANLP). *Borovets, Bulgaria.*

Chin-Yew Lin, and Eduard Hovy. 2003. *Automatic evaluation of summaries using n-gram co-occurrence statistics.* In: 2003 Conference of the North American Chapter of the Association for Computational Linguistics on Human Language Technology-Volume 1, pp. 71-78, Association for Computational Linguistics.

Daoud Clarke. 2006. *Meaning as Context and Subsequence Analysis for Entailment.* In: the Second PASCAL Recognising Textual Entailment Challenge, Venice, Italy.

Debarghya Majumdar, and Pushpak Bhattacharyya. 2010. *Lexical Based Text Entailment System for Summarization Settings of RTE6.* In: the Text Analysis Conference (TAC 2010), National Institute of Standards and Technology Gaithersburg, Maryland, USA.

Eamonn Newman, John Dunnion, and Joe Carthy. 2006. *Constructing a Decision Tree Classifier using Lexical and Syntactic Features.* In: the Second PASCAL Recognising Textual Entailment Challenge.

Jesús Herrera, Anselmo Peñas, and Felisa Verdejo. 2005. *Textual Entailment Recognition Based on Dependency Analysis and WordNet.* In: the First Challenge Workshop Recognising Textual Entailment, pp. 21-24, 33–36 Southampton, U.K.

Ken Litkowski. 2009. *Overlap Analysis in Textual Entailment Recognition.* In: TAC 2009 Workshop, National Institute of Standards and Technology Gaithersburg, Maryland USA.

Lucy Vanderwende, Arul Menezes, and Rion Snow. 2006. *Microsoft Research at RTE-2: Syntactic Contributions in the Entailment Task: an implementation.* In: the Second PASCALChallenges Workshop.

Masaaki Tsuchida, and Kai Ishikawa. 2011. *IKOMA at TAC2011: A Method for Recognizing Textual Entailment using Lexical-level and Sentence Structure-level features.* In: TAC 2011 Notebook Proceedings.

Milen Kouylekov, Bernardo Magnini. 2005. *Recognizing Textual Entailment with Tree Edit Distance Algorithms.* In: the First PASCAL Recognizing Textual Entailment Workshop.

Orlando Montalvo-Huhn, and Stephen Taylor. 2008. *Textual Entailment – Fitchburg State College.* In: TAC08, Fourth PASCAL Challenges Workshop on Recognising Textual Entailment.

Partha Pakray, Pinaki Bhaskar, Santanu Pal, Dipankar Das, Sivaji Bandyopadhyay, and Alexander Gelbukh. 2010. *JU_CSE_TE: System Description QA@CLEF 2010 – ResPubliQA.* In: CLEF 2010 Workshop on Multiple Language Question Answering (MLQA 2010), Padua, Italy.

Partha Pakray, Pinaki Bhaskar, Somnath Banerjee, Bidhan Chandra Pal, Alexander Gelbukh, and Sivaji Bandyopadhyay. 2011a. *A Hybrid Question Answering System based on Information Retrieval and Answer Validation.* In: Question Answering for Machine Reading Evaluation (QA4MRE) at CLEF 2011, Amsterdam.

Partha Pakray, Snehasis Neogi, Pinaki Bhaskar, Soujanya Poria, Sivaji Bandyopadhyay, Alexander Gelbukh. 2011b. *A Textual Entailment System using Anaphora Resolution.* In: the Text Analysis Conference Recognizing Textual Entailment Track (TAC RTE) Notebook.

Pinaki Bhaskar, and Sivaji Bandyopadhyay. 2010a. *A Query Focused Automatic Multi Document Summarizer.* In: the proceeding of the 8th International Conference on Natural Language Processing (ICON 2010), pp. 241-250, India.

Pinaki Bhaskar, and Sivaji Bandyopadhyay. 2010b. *A Query Focused Multi Document Automatic Summarization.* In: the proceeding of the 24th Pacific Asia Conference on Language, Information and Computation (PACLIC 24), pp 545-554, Japan.

Pinaki Bhaskar, Amitava Das, Partha Pakray, and Sivaji Bandyopadhyay. 2010c. *Theme Based English and Bengali Ad-hoc Monolingual Information Retrieval in FIRE 2010.* In: the Forum for Information Retrieval Evaluation (FIRE) – 2010, Gandhinagar, India.

Pinaki Bhaskar, Somnath Banerjee, Snehasis Neogi, and Sivaji Bandyopadhyay. 2012a. *A Hybrid QA System with Focused IR and Automatic Summarization for INEX 2011.* In: Geva, S., Kamps, J., Schenkel, R.(eds.): Focused Retrieval of Content and Structure: 10th International Workshop of the Initiative for the Evaluation of XML Retrieval, INEX 2011. Lecture Notes in Computer Science, vol. 7424. Springer Verlag, Berlin, Heidelberg

Pinaki Bhaskar, and Sivaji Bandyopadhyay. 2012b. *Cross Lingual Query Dependent Snippet Generation.* In: International Journal of Computer Science and Information Technologies (IJCSIT), ISSN: 0975-9646, Vol. 3, Issue 4, pp. 4603 – 4609.

Pinaki Bhaskar, and Sivaji Bandyopadhyay. 2012c. *Language Independent Query Focused Snippet Generation.* In: T. Catarci et al. (Eds.): Information Access Evaluation. Multilinguality, Multimodality, and Visual Analytics: Third International Conference of the CLEF Initiative, CLEF 2012, Rome, Italy, Proceedings, Lecture Notes in Computer Science Volume 7488, 2012, pp 138-140, DOI 10.1007/978-3-642-33247-0_16, ISBN 978-3-642-33246-3, ISSN 0302-9743, Springer Verlag, Berlin, Heidelberg, Germany.

Pinaki Bhaskar, Somnath Banerjee, and Sivaji Bandyopadhyay. 2012d. *A Hybrid Tweet Contextualization System using IR and Summarization.* In: the Initiative for the Evaluation of XML Retrieval, INEX 2012 at Conference and Labs of the Evaluation Forum (CLEF) 2012, Pamela Forner, Jussi Karlgren, Christa Womser-Hacker (Eds.): CLEF 2012 Evaluation Labs and Workshop, pp. 164-175, ISBN 978-88-904810-3-1, ISSN 2038-4963, Rome, Italy.

Pinaki Bhaskar, Partha Pakray, Somnath Banerjee, Samadrita Banerjee, Sivaji Bandyopadhyay, and Alexander Gelbukh. 2012e. *Question Answering System for QA4MRE@CLEF 2012.* In: Question Answering for Machine Reading Evaluation (QA4MRE) at Conference and Labs of the Evaluation Forum (CLEF) 2012, Rome, Italy.

Pinaki Bhaskar, Kishorjit Nongmeikapam, and Sivaji Bandyopadhyay. 2012f. *Keyphrase Extraction in Scientific Articles: A Supervised Approach.* In: the proceedings of 24th International Conference on Computational Linguastics (Coling 2012), pp. 17-24, India.

Pinaki Bhaskar. 2013a. *A Query Focused Language Independent Multi-document Summarization.* Jian, A. (Eds.), ISBN 978-3-8484-0089-8, LAMBERT Academic Publishing, Saarbrücken, Germany.

Pinaki Bhaskar. 2013b. *Answering Questions from Multiple Documents – the Role of Multi-Document Summarization.* In: Student Research Workshop in the Recent Advances in Natural Language Processing (RANLP), Hissar, Bulgaria.

Pinaki Bhaskar 2013c. *Multi-Document Summarization using Automatic Key-Phrase Extraction.* In: Student Research Workshop in the Recent Advances in Natural Language Processing (RANLP), Hissar, Bulgaria.

Pinaki Bhaskar, Somnath Banerjee, and Sivaji Bandyopadhyay. 2013d. *Tweet Contextualization (Answering Tweet Question) – the Role of Multi-document Summarization.* In: the Initiative for the Evaluation of XML Retrieval, INEX 2013 at CLEF 2013 Conference and Labs of the Evaluation Forum, Valencia, Spain.

Pinaki Bhaskar, Somnath Banerjee, Partha Pakray, Samadrita Banerjee, Sivaji Bandyopadhyay, and Alexander Gelbukh. 2013e. *A Hybrid Question Answering System for Multiple Choice Question (MCQ).* In: Question Answering for Machine Reading Evaluation (QA4MRE) at CLEF 2013 Conference and Labs of the Evaluation Forum, Valencia, Spain.

Sivaji Bandyopadhyay, Amitava Das, and Pinaki Bhaskar. 2008. *English Bengali Ad-hoc Monolingual Information Retrieval Task Result at FIRE 2008.* In: the Forum for Information Retrieval Evaluation (FIRE) - 2008, Kolkata, India.

Somnath Banerjee, Partha Pakray, Pinaki Bhaskar, and Sivaji Bandyopadhyay, Alexander Gelbukh. 2013. *Multiple Choice Question (MCQ) Answering System for Entrance Examination.* In: Question Answering for Machine Reading Evaluation (QA4MRE) at CLEF 2013 Conference and Labs of the Evaluation Forum, Valencia, Spain.

Rod Adams, Gabriel Nicolae, Cristina Nicolae, and Sanda Harabagiu. 2007. *Textual Entailment Through Extended Lexical Overlap and Lexico-Semantic Matching.* In: ACL PASCAL Workshop on Textual Entailment and Paraphrasing. pp.119-124. 28-29, Prague, Czech Republic.

Rui Wang, and Günter Neumannm. 2007. *Recognizing Textual Entailment Using Sentence Similarity based on Dependency Tree Skeletons.* In: the third PASCAL Recognising Textual Entailment Challenge.

Vasudeva Varma, Vijay Bharat, Sudheer Kovelamudi, Praveen Bysani, Santosh GSK, Kiran Kumar N, Kranthi Reddy, Karuna Kumar, and Nitin Maganti. 2009. *IIIT Hyderabad at TAC 2009.* In: TAC 2009 Workshop, National Institute of Standards and Technology Gaithersburg, Maryland USA.

Towards a Discourse Model for Knowledge Elicitation

Eugeniu Costetchi
CRP Henri Tudor, Luxembourg, 29, J.F. Kennedy, 1855, Luxembourg
Eugeniu.Costetchi@Tudor.lu

Abstract

Knowledge acquisition has been and still remains a hard problem. When it comes to eliciting knowledge from human subjects, an artificial interviewer can be of tremendous benefit. In this paper we present a discourse model for representing the explicit propositional content of a text along with question raising mechanism based on it. This feature is perfectly aligned with the purpose of acquiring more knowledge from the human respondent and acting as a self-extending knowledge base.

1 Introduction

In ontology engineering field, one of the main goals is building an ontology (knowledge base) of a particular domain. The ontology in this case represents a *commonly agreed "specification of a conceptualization"* (Gruber, 1993) within a group of domain experts.

There have been proposed many methodologies to build ontologies e.g. (Ferndndez, Gmez-p, & Juristo, 1997; Noy & Mcguinness, 2000; Uschold & King, 1995). Some are manual, some others are semi-automatic, however, the main burden of interviewing (or eliciting knowledge from) the domain experts, conceptualizing and then encoding the knowledge with a formal language is left on the shoulders of the ontology engineer. Therefore, the process is slow, expensive, non-scalable and biased by the ontology engineer's understanding of the domain.

A solution to knowledge acquisition problem in ontology engineering is envisioned in (Costetchi, Ras, & Latour, 2011). They present a system that could take the role of a human interviewer in the process of knowledge elicitation for the purpose of creating the ontology of the discussed topic. In their vision, one crucial difference to ontology definition is the fact that the created ontology is not shared but it is an *individual "specification of conceptualization"* which captures the text propositional content without assuming any prior knowledge of the domain of discourse.

We embark on this idea of artificial interviewer for the purpose of knowledge acquisition as a topic or domain ontology. The proposal is to start from a syntactic and semantic analysis of text (parsing) and interpret the parsed information, through the lens of the Systemic Functional Linguistics (Halliday & Matthiessen, 2004), into a coherent and consistent discourse model. Then it can serve as basis for question generation in order to drive further the knowledge elicitation process. The system, therefore, is intended to act as a self-extending knowledge base by means of written interaction with a human respondent.

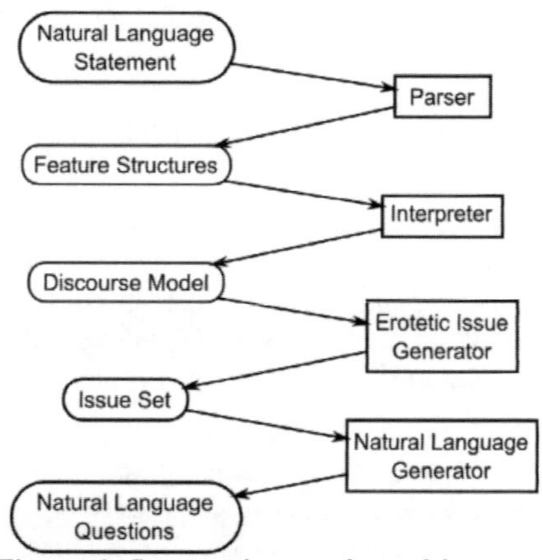

Figure 1: Interaction cycle architecture.

Figure 1 presents the simplified architecture for one interaction. Rounded boxes on the left-hand side represent the data structures; the boxes on the right-hand side represent operational modules and the arrows represent input-output data flows. The *parser* takes natural language text and provides a syntactic and semantic analysis in terms of *feature structures* which are sets of attribute-value pairs. The content of feature structures is systematized according to SFL theory. The *interpreter* instantiates the *discourse model* from the feature structures. The discourse model serves as the central knowledge repository. Based on it and its instantiation the *erotetic issue generator* creates all possible issues that can be raised, given a particular instance of discourse model. An issue is a formal representation of a question. The issues serve as an *expansion mechanism* of the discourse model. The model extends by accommodating answers (statements) that resolve the issue. Then natural language generator translates formally expressed issues into natural language questions.

The scope of this paper is limited to the discussion of the discourse model and how it can serve as a basis for question raising. Other challenges are just briefly mentioned and left out of the discussion scope.

In next section of the paper is presented the general approach to the problem followed by a section describing the SFL parser. In section 4 we present the discourse model and an example text interpretation. Section 5 provides an example axiomatization employed for question rising which is presented in Section 6. Final remarks and conclusions are drawn in Section 7.

2 The Approach

An interaction cycle between human and system starts with the natural language statement written by human and ends with a set natural language questions generated by the system. The statements are parsed and interpreted in terms of a discourse model which serves as a formal semantic representation of what has been said in the text. The same model serves as a foundation to raise questions (as issues). The raised questions are transformed into natural language text.

For text analysis is employed a systemic functional parser (Costetchi, 2013). It employs a graph-based transformation from dependency parse into a set of feature structures.

The interpretation process consists of instantiating the of discourse model from the feature structures produced by the SFL parser therefore it relied only on linguistic semantics. Pragmatic interpretations like implicatures (Grice, 1975) will not be interpreted as that would require (prior) world knowledge (which is avoided within the system).

SFL adopts a semiotic perspective on language and distinguishes different meaning-lines fused in the text. It provides, among others, linguistic semantics that resembles *frame semantics* (Fillmore, 1985; Minsky, 1974) at the clause level (in terms of processes and their participants) and also *taxis semantics* at the inter-clause level (in terms of logico-semantic relations) which resemble Rhetoric Structure Theory relations (Mann & Thompson, 1988).

To parse in terms of full SFG grammar is computationally unfeasible (Bateman, 2008; Kay, 1985; Robert Kasper, 1988), but it is possible to parse with parts of grammar which provide semantic account of the clause (Costetchi, 2013; Michael O'Donnell, 2012) and inter-clause relations.

The discourse model serves as a foundation for generating questions. If we compare the expansion of the model to a growing plant, then the plant would have buds from which a new leaf, branch or flower can grow. Within the model we define *question raising buds* as "places" in the model where new knowledge can be integrated. And since it is not priory known what that knowledge is going to be, the expansion of the bud is resolved by raising a question and accommodating the answer.

The next section describes the discourse model and provides an example text interpretation.

3 The SFL Parser

The parser (Costetchi, 2013) employs a graph-based approach to generate Systemic Functional Grammar *mood* (chunked functional constituency parse) and *transitivity* (frame semantic account of process type and participant roles) parses from the Stanford Dependency parse (Marneffe, MacCartney, & Manning, 2006; Marneffe & Manning, 2008) and Process Type Database (Neale, 2002). It is a computationally and linguistically viable text parsing approach for natural language which encompasses framed semantic roles together with an adequate syntactic structure to support those semantic roles. An example analysis generated by the parser is presented in Table 1.

example 1	**the duke**	**had**	**given**	**the teapot**	**to my aunt.**
Mood	clause: [mood type: declarative; tense: past perfect simple; voice: active; polarity: positive]				
	subject	predicate: finite	predicate: predicator	complement	complement
transitivity	agent-carrier	possessive process		possessed	beneficiary
example 2	**the lion**	**caught**		**the tourist**	**yesterday.**
Mood	clause: [mood type: declarative; tense: past perfect simple; voice: active; polarity: positive]				
	subject	predicator/finite		complement	adjunct
transitivity	agent-carrier	possessive process		affected-possessed	temporal location

Table 1: Mood and transitivity example.

The parser produces feature structures representing syntactic and semantic analysis of text. Among the clause *syntactic features* are: *mood, tense, voice* and *polarity* while the clause *semantic features* are the *process type* and *participant roles*. In Figure 2 is presented an example of semantic feature structure.

$$\begin{bmatrix} \text{process type: possesive} \\ \text{process: catch} \\ \text{Ag-Ca: lion} \\ \text{Af-Pos: tourist} \end{bmatrix}$$

Figure 2: Feature structure example.

The parser distinguishes among 16 process types (Figure 3) and 29 participant roles where 17 are simple and 12 are compound. In (Fawcett, 2009) are proposed 65 configurations of process types and participant roles. The semantics of such configurations is captured by GUM ontology (Bateman, Henschel, & Rinaldi, 1995). However the process type and participant role classifications are different, therefore a structural adaptation is required to provide compatibility. We describe the adaptation in the next section.

4 The Discourse Model

The discourse model proposed here draws mainly on GUM. Generalized Upper Model (Bateman et al., 1995) is a linguistically motivated upper level ontology that is domain and task independent. It serves an interface between the linguistic and conceptual forms. This model is compatible with SFL experiential line of meaning which deals with semantic content of text. We further propose a temporal extension and two structural modification of GUM.

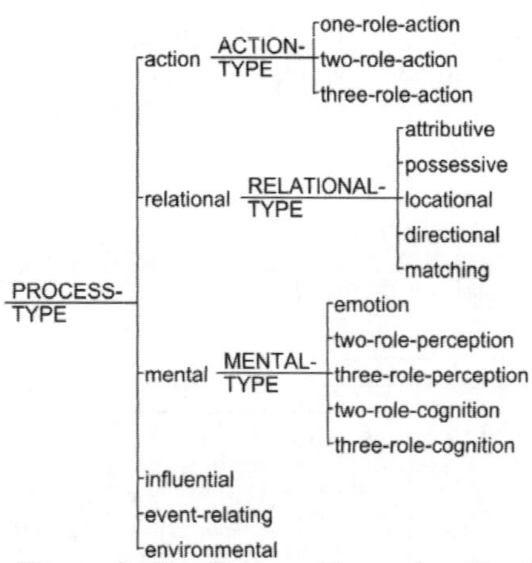

Figure 3: The Process Type classification.

The first structural modification consists in adaptation of process type and participant role classifications. GUM is build based on Hallidayan classification (Halliday & Matthiessen, 2004) whereas we propose to use the one described in (Fawcett, 2009). The main reason for such adaptation is the SFL parser which produces semantic descriptions according to the latter classification. The top level classification of Fawcett's process types is presented in Figure 3.

The second structural modification consists in dividing the process types into *eventive* and *stative* processes. This distinction is metaphysically motivated in DOLCE upper level ontology (Borgo & Masolo, 2009) and linguistically motivated by Bach (1986). This distinction is necessary for the temporal extension of the model. So we propose that *attributive, possessive, locational, emotion and environmental* processes to correspond to states while the *action, directional, matching, perception and cognition* processes to be classified as events. This is an intuitive distinction among the process types based on their description and more fine grained division shall be proposed that will, for example, take into consideration the participant roles as well.

In natural language a finite clause is anchored into the "*here and now*", so to speak, bringing the clause into the context of the speech event. This is achieved either by reference to *the time of speaking* (via tense) or by reference to the *judgment of the speaker* (via modality). We hold the view that, in a narrative, each participant can be described via a temporal evolution complemented by atemporal descriptions (e.g. modal, conditional, causal, concessive, etc.) We focus on the former one and the atemporal one is left for future works.

The temporal dimension provides a linear layout for events and states. Each *participant* has one or more time-lines. The events are distributed along the timeline(s) of the participants. The *events* happen in time and are assumed to be bound by start and end time-points. The *states* last in time and correspond to the conditions and properties of participants along a time interval. They are assumed to be unbound unless a start/end time points and/or duration are specified. Allen (1983) proposes seven basic relations to relate intervals: *before, meets, overlaps, starts, finishes, during and equal.* We incorporate these relations into the model as means to provide a partial ordering to the events and states on the participant timelines. The choice of the temporal relation between two events/states is based on the tense, aspect and temporal circumstances. We do not provide yet a description of the selection conditions but rather focus on motivating their role in a discourse model and in question generation.

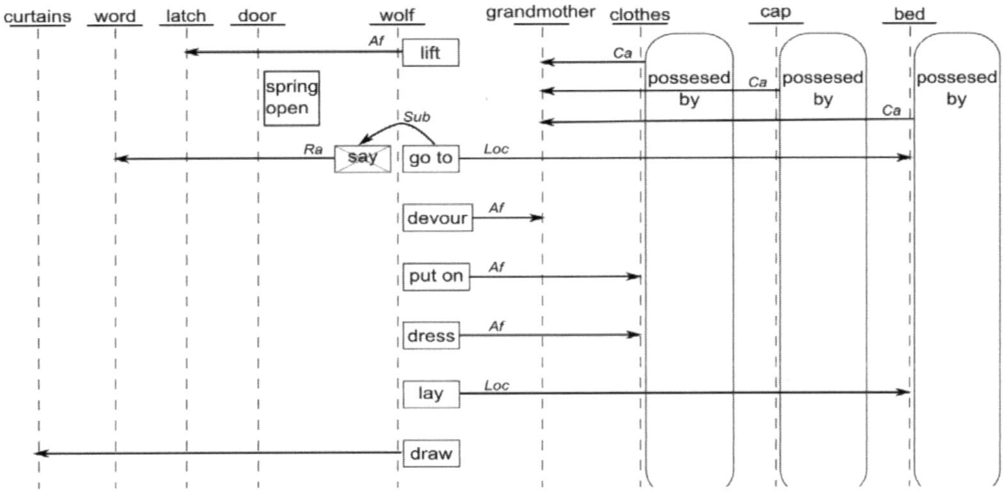

Figure 4: The wolf example from "Little Red Riding Hood".

As mentioned before, not all statements can be integrated into a timeline for they are *atemporal.* For example some present simple clauses cannot be (easily) located in time when they express facts or generalizations. In this case the events are placed on "*atemporal timelines*". In the same manner are treated the conditional or causal relations. The decision to place them on atemporal timelines is merely pragmatic and aims to keep a uniform representation of events and states.

In Figure 4, is provided an example from *"Little Red Riding Hood".* It is a graphical representation of a paragraph interpreted into the discourse model.

"The wolf lifted the latch, the door sprang open, and without saying a word he went straight to the grandmother's bed, and devoured her. Then he put on her clothes, dressed himself in her cap, laid himself in bed and drew the curtains."

At the top of the schema are all the participants mentioned in the discourse ordered arbitrarily. Each of them has a timeline depicted by a dotted vertical line. The events are drawn by squared boxes while the states by rounded boxes. The events are temporally delimited, positioned and ordered as they flow in the discourse, while the states stretch along the entire duration of the discourse. The temporal interval relations between events are implicit in the graphical representation.

The events are placed on the timeline of the subject participant, e.g. *Agent* that brings about the event or the possessed thing which is the head noun in possessive nominal phrases. Whether it is a state or event (e.g. *wolf lifted the latch*) is decided according to the earlier classification. Note that we treat possessive pronouns in nominal phrases as nominalised possessive processes. For example "*grandmother's bed*" is semantically equivalent to "*grandmother has a bed*" where the *grandmother* is the carrier and the *bed* is the possessed thing.

The participant roles become orthogonal relations from events or states to other participants (and sometimes to events or states, e.g. phenomenon participant role occurring in mental or influential processes). For example in Table 1, the frame semantic relations are the *agent-carrier*, *possessed* and *beneficiary.* So the event of giving is placed on the *lion*'s timeline and from this event there are two orthogonal relations to the *teapot* and *aunt.* Another example is in Figure 4 where *lift* is placed on *wolf's* timeline but it has the second participant *latch* which has the role of affected.

In current model only noun participants are considered. Therefore the pronouns (*he, her*) have to be anaphorically resolved. We assume that there is already a mechanism to resolve anaphora as correference indexing in order to trace the identity of participants and have a concise instance of the model.

This is just a preliminary attempt to characterize the discourse model since it is still a work in progress we do not yet provide a formal characterisation of it.

5 Axiomatization of Process Types and Participant Roles

In SFL, the classification of participants and process types is linguistically motivated. However some common sense principles surface as supporting models. We provide an example axiomatization for a process type and its participant roles. Such axiomatization will also serve as foundation in question generation process.

For example *action* processes are distinguished from *mental* processes as the first one occurs in physical realm while the second one in mental realm. The *actions* are considered to express quanta of change in the world occurring over time and they fall under the *event* category. In other words, the world transitions from an initial state s_i through event *e* to a final state s_f.

```
Action(e) -> si <before e <before sf
```

The actions can take a limited number of participant roles: *agent, affected, carrier* and *created.* For example *agent* role is given to the participant that brings about the event. We can say that agent *x* does the action *e*. The *affected* role is given to the participant that receives some change through action *e*. The *created* role is given to the participant that did not exist before the action *e* and it came about as a result of action *e*. We propose new relations to distinguish between the linguistic semantic and the common sense axiomatization which is of a conceptual nature. Below is the formal expression of relations between participants and the event.

```
Agent(x) -> do(x,e)
Affected(y) -> change(e,y)
Created(z) -> create(e,z)
```

If we put together all the above axioms, we can say that in the world can occur an event which may be a happening (no agent involved) or a doing of an agent. As a consequence there is a state change in the affected participant or creation of a new participant that did not exist before. Also the agent is relevant for pre-event state s_i while the affected and created are relevant for post-event state s_f.

```
Action(e) -> (do(x,e) OR happen(e)) AND
             (change(e,y) OR cre-
              ate(e,z))
```

A similar common sense axiomatization is proposed for *relational* processes. They stand in the opposition to both actions and mental processes and describe the state of affairs. For example, in an *attributive* process, the *carrier* is ascribed an *attribute* which can be either quality, identity, class or an abstract role from the domain model. The attributive processes do not denote any change so they fall into state category. We can say that in a particular state of the world *s* there is a carrier *c* that can be characterized by its attribute *a*.

```
Attributive(s) AND Carrier(c) AND
    Attribute(a)  -> is(c,a,s)
```

Similar reasoning applies to possessive relational processes.

```
Posessive(s) AND Carrier(c) AND
    Posessed(p)  -> have(c,p,s)
```

Now we can say that a state of the world *s* is characterized by the sum of relations that hold between carriers and their ascribed attributes, possessions, matches etc.

Such axiomatizations fall beyond the discourse model because they are of conceptual nature even if they are derived from a linguistic model. In the next section we describe how questions can be generated from discourse model based on such common sense axiomatizations.

6 On Question Raising

We take a situated and context-bound perspective on knowledge and language. SFL, through semantic frames, provides a linguistic support to situated knowledge while formal representation is provided through situation semantics (Barwise & Perry, 1983).

Given a relation $rel(p_1,p_2 \ldots p_n)$ where all parameters are known we generate an issue by assuming that there exist an alternative value for a parameter p_k where $1 \leq k \leq n$. We formally represent a question via lambda notation as follows:

$$\lambda p_k \ rel(p_1, \ p_2 \ldots p_k \ldots p_n)$$

In the following we illustrate the question rising mechanisms by using as seeds the below examples.

a. *[The wolf]$_{ag}$ [lifted]$_{action}$ [the latch]$_{aff}$*
b. *[grandmother's]$_{car}$ [bed]$_{poss}$*

They can be represented as common sense axiomatization from above, as follows:

```
a. Action(lift) -> do(wolf,lift) AND
                   change(lift, latch)
   si <before lift <before sf

b. Posessive(s) AND
   Carrier(grandmother) AND
   Posessed(bed) ->
            have(grandmother,bed,s)
```

Alternative participant questions are questions aiming to elicit alternative participants given the context of a particular event or state. So we can ask for alternative participants in *do* and *change* relations as follows:

```
λx do(x,lift); λy change(lift,y);
        λc has(c,bed,s)
```

This can be translated into natural language as

"Who else can lift a latch?"
"What else can a wolf lift?"
"Who else has a bed?"

Alternative event questions are questions aiming to elicit in what events the current participants can be in.

```
λe do(wolf,e); λe change(e,latch)
```

Correspondingly, the natural language expression is:

"What else a wolf can do?"
"What else can happen to a latch?"

State elicitation questions seek to receive new attributes for a given participant:

```
λa has(grandmother,a,s)
```

"What else does the grandmother have?"

Now taking into consideration change-based axiomatization for actions we can formulate questions about initial and final states even if they are not mentioned in the discourse. To do so we appeal to temporal relations to specify the position of the targeted state relative to the event.

Consequence elicitation questions seek to identify the affected participants and their corresponding post-event attributes. For example if we want to elicit how the latch changed after the event we write it as follows:

λa is(latch,a,s_f) AND $s_f >_{after}$ lift

"How is the latch after the lift?" or
"How did the latch change after the lift?"

Temporal elicitation questions aim to elicit new events or states related to a target event. For example, an event e_1 is mentioned in the discourse. Then, for a given an interval relation, e.g. *before*, assume there is an unknown state or event e_2 that stands in this relation to e_1. In natural language, this hypothesis can be translated into a question "*What happened before e_1*?" The satisfiable answer to this question will bring the new event or state statement e_2 into the discourse model. And it will be placed into a *before* relation with e_1.

When decontextualized, the above questions might sound odd or unnatural. Therefore a question selection mechanism would need to be build based on questioning sequences found in natural language dialogues that follow a predictable goal and focus of attention. We do not cover such a mechanism here, but rather are interested to explore means for finding possible question classes. When questions raising methods are clear and the possible classes are known then the selection algorithm can employ them to simulate coherent questioning sequence. So far we have provided some examples of question classes that can be generated from the discourse model, but it is neither an exhaustive nor systematic enumeration of question classes and more work needs to be done in this area. We conclude now on the proposed discourse model and question raising mechanism.

7 Discussion and Conclusions

The current paper is motivated by the idea of an automatic interviewing system. We discuss a preliminary description of a discourse model and question generation mechanism. The discourse model takes as foundation GUM ontology and can represent linguistically motivated semantic relations between entities and events and states in which they participate. However those relations are general enough as to enable further transformation into domain ontology. The model is also temporally imbued so the events and states can be ordered along the timelines of entities. In the last part of the paper we show how questions can be generated for the knowledge elicitation process.

The automatic interviewing system is motivated by ontology building process. The instances of the presented discourse model can be transformed into the topic/domain ontologies once the elicitation process if over. This challenge shall be addressed in the future work.

There are many unaddressed challenges. A few important ones are: reference tracking of participants and events, accommodation of received answers and knowledge update, question selection and sequencing along the interview session, dialogue management and turn taking, natural language generation for questions (either by employing a fully-fledged natural language generation system or a template-based approach suffices for this task).

The discourse model is intended for interactive discourses but it can be employed equally successful on non-interactive discourses with suitable adaptations of the parsing and interpretation modules to the text type. The model could be of prodigious benefit, beyond its intended meaning, for text mining, knowledge acquisition, information extraction, sentiment analysis, expert systems, semantic web and ontology building communities.

References

James F. Allen. 1983. Maintaining knowledge about temporal intervals. *Communications of the ACM*, *26*, 832–843.

Emmon Bach. 1986. The algebra of events. *Linguistics and Philosophy*, *9*, 5–16.

Jon Barwise, & John Perry. 1983. *Situations and Attitudes. Semantics A Reader* (p. 352). MIT Press.

John A. Bateman. 2008. Systemic-Functional Linguistics and the Notion of Linguistic Structure: Unanswered Questions, New Possibilities. In Jonathan J. Webster (Ed.), *Meaning in Context: Implementing Intelligent Applications of Language Studies* (pp. 24–58). London, New York: Continuum.

John A. Bateman, Renate Henschel, & Fabio Rinaldi. 1995. *The Generalized Upper Model* . Retrieved from http://www.fb10.uni-bremen.de/anglistik/langpro/webspace/jb/gum/gum-2.pdf

Stefano Borgo, & Claudio Masolo. 2009. Foundational choices in DOLCE. *Handbook on Ontologies*, *2*, 361–381.

Eugeniu Costetchi. 2013. A method to generate simplified Systemic Functional Parses from Dependency Parses. In *Proceedings of DepLing2013 [forthcoming]*. Prague.

Eugeniu Costetchi, Eric Ras, & Thibaud Latour. 2011. Automated Dialogue-Based Ontology Elicitation. *Procedia Computer Science*, *7*, 185–186.

Robin P. Fawcett. 2009. How to Analyze Process and Participant Roles. In *The Functional Semantics Handbook: Analyzing English at the level of meaning*. London: Continuum.

Mariano Ferndndez, Asuncin Gmez-p, & Natalia Juristo. 1997. METHONTOLOGY : From Ontological Art Towards Ontological Engineering. In *Assessment* (Vol. SS-97-06, pp. 33–40). AAAI Press.

Charles J. Fillmore. 1985. Frames and the semantics of understanding. *Quaderni di Semantica*, *6*, 222–254.

Paul H. Grice. 1975. Logic and Conversation. In P. Cole & J. L. Morgan (Eds.), *Syntax And Semantics* (Vol. 3, pp. 41–58). Academic Press.

Thomas R. Gruber. 1993. Towards Principles for the Design of Ontologies Used for Knowledge Sharing. *Formal Ontology in Conceptual Analysis and Knowledge Representation*, *43*, 907–928.

Michael A. K. Halliday, & Christian Matthiessen. 2004. *An introduction to functional grammar*. London: Hodder Education.

Martin Kay. 1985. Parsing In Functional Unification Grammar. In D.Dowty, L. Karttunen, & A. Zwicky (Eds.), *Natural Language Parsing*. Cambridge University Press.

William C. Mann, & Sandra A. Thompson. 1988. Rhetorical structure theory: Toward a functional theory of text organization. *Text*, *8*, 243–281.

Marie-Catherine Marneffe, Bill MacCartney, & Christopher D. Manning. 2006. Generating Typed Dependency Parses from Phrase Structure Parses. In *LREC 2006* (Vol. 6, pp. 449–454).

Marie-Catherine Marneffe, & Christopher D. Manning. 2008. The Stanford typed dependencies representation. *Coling 2008 Proceedings of the workshop on CrossFramework and CrossDomain Parser Evaluation CrossParser 08*, *1*, 1–8.

Michael O'Donnell. 2012. Transitivity Development in Spanish Learners of English. In *Proceedings of 39th International Systemic Functional Linguistics Conference*. Sydney, Australia.

Marvin Minsky. 1974. A framework for representing knowledge. In P. Winston (Ed.), *The Psychology of Computer Vision* (Vol. 20, pp. 211–277). McGraw-Hill.

Amy C. Neale. 2002. *More Delicate TRANSITIVITY: Extending the PROCESS TYPE for English to include full semantic classifications*. Cardiff.

Natalya F. Noy, & Deborah L. Mcguinness. 2000. Ontology Development 101 : A Guide to Creating Your First Ontology. *Development*, *32*, 1–25.

Robert Kasper. 1988. An Experimental Parser for Systemic Grammars. In *Proceedings of the 12th Int. Conf. on Computational Linguistics*. Budapest.

Mike Uschold, & Martin King. 1995. Towards a Methodology for Building Ontologies. In D. Skuce (Ed.), *Methodology* (Vol. 80, pp. 275–280). Citeseer.

Detecting Negated and Uncertain Information in Biomedical and Review Texts

Noa P. Cruz Díaz
Universidad de Huelva
E.T.S. de ingeniería. Ctra. Palos de la Frontera s/n. 21819
Palos de la Frontera (Huelva)
noa.cruz@dti.uhu.es

Abstract

The thesis proposed here intends to assist Natural Language Processing tasks through the negation and speculation detection. We are focusing on the biomedical and review domain in which it has been proven that the treatment of these language forms helps to improve the performance of the main task. In the biomedical domain, the existence of a corpus annotated for negation, speculation and their scope has made it possible for the development of a machine learning system to automatically detect these language forms. Although the performance for clinical documents is high, we need to continue working on it to improve the efficiency of the system for scientific papers. On the other hand, in the review domain, the absence of an annotated corpus with this kind of information has led us to carry out the annotation for negation, speculation and their scope of a set of reviews. The next step in this direction will be to adapt it to this domain for the system developed by the biomedical area.

1 Introduction

Negation and speculation are complex expressive linguistic phenomena which have been extensively studied both in linguistic and philosophy (Saurí, 2008). They modify the meaning of the phrases in their scope. This means, negation denies or rejects statements transforming a positive sentence into a negative one, e.g., "*Mildly hyperinflated lungs without focal opacity*". Speculation is used to express that some fact is not known with certainty, e.g., "*Atelectasis in the right mid zone is, however, possible*". These two phenomena are interrelated (de Haan, 1997) and have similar characteristics in the text.

From a natural language processing (NLP) perspective, identification of negation and speculation is a very important problem for a wide range of applications such as information extraction, interaction detection, opinion mining, sentiment analysis, paraphrasing and recognizing textual entailment.

For all of these tasks it is crucial to know when a part of the text should have the opposite meaning (in the case of negation) or should be treated as subjective and non-factual (in the case of speculation). This implies that a simple approach like a bag of words could be not enough so an in-depth analysis of the text would be necessary. Therefore, for improving the effectiveness of these kinds of applications, we aim to develop negation/speculation detection systems based on machine learning techniques. We focus on two domains of preference: biomedical domain and review domain.

In the biomedical domain, there are many machine learning approaches developed on detecting negative and speculative information due to the availability of the BioScope corpus, a collection of clinical documents, full papers and abstracts annotated for negation, speculation and their scope (Vincze et al., 2008), which is the same collection used in our experiments.
Our combination of novel features together with the classification algorithm choice improves the results to date for the sub-collection of clinical documents (Cruz et al., 2012).

However, the research community is trying to explore other areas such as sentiment analysis where distinguishes between objective and subjective information is also crucial and therefore must be taken into account. For example, Morante et al. (2011) discuss the need for corpora which covers different domains apart from biomedical. In fact, we are not aware of any available standard corpora of reasonable size annotated with negation and speculation in this area. This issue together with the fact that identification of this kind of information in reviews can help the opinion mining task motivated our work of annotation of the SFU Review Corpus (Konstantinova et al., 2012). This means that this corpus is the first one with an annotation of negative/speculative information and their linguistic scope in the review domain. In addition, it will allow us to develop a negation/speculation detection system in the same way we did for the biomedical domain.

With the aim of presenting the work carried out and the further work to be done, in my thesis in this respect, the structure of the paper has been divided in the following: Section 2 outlines related research; Section 3 describes the goals achieved in the biomedical and review domain. Section 4 discusses the future research directions in both domains. The paper finishes with the conclusions (Section 5).

2 Related Work

In the biomedical domain, which is the main focus of the thesis, there are many approaches developed on detecting negative and speculative information because of their benefits to the NLP applications. These approaches evolve from rule-based ones to machine learning techniques.

Among the first types of research, the one developed by Chapman et al. (2001) stands out. Their algorithm, NegEx, which is based on regular expressions, determines whether a finding or disease mentioned within narrative medical reports is present or absent. Although the algorithm is defined by the authors themselves as simple, it has proven to be powerful in negation detection in discharge summaries. The reported results of NegEx showed a precision of 84.5%, recall of 77.8% and a specificity of 94.5%. In 2007, the authors developed an algorithm called ConText (Chapman et al., 2007), an extension of the NegEx negation algorithm, which identify the values of three contextual features (negated, historical or hypothetical and experienced). In spite of its simplicity, the system performed well at identifying negation and hypothetical status.
Other interesting research works based on regular expressions are that of Mutalik et al. (2001), Elkin et al. (2005) and Huang and Lowe (2007) who were aware that negated terms may be difficult to identify if negation cues are more than a few words away from them. To address this limitation in automatically detecting negations in clinical radiology reports, they proposed a novel hybrid approach, combining regular expression matching with grammatical parsing. The sensitivity of negation detection was 92.6%, the PPV was 98.6% and the specificity was 99.8%.

However, the most recent works are based on machine-learning approaches. In addition, most of them use the BioScope corpus which is the same collection used in our experiments.
One of the most representative works in this regard is the research conducted by Morante and Daelemans (2009a). Their machine-learning system consists of five classifiers. The first one decides if the tokens in a sentence are negation cues or not. Four classifiers are used to predict the scope. Exactly, three of them determine whether a token is the first token, the last, or neither in the scope sequence and the last one uses these predictions to determine the scope classes. The set of documents used for experimentation was the BioScope corpus. The performance showed for the system in all the sub-collection of the corpus was high, especially in the case of clinical reports. The authors (2009b) extended their research to include speculation detection. They showed that the same scope-finding approach can be applied to both negation and speculation. Another recent work is that developed by Agarwal and Yu (2010). In this work, the authors detected negation cue phrases and their scope in clinical notes and biological literature from the BioScope corpus using conditional random fields (CRF) as machine-learning algorithm. The best CRF-based model obtained good results in terms of F-score both for negation and speculation detection task. Also using the BioScope corpus, recently, Velldal et al. (2012) explored two different syntactic approaches to resolve the task. One of them uses manually crafted rules operating over dependency structures while the other automatically learns a discriminative ranking function over nodes in constituent trees. The results obtained by the combination of the 2 approaches can be considered as the state-of-the-art.

On the other hand, the impact of negation and speculation detection on sentiment analysis, which is the other goal of this thesis, has not been sufficiently considered compared to the biomedical domain.

Some authors have studied the role of negation. For example, Councill et al. (2010) described a system that can exactly identify the scope of negation in free text. The authors concluded that the performance was improved dramatically by introducing negation scope detection. In more recent work, Dadvar et al. (2011) investigated the problem of determining the polarity of sentiment in movie reviews when negation words occur in the sentences. The authors also observed significant improvements on the classification of the documents after applying negation detection. Lapponi et al. (2012) reviewed different schemes for representing negation and presented a state-of-the-art system for negation detection. By employing different configurations of their system as a component in a testbed for lexical-based sentiment classification, they demonstrated that the choice of representation has a significant effect on the performance.

For its part, speculation has not received much attention perhaps because of the absence up to this point of a corpus annotated with this information. However, it should be treated in the future because authors such as Pang and Lee (2004) showed that subjectivity detection in the review domain helps to improve polarity classification.

3 Work Done

3.1 Biomedical Domain

The machine-learning system developed for negation and speculation detection was trained and evaluated on the clinical texts of the BioScope corpus. This is a freely available resource consisting of clinical documents, full articles and abstracts with annotation of negative and speculative cues and their scope. The sub-collection of clinical documents represents the major portion of the corpus and is the densest in negative and speculative information. More specifically, it contains 1,954 documents formed by a clinical history section and an impression section, the latter, used by the radiologist to describe the diagnosis obtained from the radiographies. In terms of the percentage of negation and speculation cues, it represents 4.78% of the total of words in the sub-collection. In the others, this percentage is only about 1.7%.

Our system was modeled in two consecutive classification phases. In the first one, a classifier decided whether each token in a sentence was a cue or not. More specifically, with the aim of finding complex negation cues formed by more than one word, the classifier determined if the tokens ere at the beginning, inside or outside of the cue. In the second phase, another classifier decided, for every sentence that had cues, if the other words in the sentence were inside or outside the scope of the cue. This means repeating the process as many times as cues appeared in the sentence.

We used different sets of novel features in each of the two phases into which the task was divided. They encoded information about the cue, the paired token, their contexts and the tokens between.

As classification algorithms, we experimented with Naïve Bayes and C4.5 (Quinlan, 1986) implemented in Weka (Witten & Frank, 2005). Authors such as Garcia, Fernandez and Herrera (2009) have shown its competitiveness in terms of accuracy and its adequacy for imbalanced problems. We also used Support Vector Machine (SVM) implemented in LIBSVM (Chang and Lin, 2001) because this classifier has proven to be very powerful in text classification tasks as described by Sebastiani (2002).

We trained and evaluated the system with the sub-collection of clinical documents of the BioScope corpus. This was done by randomly dividing the sub-collection into three parts, using two thirds for training and one third for evaluating.

The results obtained in negation, due to the complexity of the speculation detection task, are higher than those obtained in speculation. However, our combination of novel features together with the classification algorithm choice achieves good performance values in both cases. What's more, these results are higher than those previously published.

Cruz et al. (2012) show a complete description of the system and an extensive analysis of these results.

3.2 Review Domain

The novelty in this work is derived from the annotation of the SFU Review Corpus with negation and speculation information.

This corpus is widely used in the field of sentiment analysis and opinion mining and consists of 400 documents (50 of each type) of movie, book, and consumer product reviews from the website Epinions.com. All the texts differ in size, are written by different people and have been assigned a label based on whether it is a positive or negative review. In total, more than 17,000 sentences were annotated by one linguistic who followed the general principles used to annotate the BioScope corpus. However, in order to fit the needs of the review domain, we introduced main changes which are summarized below:

- Keywords: Unlike the BioScope corpus, where the cue words are annotated as part of the scope, for the SFU corpus we decided not to include the cue words in the scope.

- Scope: When the annotator was unsure of the scope of a keyword only the keyword was annotated.
- Type of keyword: When the annotator was unsure what type the keyword should be assigned to (whether it expresses negation or speculation), nothing was annotated.
- Coordination: The BioScope guidelines suggest extending the scope for speculation and negation keywords to all members of the coordination. However, in the case of the review domain as the keywords were not included in the scope, the scopes were annotated separately and then linked to the keywords.
- Embedded scopes: Although keywords are not included in their own scope, a keyword can be included in the scope of other keywords and situations of embedded scopes are possible. There were also cases when the combination of different types of keywords (i.e. negation and speculation ones) resulted in the embedded scopes.
- No scope: Unlike the BioScope guidelines which mention only the cases of negation keywords without scope, situations where speculation keywords had no scope were encountered as well in the review domain.

Konstantinova & de Sousa (2011) provide an extensive description of all different cases and also give examples illustrating these rules.

In addition, the nature of the review domain texts introduces a greater possibility of encountering difficult cases than in the biomedical domain. With the aim of measuring inter-annotator agreement and correcting these problematic cases, a second linguist annotated 10% of the documents, randomly selected and in a stratified way. This annotation was done according to the guidelines used by the first annotator. During the annotation process, the annotators were not allowed to communicate with each other. After the annotation was finished a disagreement analysis was carried out and the two annotators met to discuss the guidelines and the most problematic cases.

Most of the disagreement cases were simply the result of human error, when one of the annotators accidentally missed a word or included a word that did not belong either in the scope or as a part of a cue word. However, other cases of disagreement can be explained mostly by the lack of clear guidelines. More detail about theses special cases can be found in Konstantinova & de Sousa (2012).

The agreement between annotators is consider high so we can be confident that the corpus is annotated correctly and that the annotation is reproducible.

This corpus is freely downloadable[1] and the annotation guidelines are fully available as well.

4 Future Work

So far, the work done in the biomedical domain includes the development of a machine-learning system to detect speculation, negation and their linguistic scope in clinical texts. As we have mentioned, the result for this sub-collection is very good, especially for negation. However, the system is not so efficient for the other sub-collections of documents due to the fact that scientific literature presents more ambiguity and complex expressions.

Therefore, future research directions include, improving the performance of the system in this case. We will carry this out in two aspects. Firstly, in the cue detection phase we plan to use external sources of information which could include external lexicon such as WordNet or Freebase. Secondly, in the scope detection phase, it will be necessary to explore new features derived from deeper syntactic analysis because as Huang and Lowe notes (2007), structure information stored in parse trees helps identifying the scope or as Vincze (2008) points out, the scope of a cue can be determined on the basics of syntax. In fact, initial results obtained with the SFU corpus using features extracted via dependency graphs are competitive and improvable in the future by adding more syntactic information.

In addition, we plan to integrate negation/speculation detection in a clinical record retrieval system. An initial work in this regard can be found in Cordoba et al. (2011).

We also intend to broaden this work into different areas such as sentiment analysis where the corpus annotation described in the previous section will facilitate the training of a system to automatically detect negation and speculation in the same way as we did for the biomedical domain.

---

[1]http://www.sfu.ca/~mtaboada/research/SFU_Review_Corpus.html

As a last point, we intend to explore if correct annotation of negation/speculation improves the results of the SO-CAL system (Taboada et al., 2008; Taboada et al., 2011) using our system as a recognizer for this kind of information, rather than the search heuristics that the SO-CAL system is currently using. Thus, we could measure the practical impact of accurate negation/speculation detection and check as authors like Councill (2010) affirms it helps to improve the performance in sentiment predictions.

5 Conclusions

The aim of the thesis here described is to develop a system to automatically detect negation, speculation and their scope in the biomedical domain as well as in the review domain for improving NLP effectiveness. In the case of clinical documents, the system obtains a high level of performance, especially in negation. The ambiguity in scientific papers is greater and the detection becomes more complicated. Therefore, an in-depth analysis of the text is necessary to improve performance in this case.

Finally, we plan to adapt the system developed for the biomedical area to the review domain. The first step in this aspect has been the annotation of the SFU Review Corpus (Taboada et al., 2006) with negation and speculation information.

References

Shashank Agarwal and Yu Hong. 2010. Biomedical negation scope detection with conditional random fields. *Journal of the American Medical Information Association*, 17(6), pages 696–701.

Chih-Chung Chang and Chih-Jen Lin. 2001. LIBSVM: A library for support vector machines. *ACM Transactions on Intelligent Systems and Technology*, 2(27), pages 1–27.

Wendy Chapman, Will Bridewell, Paul Hanbury, Gegory Cooper and Bruce Buchanan. 2001. A simple algorithm for identifying negated findings and diseases in discharge summaries. *Journal of Biomedical Information*, 34(5), pages 301–310.

Wendy Chapman, David Chu, John Dowling. ConText: An algorithm for identifying contextual features from clinical text. 2007. *Proceedings of the Workshop on BioNLP 2007: Biological, Translational, and Clinical Language Processing*, pages 81-88.

Jose Manuel Córdoba et al. Medical-Miner at TREC 2011 Medical Records Track. TREC, 2011.

Isaac Councill, Ryan McDonald and Leonid Velikovich. 2010. What's great and what's not: Learning to classify the scope of negation for improved sentiment analysis. *Proceedings of the Workshop on Negation and Speculation in Natural Language Processing (NeSp-NLP'10)*, pages 51–59.

Noa P. Cruz Díaz, Manuel J. Maña López, Jacinto Mata Vázquez and Victoria Pachón Álvarez. 2012. A machine-learning approach to negation and speculation detection in clinical texts. *Journal of the American society for information science and technology*, 63(7), pages 1398–1410.

Maral Dadvar, Claudia Hauff and F.M.G de Jong. 2011. Scope of negation detection in sentiment analysis. *11th Dutch-Belgian Information Retrieval Workshop (DIR 2011)*, pages 16–19.

Ferdinand de Haan. 1997. *The interaction of modality and negation: a typological study*. Garland Publishing, New York, USA.

Peter Elkin, Steven Brown, Brent Bauer, Casey Husser, William Carruth, Larry Bergstrom and Dietlind Wahner-Roedler. 2005. A controlled trial of automated classification of negation from clinical notes. *BMC Medical Information Decision Making*, 5(1), 13.

Salvador García, Alberto Fernández and Francisco Herrera. 2009. Enhancing the effectiveness and interpretability of decision tree and rule induction classifiers with evolutionary training set selection over imbalanced problems. *Applied Soft Computing*, volume 9, pages 1304–1314.

Yang Huang and Henry Lowe. 2007. A novel hybrid approach to automated negation detection in clinical radiology reports. *Journal of the American Medical Information Association*, 14(3), pages 304–311.

Natalia Konstantinova and Sheila de Sousa. Annotating Negation and Speculation: the Case of the Review Domain. *Proceedings of the Second Student Research Workshop associated with RANLP 2011*, pages 139-144

Natalia Konstantinova, Sheila de Sousa, Noa Cruz, Manuel Maña, Maite Taboada and Ruslan Mitkov. 2012. A review corpus annotated for negation, speculation and their scope. *Proceedings of the Eight International Conference on Language Resources and Evaluation (LREC).*

Emanuel Lapponi, Jonathon Read, Lilja Øvrelid. 2012. Representing and resolving negation for sentiment analysis. *Proceedings of the 2012 ICDM Workshop on Sentiment Elicitation from Natural Text for Information Retrieval and Extraction.*

Roser Morante and Walter Daelemans. 2009a. A metalearning approach to processing the scope of negation. *Proceedings of the 13th Conference on*

Computational Natural Language Learning, pages 21–29.

Roser Morante and Walter Daelemans. 2009b. Learning the scope of hedge cues in biomedical texts. *Proceedings of the Workshop on BioNLP*, pages 28–36.

Roser Morante, Sarah Schrauwen and Walter Daelemans. 2011. Corpus-based approaches to processing the scope of negation cues: an evaluation of the state of the art. *Proceedings of the Ninth International Conference on Computational Semantics*, pages 350–354.

Pradeep G. Mutalik, Aniruddha Deshpande and Prakash M. Nadkarni. 2001. Use of general purpose negation detection to augment concept indexing of medical documents: A quantitative study using the UMLS. *Journal of the American Medical Information Association*, 8(6), pages 598–609.

Bo Pang and Lillian Lee. 2004. A Sentimental Education: Sentiment Analysis Using Subjectivity Summarization Based on Minimum Cuts. *Proceedings of the ACL*, pages 271-278.

John Ross Quinlan. 1986. Induction of decision trees. *Machine Learning*, volume 1, pages 81–106.

Roser Saurí. 2008. A factuality profiler for eventualities in text. *Ph.D. thesis*, Waltham, MA, USA.

Fabrizio Sebastiani. 2002. Machine learning in automated text categorization. *ACM Computing Survey*, 34(1), pages 1–47.

Maite Taboada, Caroline Anthony and Kemberly Voll. 2006. Methods for creating semantic orientation dictionaries. *Proceedings of 5th International Conference on Language Resources and Evaluation (LREC)*, pages 427–432.

Maite Taboada, Caroline Anthony, Julian Brooke, Jack Grieve and Kemberly Voll. 2008. SO-CAL: *Semantic Orientation CALculator*. Simon Fraser University, Vancouver.

Taboada, Julian Brooke, Milan Tofiloski, Kemberly Voll and Manfred Stede 2011. Lexicon-Based Methods for Sentiment Analysis. *Computational Linguistics* 37 (2), pages 267-307.

Eric Velldal, Lilja Ovrelid, Jonathon Read and Stephan Oepen S. 2012. Speculation and negation: Rules, rankers, and the role of syntax. *Computational Linguistics*.

Veronica Vincze, György Szarvas, Richárd Farkas and János Csirik. 2008. The Bio-Scope corpus: biomedical texts annotated for uncertainty, negation and their scopes. *BMC Bioinformatics*, 9(Suppl 11):S9+.

Ian H. Witten and Eibe Frank. 2005. *Data mining: Practical machine learning tools and techniques* (2nd ed.). Waltham, MA: Morgan Kaufmann.

Cross-Language Plagiarism Detection Methods

Vera Danilova
Dept. of Romance Languages, Autonomous University of Barcelona, Spain
maolve@gmail.com

Abstract

The present paper provides a summary on the existing approaches to plagiarism detection in multilingual context. Our aim is to organize the available data for the further research. Considering distant language pairs is of a particular interest for us. Cross-language plagiarism detection issue has acquired pronounced importance lately, since semantic contents of a document can be easily and discreetly plagiarized through the use of translation (human or machine-based). We attempt to show the development of detection approaches from the first experiments based on machine translation pre-processing to the up-to-date knowledge-based systems that proved to obtain reliable results on various corpora.

1 Introduction

According to Barrón-Cedeño *et al.* (2008), cross-language plagiarism detection (CLPD) consists in discriminating semantically similar texts independent of the languages they are written in, when no reference to the original source is given. However, here *similar* means that the objects (texts) share only certain characteristics and are comparable, whereas plagiarism has to do with the cases when author's original words and ideas are copied (with or without formal modifications). As follows from an updated version of the definition in Barrón-Cedeño (2012) a cross-language plagiarism case takes place when we deal with unacknowledged reuse of a text involving its translation from one language to another.

As indicated by Barrón Cedeño (2012) no technologies were developed for CLPD purposes before 2008. Since the establishment of the International Competition on Plagiarism Detection as a part of the workshop PAN (*Uncovering Plagiarism, Authorship and Social Software Misuse*) in 2009, cross-lingual issues started to draw attention of the participants. In 2010 there were attempts of using machine translation (MT) at the document pre-processing step in order to deal with non-English documents as possible sources of plagiarism. The detailed comparison of sections was implemented using traditional monolingual methods. The main problems that manifested themselves immediately were computational cost and quality of MT that is so far unable to permit reliable comparison of suspicious texts and sources. Moreover, authors tend to modify translated texts using paraphrases, which makes the discrimination process even more complicated. Also, one of the main challenges is the presence of salient distinctions in syntactic structures of languages belonging to different families.

It was already in 2008 that the researchers started to come up with new strategies for avoiding the MT step. Barrón Cedeño (2008) proposed a statistical approach based on parallel corpora for the CLPD. In Lee *et al.* (2008), a text categorization approach was posited. Domain-specific classification was performed using support vector machine model and parallel corpora containing Chinese-English text pairs. Similarity measurement was carried out by means of language-neutral clustering based on Self-Organizing Maps (SOM). Ceska *et al.* (2008) proposed a tool named MLPlag based on the word location analysis. EuroWordNet thesaurus was used for language-independent text representation (synonym normalization). Detailed comparison was performed by computing both symmetric (VSM-based) and asymmetric similarity measures, which required a preliminary calculation of occurrence frequency of plagiarized words. Multilingual pre-processing involving lemmatization and inter-lingual indexing anticipated the comparison.

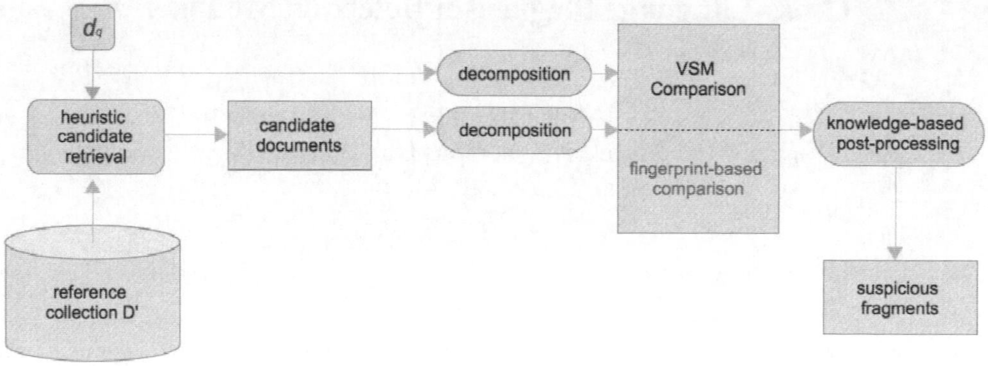

Figure 1: Plagiarism detection process (adapted from Potthast *et al.* (2011).

Despite of the disadvantages of MT-based approach, it was not discarded by the researchers. As Meuschke and Gipp (2013) point out, it is suitable for small document collections. In the subsequent sections we describe the application of MT and other approaches more in detail.

2 Related Work

The surveys by Potthast *et al.* (2011) and Barrón Cedeño *et al.* (2013) were dedicated exclusively to the classification and evaluation of CLPD methods. Also, a large description of CLPD technology is provided in the doctoral thesis by Barrón Cedeño (2012). Potthast *et al.* (2011) outline the steps of CLPD process, provide some strategies of heuristic retrieval and evaluate the performance of three models for the detailed analysis. Barrón Cedeño *et al.* (2013) enrich this survey by describing the whole architecture of plagiarism analysis. Also, a modification to the classification of detailed analysis methods is introduced and an evaluation of three other models is provided.

The rest of the article is organized as follows: Section 3 introduces the main approaches to CLPD, explains the prototypical structure of analysis and outlines the performance evaluation, presented in the previous surveys; Section 4 concludes the paper.

3 Approaches to CLPD

3.1 Intrinsic VS External CLPD

Barrón Cedeño (2012) divides CLPD methods into intrinsic and external, because, as shown in the literature, intrinsic plagiarism detection techniques allow to discriminate the so called *effects of translation process* inside the text. Some of the relevant indicators found by researchers are as follows: function words, morphosyntactic categories, personal pronouns, adverbs (in 2006 by Baroni and Bernardini); animate pronouns, such as *I, we, he*, cohesive markers, such as *therefore, thus* (in 2011 by Koppel and Ordan); a high number of *hapax legomena* (in 2006 by Somers).

Some researchers, cited in Pataki (2012), argue that no regularities indicating MT within texts were revealed as a result of a series of experiments with German-English translation, which is one of the best qualities. Thus, they regard this solution as infeasible due to the randomness and variable nature of features.

3.2 CLPD Process Structure

The majority of authors attribute CLPD to the external PD approach, as in Meuschke and Gipp (2013), therefore, the same conventional detection steps, namely, candidate retrieval, detailed comparison and knowledge-based post-processing are distinguished and remain unchanged, as shown in the surveys by Potthast *et al.* (2011) and Barrón Cedeño *et al.* (2013). The standard plagiarism detection workflow is presented in Fig. 1.

3.3 Retrieval and Comparison

The candidate retrieval stage applies heuristics in order to reduce the search space (included topic/genre filtering of the potential source documents). Potthast *et al.* (2011) outlined three approaches: the first one implies query formulation on the basis of keywords extracted from the suspicious document and translated into the corresponding language (a CLIR solution); the next two approaches rely on the results of machine translation and make use of either standard keyword retrieval (an IR solution) or hash coding. Detailed comparison step includes measuring the similarity between suspicious text and the potential source documents resulting from the candidate retrieval step. The corresponding methods outlined in Potthast *et al.* (2011) are as follows: syntax-based (CL-CNG), dictionary-based (Eurovoc thesaurus-based, CL-VSM), parallel corpora based (CL-ASA, CL-LSI, CL-KCCA) and comparable corpora-based (CL-ESA). Some of them rely on the use of tools, containing language- and topic-specific information, e.g. dictionary based, parallel corpora-based, comparable corpora-based and some of them do not, such as syntax-based. In what follows a detailed explanation is provided for each one of the comparison models.

Syntax-Based Models

CL-CNG or Cross-Language Character N-Gram model uses overlapping character 4-gram tokenization on the basis of the Hopkins Automated Information Retriever for Combing Unstructured Text (HAIRCUT) system and was created by McNamee and Mayfield (2004). The key distinction of this approach lies in the possibility of comparing multilingual documents without translation. The best results were achieved for the languages sharing similar syntactic structure and international lexicon (e.g., related European language pairs).

The rest of the methods depends on the use of lexico-conceptual knowledge bases, corpora and dictionaries.

Dictionary-Based Models

CL-VSM (Cross-Language Vector Space Model) approach consists in constructing vector space models of the documents using indexed thesauri, dictionaries and other concept spaces. Eurovoc and corpora developed in the JRC(Joint Research Centre), e.g. JRC-Acquis Multilingual Parallel Corpus, presented in Steinberger (2012) link texts through the so called "language-independent anchors", multilingual pairs of words that denote entity names, locations, dates, measurement units etc.. In Gupta (2012) CL-CTS, Cross-Language Conceptual Thesaurus-Based Similarity method, is proposed, which is an algorithm that measures the similarity between texts written in different languages (English, German and Spanish in that particular case) on the basis of the domain-specific mapping presented in Eurovoc. An *ad-hoc* function defines whether a document belongs to some thesaurus concept *id*, represented by vector dimension in multidimensional vector space. The main advantage of this method lies in robustness to topic variance. In Pataki (2012) a dictionary-based language-independent approach is presented that consists of three main stages, namely, search space reduction, similarity estimation and filtering of results. Retrieval space is reduced by means of document pre-processing (fragmentation, stemming, elimination of stop-words), key words extraction and translation of their lemmas. It was estimated that the optimum number of translations equals to five. The main distinction of the present method lies in the use of an *ad-hoc* metric based on the minimum function, which allows to discard word number variance. Its purpose is to verify whether the compared documents are likely to be translations of one another. Post-processing step is rule-based and considers two thresholds for the obtained similarities. In order to reduce the computational cost of candidate retrieval and similarity analysis it was proposed in Pataki and Marosi (2012) to use SZTAKI desktop grid. It dynamically uploads and preprocesses information from the Wikipedia database and stores it to the KOPI system. Torrejón and Ramos (2011) presented a combination of n-gram and dictionary-based approach as an extension to "CoReMo" System developed earlier for external plagiarism detection purposes. ***Direct2stem*** and ***stem2stem*** dictionaries are integrated into the system and are based on Wiktionary and Wikipedia interlanguage links dictionaries. ***Direct2stem*** takes full words as entries and provides translations of the most frequent stems as output. ***Stem2stem*** gets activated in case the previous dictionary could not find any translation variant: original roots are taken as input in this case. If both dictionaries fail, the word gets stemmed by the English rules. CoReMo System's core rests on CTNG or *Contextual n-grams*, and RM, *Referential Monotony*. Contextual n-gram modelling is used to obtain the inverted index and uncover plagiarized fragments, which is performed by alphabetic ordering of overlapping 1-grams. Pre-processing includes case folding, elimination of stopwords, Porter stemming and internal sorting. Referential monotony is an algorithm that selects the longest sequences of text splits that indicate possible plagiarism and compares them to the whole source text. CoReMo system algorithm's advantages, as observed by the authors, are good runtime performance (obtaining of global results in 30 minutes), integrated dictionary and low computer requirements.

Comparable Corpora-Based Models

CL-ESA or Cross-Language Explicit Similarity Analysis, as reported in Potthast *et al.* (2011) represents approaches based on comparable corpora. According to Talvensaari (2008), as opposed to parallel corpora (CL-LSI, CL-KCCA and CL-ASA models), comparable corpora concept does not involve sentence-aligned translations. It is represented by topic-related texts with common vocabulary. Wikipedia encyclopedia and similar resources can serve as an example. These corpora are noisier, but at the same time more flexible. CL-ESA approach implies automatic creation of word associations for bilingual document representation in order to perform comparison of vocabulary correlation. As explained in Cimiano *et al.* (2009), concept space C is associated precisely to the article space in Wikipedia, therefore the approach is called "explicit". The association strength between the suspicious document and the concept space is evaluated by calculating the sum of the *tf-idf* values of the article for all words of the analysed text. Later, for cross-language retrieval purposes, the method was extended by the employment of Wikipedia language links to index the document with respect to the corresponding articles in any language.

Parallel Corpora-Based Models

CL-ASA or Cross-Language Alignment Similarity Analysis introduced by Barrón Cedeño *et al.* (2008) implies creation of bilingual statistical dictionary (core of CLiPA (Cross-Lingual Plagiarism Analysis) system) on the basis of parallel corpus being aligned using the well-known IBM Model 1. As observed in Ceska *et al.* (2008) word positions are taken into account. At the second step expectation maximization algorithm is applied in order to calculate statistical dictionary probabilities. The model was modified, as presented in Potthast *et al.* (2011): translation model probability $p(d_q/d')$ was changed to weight measure $w(d_q/d')$ and language model probability $p(d')$ was substituted by a length model in order to apply it similarity analysis of full-scale documents of variable length.

CL-LSI or Cross-Language Latent Semantic Indexing also uses parallel corpora. It is a common strategy applied in IR systems for term-document association. It is "latent" in the way that it extracts topic-related lexemes from the data itself and not from the external sources as opposed to CL-ESA. In Potthast *et al.* (2011) it is observed that CL-LSI is characterized by poor runtime performance due to the use of linear algebra technique, singular value decomposition of the original term-document matrix, as the core of the algorithm. According to Cimiano *et al.* (2009), concepts are latently contained in the columns of one of the orthogonal matrices (term-concept correlation weights) resulting from the main matrix decomposition.

CL-KCCA or Cross-Language Kernel Canonical Correlation Analysis performs much better than LSI on the same datasets, although it is based on SVD as well, according to Vinokourov *et al.* (2002). However, Potthast *et al.* (2011) observe that for the same reasons of runtime performance this approach cannot compete with CL-CNG and CL-ASA. As explained in Vinokourov *et al.* (2002), CL-KCCA analyses the correspondence of points in two embedding spaces that represent bilingual document pair and measures the correlation of the respective projection values. It provides detection of certain semantic similarities, represented by word sets with the same patterns of occurrence values for given bilingual document pairs.

One of more recent approaches named CL-KGA was not included into this classification. It can be considered both dictionary- and comparable corpora-based. It is described as follows. CL-KGA or Cross-Language Knowledge Graph Analysis, presented in Franco-Salvador *et al.* (2013), is substantially new in that it involves the use of the recently created multilingual semantic network BabelNet and graph-based text representation and comparison. In BabelNet, WordNet synsets and Wikipedia pages form concepts (nodes), meanwhile semantic pointers and hyperlinks constitute relations (edges) respectively, as explained in Navigli (2012). This structure enhances word-sense disambiguation and concept mapping of the analysed documents. However, any other knowledge base can be integrated into this system, as pointed out by the authors. Text fragmentation at the pre-processing step is performed using 5-sentence sliding window, grammatical categories are tagged with the TreeTagger tool. Similarity is measured basing on relation and concept weight values. CL-KGA, as observed by Franco-Salvador *et al.* (2013), refines the results of the other state-of-the-art approaches, according to plagdet evaluation results.

Barrón Cedeño *et al.* (2013) update this classification by adding the fifth model (MT-based) and attributing the whole set to the retrieval step, not the detailed comparison. Thus, as a result we have five families of retrieval models: lexicon-based, thesaurus-based, comparable corpus-based, parallel corpus-based and MT-based. Authors define them as *systems*. Lexicon-based systems (an amplified version syntax-based model class, presented in Potthast *et al.* (2011)) comprise the following techniques: *cognateness*, based on prefixes and other tokens; *dot-plot* model, based on character *n*-grams; CL-CNG (Cross-Language Character N-Grams). The rest of the models, except the MT-based one, are identical to those described in Potthast *et al.* (2011). MT-based model (or *T+MA*) involves determination of the suspicious document language with a language detector, translation and monolingual analysis. In Barrón Cedeño (2012) T+MA includes *web-based CL models* and *multiple translations*. The approach by Kent and Salim (2009 and 2010) belongs to the first type. They use Google Translate API to obtain English versions of texts that were originally written in Malay, with that the further pre-processing and comparison using three least-frequent four-grams fingerprint matching are performed. The approach by Muhr *et al.* (2010) is attributed to the second type. Instead of a full-scale automatic translation, they make use only of the main component of the corresponding systems: word alignment algorithm. German and Spanish texts form the corpus for the subsequent experiments. The words are aligned using BerkeleyAligner and 5 translation candidates are assigned on the basis of the Europarl corpus. As observed in Barrón Cedeño *et al.* (2013), T+MA proved its efficiency in PAN 2011, however, the same translation system (Google Translator) was used for generation and analysis. Therefore, an evaluation of T+MA performance using other translation systems was implemented.

3.4 Results of Performance Evaluation

In Potthast *et al.* (2011) the performance of CL-C3G (based on 3-grams), CL-ESA and CL-ASA was compared. Three experiments (cross-language ranking, bilingual rank correlation and cross-language similarity distribution) were carried out on the basis of two aligned corpora: comparable Wikipedia and parallel JRC-Acquis corpus (legal documents of the European Union aligned in 22 languages). Language pairs included English as the first language and Spanish, German, French, Dutch, or Polish as the second one. CL-C3G and CL-ESA show better results when suspicious and original documents share topic-specific information, whereas CL-ASA performs better with professional and automatic translations (due to the nature of the corpora used). CL-ASA and CL-ESA, as opposed to CL-CNG, can be applied for distant language pairs with alphabet and syntax unrelated, as pointed out in Barrón Cedeño (2012). CL-ESA, as compared to CL-ASA and CL-C3G, proved to be more a general purpose retrieval model, however, it depends much on the languages involved. CL-C3G outperformed the other approaches within the framework of these experiments.

In Barrón Cedeño (2012) the performance of CL-CNG, CL-ASA and CL-T+MA was compared. The author was interested in studying the behaviour of the models with respect to distant language pairs (Basque-English and Basque-Spanish). T+MA outperformed the other models, because it doesn't depend neither on corpora nor on syntactic/lexical similarities between languages. However, it is a computationally expensive method and there is still a lack of good automatic translators for most language pairs.

In Barrón Cedeño *et al.* (2013) another evaluation of CL-CNG, CL-ASA and CL-T+MA is presented, which is base on PAN-PC-11 corpus (Spanish-English). This is a standard corpus for plagiarism detection that allows for the analysis of plagiarism cases from exact copy to paraphrase and translation. Three experiments are carried out in order to assess the models performance with respect to precision and recall values. The respective scenarios are as follows. In Experiment A the suspicious document is an exact copy of a reference collection document. This experiment is designed to adjust the parameters of CL-ASA. In Experiment B the candidate and source are known and the aim is to detect plagiarized fragments. In Experiment C plagiarized fragments shall be retrieved from the noisy set of reference collection documents. According to the results of Experiment A, performance of the models depends on the document length: when considering an exact copy case, CL-CNG and T+MA work better with longer documents as opposed to CL-ASA (due to the use of length model). CL-CNG appears to outperform the other models in paraphrase uncovering. As to the results of Experiment B, T+MA shows the best recall in fragment detection, whereas CL-ASA provides the highest precision values, particularly in case of long texts (chunks have a fixed length of 5 sentences). Short plagiarism cases appear to be the hardest to detect. Within the framework of the Experiment C, CL-ASA provided better values of F-measure on short texts than T+MA model. Those obtained using CL-CNG, despite of not being influenced by the length and nature of plagiarism, turned out to be the worst ones. On the basis of the experiments performed authors conclude that T+MA and CL-CNG can be considered as recall-oriented systems and CL-ASA as a precision-oriented one.

4 Conclusions

The paper in hand outlines the existing approaches to translated plagiarism detection for the purposes of further research in the context of distant language pairs. The problem-oriented surveys by Potthast *et al.* (2011) and Barrón Cedeño *et al.* (2013) are summarized. It can be seen that the prototypical detection process remains unchanged: it includes heuristic retrieval, detailed comparison and knowledge-based filtering. Retrieval and comparison algorithms are being modified and knowledge bases are being expanded. CL-CNG was developed in 2004 and it is still one of the best-performing approaches that does not require the availability of any concept bases, such as dictionaries, thesauri, semantic networks or corpora, however it performs well only for languages sharing syntactic and lexical similarities (Indoeuropean families). All of the other analysis approaches depend on the availability of knowledge bases. In Torrejón and Ramos (2011) and Pataki (2012) *ad-hoc* dictionaries are used; Steinberger (2012) and Gupta (2012) describe the application of Eurovoc thesaurus; CL-ESA makes use of comparable corpora and such models as CL-ASA, CL-KCCA, CL-LSI require the availability of parallel corpora to properly perform the analysis; CL-KGA approach relies on the use of large semantic network BabelNet that combines WordNet synsets with Wikipedia articles, thus ensuring a more precise concept mapping. MT+A, according to the comparison by Barrón Cedeño *et al.* (2013), provides the best results, however, the translation of the whole reference collection is too costly and the corresponding translation services are far from being perfect, particularly for the cases of distant language pairs. Within the framework of the considered approaches, linguistic features are taken into account at the pre-processing step (lemmatization, case-folding, grammatical categories tagging etc.). Due to the variation in languages structures, their analysis is being avoided at the comparison step for the purposes of preserving runtime characteristics. The core analysis unit for the present methods is either character (CL-CNG) or word with the underlying concepts and connections.

References

Alberto Barrón-Cedeño, Paolo Rosso, David Pinto, and Alfons Juan. 2008. *On cross-lingual plagiarism analysis using a statistical model.* Proceedings of the ECAI'08 PAN Workshop: Uncovering Plagiarism, Authorship and Social Software Misuse, pp. 9-13. Patras, Greece.

Alberto Barrón-Cedeño. 2012. *On the Mono- and Cross-Language Detection of Text Re-Use and Plagiarism (Thesis).* Departmento de Sistemas Informáticos y Computación, Universidad Politécnica de Valencia.

Alberto Barrón-Cedeño, Parth Gupta, and Paolo Rosso. 2013 *Methods for cross-language plagiarism detection.* Knowledge-Based Systems 50, 211-217.

Zdenek Ceska, Michal Toman, and Karel Jezek. 2008. *Multilingual Plagiarism Detection.* AIMSA 2008, LNAI 5253, pp. 83-92, 2008.

Philipp Cimiano, Antje Schultz, Sergey Sizov, Philipp Sorg, and Steffen Staab 2009. *Explicit Versus Latent Concept Models for Cross-Language Information Retrieval.* Proceedings of the Twenty-First International Joint Conference on Artificial Intelligence (IJCAI-09).

Marc Franco-Salvador, Parth Gupta, and Paolo Rosso. 2013. *Cross-Language Plagiarism Detection Using a Multilingual Semantic Network.* IECIR 2013, LNCS 7814, pp. 710-713.

Parth Gupta, Alberto Barrón-Cedeño, and Paolo Rosso. 2012. *Cross-Language High Similarity Search Us-*

ing a Conceptual Thesaurus. ACLEF 2012, LNCS 7488, pp. 67-75, 2012.

Chow Kok Kent, and Naomie Salim. 2009. *Web Based Cross Language Plagiarism Detection*. Journal of Computing, Volume 1, Issue 1.

Chow Kok Kent, and Naomie Salim. 2010. *Web Based Cross Language Plagiarism Detection*. Second International Conference on Computational Intelligence, Modelling and Simulation, pages 199-204, IEEE.

Chung-Hong Lee, Chih-Hong Wu, and Hsin-Chang Yang. 2008. *A Platform Framework for Cross-lingual Text Relatedness Evaluation and Plagiarism Detection*. The 3rd International Conference on Innovative Computing Information and Control (ICICIC'08).

Paul McNamee, and James Mayfield. 2004. *Character N-Gram Tokenization for European Language Text Retrieval*. Information Retrieval,7,773-97.

Norman Meuschke, and Bela Gipp 2013. *State-of-the-art in detecting academic plagiarism*. International Journal for Educational Integrity Vol. 9 No.1, pp. 50-71 .

Markus Muhr, Roman Kern, Mario Zechner, and Michael Granitzer. 2010. *External and Intrinsic Plagiarism Detection Using a Cross-Lingual Retrieval and Segmentation System*. Lab report for PAN at CLEF 2010.

Roberto Navigli 2012. *Babelplagiarism: What can BabelNet do for cross-language plagiarism detection?*. Keynotes for PAN 2012: Uncovering, Authorship, ad Social Software Misuse.

Máté Pataki. 2012. *A new approach for searching translated plagiarism*. Proceedings of the 5th International Plagiarism Conference. Newcastle, UK.

Máté Pataki, and Attila Csaba Marosi 2012. *Searching for Translated Plagiarism with the Help of Desktop Grids*. Journal of Grid Computing, 1-18.

Martin Potthast, Alberto Barrón-Cedeño, Benno Stein, and Paolo Rosso. 2011. *Cross-language plagiarism detection*. Language Resources and Evaluation 45:45-62.

Ralf Steinberger 2012. *Cross-lingual similarity calculation for plagiarism detection and more - Tools and resources*. Keynotes for PAN 2012: Uncovering, Authorship, ad Social Software Misuse.

Tuomas Talvensaari. 2008. *Comparable Corpora in Cross-Language Information Retrieval (Academic Dissertation)*. Acta Electronica Universitatis Tamperensis 779.

Diego Antonio Rodríguez Torrejón, and José Manuel Martí Ramos. 2011. *Crosslingual CoReMo System*. Notebook for PAN at CLEF 2011.

Alexei Vinokourov, John Shawe-Taylor, and Nello Cristianini. 2002. *Inferring a Semantic Representation of Text via Cross-Language Correlation Analysis*. Advances of Neural Information Processing Systems 15.

Rule-Based Named Entity Extraction For Ontology Population

Aurore de Amaral
LIASD, EA 4383, Université Paris 8
aurore.de-amaral@etud.univ-paris8.fr

Abstract

Currently, Text analysis techniques such as named entity recognition rely mainly on ontologies which represent the semantics of an application domain. To build such an ontology from specialized texts, this article presents a tool which detects proper names, locations and dates from texts by using manually written linguistic rules. The most challenging task is to extract not only entities but also interpret the information and adapt in a specific corpus in French.

Keywords

named entity extraction, information retrieval, ontology population

1 Introduction

Information extraction is fundamental since a wide variety of texts were digitized and created through Web. In this area, ontology learning is a good option to provide such information and efficiently share conceptualizations with experts and researchers. Due to this environment, it is crucial to do an efficient extraction in the texts. People and their relationships as well as locations, dates and domain terms must be discovered to create (Aussenac-Gilles et al., 2000) or complete an ontology (Magnini et al., 2006).

Because of the quantity of textual data to analyze and the continuous evolution of information (Reymonet, 2008), the extraction step should be automatically processed as much as possible. Extraction of named entities (NE) is one of the first task in ontology learning because they represent persons, names, locations and are unambiguous (Mondary, 2011). They are related to noun names like primarly defined in the MUC[1] conferences (Chinchor, 1997) and are an important part of the information retrieval domain.

This paper describes a mining method of named entities for improving the search in annotated corpora. It uses linguistic rules and lexicons. It is a qualitative method, for which the use of quantitative elements may optimize the number of results. This is the first part of an ontology learning architecture which transforms raw text data in a semantic network. From the network, a final ontology will be built, extended or populated, which will not be explained in this paper. We focus on information extraction, named entity recognition.

In section 2, the corpus that we used is described. In section 3, we present a state of art in named entity extraction. The proposed approach is exposed in section 4. In section 5, we evaluate our method of extraction and discuss it. Finally, we conclude and suggest some perspectives.

2 Domain Based Corpus

The corpus used is a digitized french dictionary, *Le dictionnaire de la Spiritualité* (the Dictionary of Spirituality), published by Éditions Beauchesne (Paris). It is an encyclopedia used by researchers in religious studies and Divinity. With more than ten thousand articles spread over a dozen volumes, it studies all the actors of Christianity. Historical events are widely represented and are a huge source of knowledge. That is why it is a reference work for all students interested in religious history of Christianity and more broadly for all historians.

The encyclopedia contains a set of entries related to other books via a number of bibliographic references that can be found at the end of each entry. Each reference contains names, places and dates.

[1] MUC: Message Understanding Conference

3 Named Entity Extraction

Currently, The systems evaluated in MUC (Poibeau, 2011) or ESTER 2 (Galliano et al., 2009) campaigns produce good results in named entity extraction, especially in newspaper articles. But the ease of use of these systems are rarely evaluated (Marrero et al., 2009), although it is important to use them at the beginning of an information extraction system.

3.1 Different Approaches

The challenges in NE recognition are found in the issue of the definition of the named entities. With the first MUC evaluation campaigns, the point was to detect persons, organization, locations, dates and numbers (ENAMEX, TIMEX and NUMEX (Chinchor, 1997)). Later, the definition of a named entity has included other categories (e.g, business concepts, also called "specfic interest entity" (Dutrey et al., 2012)) : issues involved recognition and categorisation of entities, with disambiguisation of homonymy and metonymy.

Two main approaches exist in NE extraction : linguistic approach (also called symbolic approach) (Ben Hamadou et al., 2010; Poibeau, 2003) and a statistical approach (Favre et al., 2005). The two approaches ensure satisfying results, the second one particularly on speech systems (Poibeau, 2011). The results tend to improve the precision without changing the recall of the first algorithms.

3.2 Lexicons

Our choice is to add lexical entries to expand the global lexicon. This lexicon is created with ontology concept names and their synonyms found in a dictionary on the Web[2]. Thus, the detection of people roles and locations is improved by applying lexico-syntactic rules. The method is really relevant and domain-dependent. However, the learning process admits the creation of new concept names during the searching step.

3.3 NLP Tools

In order to help this term extraction step, a natural language processing platform may be used. In (Poibeau, 2003), the author uses SYNTEX to create the grammar rules. We have chosen NooJ, which proposes syntactic parser to process and represents all types of linguistic units (Silberztein, 2009). This system is also able to show transformational analysis and export them. Finally, the ease of use with a graphical user interface tend to help the evolution of the system. In the next section, all the steps of the NE recognition method will be detailed.

[2] `http://www.crisco.unicaen.fr/des/`

4 The Proposed Approach

4.1 Lexicon Data

First, a lexicon of french cities and european countries is created. Then, a lexicon of religion domain is created. This lexicon is based on an ontology, which represents religion and other concepts validated by an expert. Classes' leaves and individuals are used to create entries. The parent's classes are used to add a semantic annotation to them. Then, morphological structures like inflectional paradigms may be manually written, for instance french plurals.

The concept names create a general lexicon. The search for synonyms of the same grammatical category automatically adds new entries to the lexicon. Without these new entries, the lexicon contains 63 entries. NooJ adds plural ones and the total is 110. There is an exemple of the NooJ dictionary showed below of french inflexional plural, when suffixes "al" become "aux" in plural :

```
cardinal,cardinal,
N+Hierarchical
+FLX=Cheval+m+s
cardinaux,cardinal,
N+Hierarchical
+FLX=Cheval+m+p
```

4.2 Syntactic Label Rules

The second step consists in manually creating global rules to delimit the main NE in the text: proper names, hierarchical names, dates, places of worship and cities. With this basic information, it will be easier to understand the relationships between actors and events. The transformational analysis shows what and where it is more suitable to annotate. Then, it shows all exceptions of predetermined rules. Tokens frequences and concordances are some of the examples of the tools the NooJ platform can perform.

The corpus contains 9466 different tokens. There is 50 entries (some of them are blank). After a syntactic parsing, named entity rules are applied. Since NooJ cannot disambiguate frequent words, a

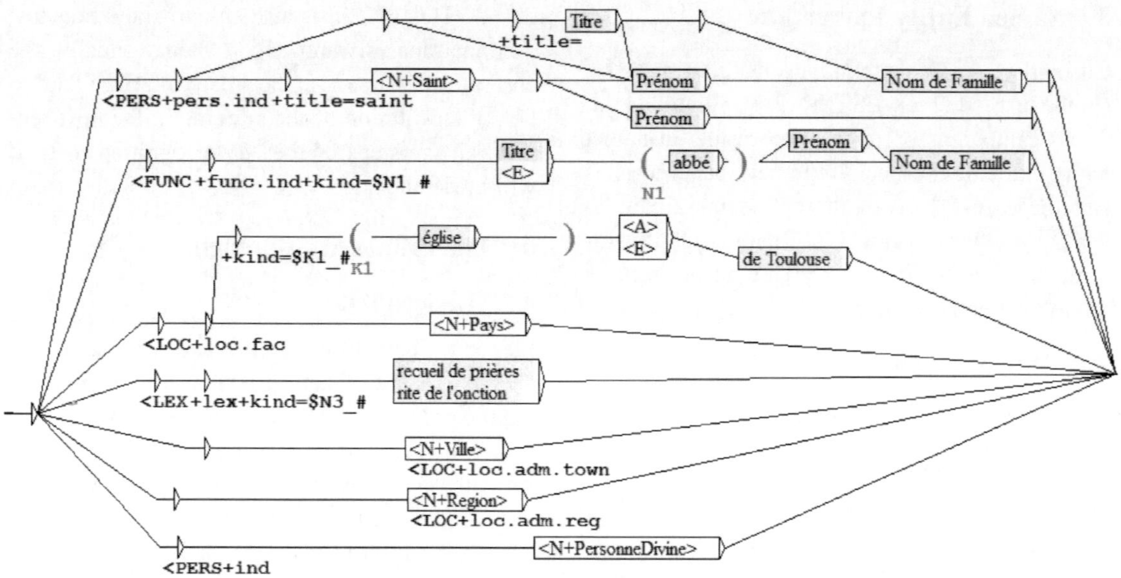

Figure 1: Main graph in NooJ

small grammar is used to identify the french grammatical more used words. There is a grammar for dates, proper names (PN) and places. The main graph in NooJ is shown in Figure 1.

The gender of the names can be identified with forenames or roles. Locations or patronyms can induce cities or place names. The nominal groups, which contain lexicon words, are also annotated. The number of results of the method is presented in Table 1.

PN	Locations	Dates
1016	985	1198

Table 1: Number of annotated text

There are different kinds of annotated proper names. The first ones and the most representative are general patronyms. A general rule distinguishes patronyms by a unique forename, which already exists in NooJ's lexicon forename or a list of uppercase words with dash followed by an other general rule for french surnames.

One of the surname's rules detects an uppercase word which may contain *de* followed by another uppercase word. *de* (of) is a french preposition which is often found in proper nouns, and can also describe functions and roles. 48 different patronyms contain a french abbreviation title (*M.* for mister, *Mme* for madam, *Melle* for unmarried womens and *Mgr* for an honorific), but other titles could be added. The number of results is shown in Table 2. Names preceded by the word *Saint* or words like priest point out a name and a religious function or a job. The compound names designates persons by their roles and not their names.

Patronyms	With functions	"saint"
832	98	86

Table 2: Number of different kinds of recognized persons

The search for locations like places of worship may identify towns, even if the lexicon of towns does not contain them. In general cases, a noun, which designates a location defined in the dictionary is followed by *de* and a first uppercase word. This uppercase word is a country or a city. A dictionary of towns and regions of France is used to disambiguate these relations.

Then, absolute dates and some kinds of relatives dates are found. There are a lot of occurrences of years.

4.3 Markup Export For The Ontology

The NooJ export file like shown in Table 3 contains several lines. This file is treated like a CSV file. The first information is the entry of the encyclopedia where the entity was found, then the entity surrounded by his left and right context. Each entity have markup tags. The markup tags used in our context take into account the general guidelines of Quaero (Rosset et al., 2011). These guidelines extend the first ones for named entities defined in MUC (Chinchor, 1997). Proper names have the *pers.ind* tag, people's function *func.ind*, locations *loc.adm.town* for towns and *loc.fac* for countries and general places. Then, dates have the *time.date* tag.

du bourg Verbe incarné, récemment rétabli a **Azérables/**LOC+loc.adm.town , elle est retenue à Limoges
du bourg ruction de la jeunesse. Elle expose ces faits l' **évêque de Limoge**s /FUNC+func.ind+kind=évêque +loc.adm.town=Limoges et lui communique son projet. Celui-ci approuve
du bourg Saint-Sacrement. Sa première communion, **le 24 juin 1800/**DATE+time.date.abs +year=1800+day=24+month=juin+year=1800 , lui laissera un souvenir qui

Table 3: Results with Quaero markup

5 Evaluation

For the system evaluation, a new corpus was created with three random articles to compare human and rule-based annotations. The evaluation results are shown in Table 4. We use F-measure which measures relevant results. Some improvements could be made by detecting more locations and adding more lexicon entries. There are 6 redundant results due to ambiguous surnames detected with NooJ. So, we could improve the proper names detection rules to eliminate some ambiguous answers and add roles in the lexicon.

	Persons	**Locations**	**Dates**
recall	0,64	0,53	0,95
precision	0,94	0,79	1
F-mesure	76%	63%	97%

Table 4: Evaluation results

6 Conclusion

The first step of the creation of an ontology learning architecture is information extraction. For this purpose, we choose to detect named entities because of the relative monosemic representation in text. Our tool uses rule-based methods and lexicons, partially created automatically with synonyms, applied on a domain-dependent corpus. The results are moderate with a good precision and relatively good performance for dates. Some improvements will be applied, especially with the detection of proper names without change the lexicons. Relations between all of this information and a parsing of bibliographic entries is the next step before the ontology learning process.

References

Nathalie Aussenac-Gilles, Brigitte Biébow, and Sylvie Szulman. 2000. Modélisation du domaine par une méthode fondée sur l'analyse de corpus. In *Actes de la 9e Conférence Francophone d'Ingénierie des Connaissances IC 2000*. Université Paul Sabatier.

Abdelmajid Ben Hamadou, Odile Piton, and Héla Fehri. 2010. Multilingual Extraction of functional relations between Arabic Named Entities using NooJ platform.

Nancy Chinchor. 1997. Muc-7 named entity task definition `http://www.itl.nist.gov/iaui/894.02/related_projects/muc/proceedings/ne_task.html`.

Camille Dutrey, Chloé Clavel, Sophie Rosset, Ioana Vasilescu, and Martine Adda-Decker. 2012. Quel est l'apport de la détection d'entités nommées pour l'extraction d'information en domaine restreint ? In *Proceedings of the Joint Conference JEP-TALN-RECITAL 2012, volume 2: TALN*, pages 359–366. ATALA/AFCP.

Benoît Favre, Frédéric Béchet, and Pascal Nocéra. 2005. Robust named entity extraction from large spoken archives. In *Proceedings of the conference on Human Language Technology and Empirical Methods in Natural Language Processing*, HLT '05, pages 491–498. Association for Computational Linguistics.

Sylvain Galliano, Guillaume Gravier, and Laura Chaubard. 2009. The ester 2 evaluation campaign for the rich transcription of french radio broadcasts. In *Interspeech 2009*.

Bernardo Magnini, Emanuele Pianta, Octavian Popescu, and Manuela Speranza. 2006. Ontology population from textual mentions: Task definition and benchmark. In *Proceedings of the 2nd Workshop on Ontology Learning and Population: Bridging the Gap between Text and Knowledge*. Association for Computational Linguistics.

Monica Marrero, Sonia Sanchez-Cuadrado, Jorge Morato, and Yorgos Andreadakis. 2009. Evaluation of Named Entity Extraction Systems. In *Research In Computer Science*, volume 41, pages 47–58. Centro de Investigación en Computación del IPN.

Thibault Mondary. 2011. *Construction d'ontologies à partir de textes. L'apport de l'analyse de concepts formels*. Ph.D. thesis, Université Paris 13 - LIPN.

Thierry Poibeau. 2003. *Extraction automatique d'information : Du texte brut au web sémantique*. Lavoisier.

Thierry Poibeau. 2011. *Traitement automatique du contenu textuel*. Lavoisier.

Axel Reymonet. 2008. *Modélisation de connaissances à partir de textes pour une recherche d'information sémantique*. Ph.D. thesis, Université Paul Sabatier.

Sophie Rosset, Cyril Grouin, and Pierre Zweigenbaum. 2011. *Entités nommées structurées: guide d'annotation Quaero*. LIMSI-Centre national de la recherche scientifique.

Max Silberztein. 2009. Syntactic parsing with NooJ.

Towards Definition Extraction Using Conditional Random Fields

Luis Espinosa Anke
Universitat Pompeu Fabra
luis.espinosa83@gmail.com

Abstract

Definition Extraction (DE) and terminology are contributing to help structuring the overwhelming amount of information available. This article presents KESSI (Knowledge Extraction System for Scientific Interviews), a multilingual domain-independent machine-learning approach to the extraction of definitional knowledge, specifically oriented to scientific interviews. The DE task was approached as both a classification and a sequential labelling task. In the latter, figures of Precision, Recall and F-Measure were similar to human annotation, and suggest that combining structural, statistical and linguistic features with Conditional Random Fields can contribute significantly to the development of DE systems.

1 Introduction

We present and discuss the process of building and evaluating a DE system for educational purposes. Aimed at exploiting the genre of scientific interviews, and envisaged as a time-saving tool for semi-automatically creating listening comprehension exercises, we present a Knowledge Extraction System for Scientific Interviews (KESSI). It is based on the theoretical and methodological foundations of DE, the task to automatically identify definitional sentences within texts (Navigli and Velardi, 2010).

KESSI is a DE system that relies solely on machine-learning techniques, which has the advantage of overcoming the domain-specificity and language dependence of rule-based methods (Del Gaudio et al., 2013). In order to train and test our model, the SMPoT (*Science Magazine Podcast Transcripts*) corpus was compiled and annotated with linguistic, terminologic and definitional information.

Two main contributions emerge from the work here presented. Firstly, it provides an analysis and discussion of the genre of scientific interviews, and examines its potential for NLP applications. We hypothesize that these interviews constitute a valuable source of information, as many scientific disciplines are covered, but dealt with in a standard register rather than the highly formal and structured register of technical manuals or scientific papers or books. Scientific interviews also present the audience with turntaking, courtesy and pragmatic elements that can prove useful for linguistic research as well as the development of Natural Language Processing tools. Secondly, promising results that border or go beyond 90% in Precision and Recall demonstrate that using CRF for DE is a viable option. These results also seem to suggest that combining linguistic information (surface forms, Part-of-Speech and syntactic functions), statistical information (word counts or tf-idf) and structural information (position of the token within the document, or whether it is the interviewer or the interviewee who speaks) can contribute to the design of DE systems.

2 Related Work

It can be argued that in general, most approaches to automatic DE rely on rule-based methods. These have ranged from verb-matching (Rebeyrolle and Tanguy, 2000; Saggion and Gaizauskas, 2004; Sarmento et al., 2006; Storrer and Wellinghoff, 2006) to punctuation (Muresan and Klavans, 2002; Malaisé et al., 2004; Sánchez and Márquez, 2005; Przepiórkowski et al., 2007; Monachesi and Westerhout, 2008) or layout features (Westerhout, 2009). It seems reasonable to argue that there are three main problems when approaching DE as a pattern-matching task (Del Gaudio et al., 2013): Firstly, it is necessary to start almost from scratch, as it is necessary to look for specific patterns which appear

Feature	Description
Pairs word-lemma	In a two-word window, we look at combinations surface form + lemma. In our example, this would be [it + ,], [it + lasts], [it + last], [last + essentially], and so on.
Pairs lemma + POS	In a two-word window, we would retrieve features like [it + V_PRES_SG3], [V_PRES_SG3 + essentially] or [essentially + ADV].
Who speaks	We focus on who mentions the current token. In our example, the interviewee.
Tf-Idf + surface form + lemma	In a two-word window, we would retrieve features like [3.32 + lasts + essentially] or [3.64 + essentially + forever]. Note that it it is possible to retrieve features from instances that are after the current token.

Table 1: Some of the features used for training the CRF model.

repeatedly in definitions. Secondly, these rules are language-dependent. Thirdly, they are also domain-dependent, making it difficult to extend them beyond the domain of application to which they were initially intended.

In order to overcome these problems, machine-learning techniques can be incorporated to the process. The most widely used algorithms have been Naïve Bayes, Maximum Entropy or Support Vector Machines, in the case of Fahmi and Bouma (2006), Naïve Bayes and Maximum Entropy (Rodríguez, 2004), genetic algorithms (Borg, 2009) or balanced random forests, in Degórski et al. (2008a; 2008b) and Westerhout (2010). Concerning unsupervised approaches, Zhang (2009) used a bootstrapping algorithm for the extraction of definitions in Chinese.

3 The SMPoT Corpus: Compilation and Annotation

We design a corpus following the criteria elicited by McEnery and Wilson (2001). The corpus consists of 50 fully annotated interview transcripts. Table 2 summarizes the size of the corpus in terms of words, sentences, terms and definitions.

Unit type	Count
Words	389293
Sentences	15315
Terms	26194
Definitions	570

Table 2: Raw counts for the SMPoT corpus

3.1 Preprocessing

After manually downloading and converting the pdf files from the *Science Magazine Website*[1], these were parsed using the dependency parser *Machinese Syntax* (Tapanainen and Järvinen, 1997). In this way, linguistic information such as lemma, Part-of-Speech, syntactic functions or a word's position in a dependency tree is provided.

Once the documents were collected, converted, pre-processed and automatically parsed, the next step was to semi-automatically annotate the terminology. For this, we benefited from an API for Python of the Yahoo! Term Extractor (also known as Yahoo! Content Analysis [2]). Terms were identified, and `<Term></Term>` tags were inserted to the xml document. Since terms can span multiple words, the `<Term></Term>` tags were introduced as parent nodes of the `<token>` tags. When queried, the Term Extractor API yields a list of terms, but its results depend on the size of the input text. This means that each document of the corpus had first to be split in sentences, and then each sentence was queried in order to preserve a high recall.

3.2 Annotating Definitions

This annotation schema builds up on previous work by Sierra et al. (2006) and Westerhout and Monachesi (2007). It is argued that in a textual genre like scientific interviews, where a certain degree of specificity and technical jargon is present,

[1] http://www.sciencemag.org/site/multimedia/podcast/
[2] http://developer.yahoo.com/contentanalysis

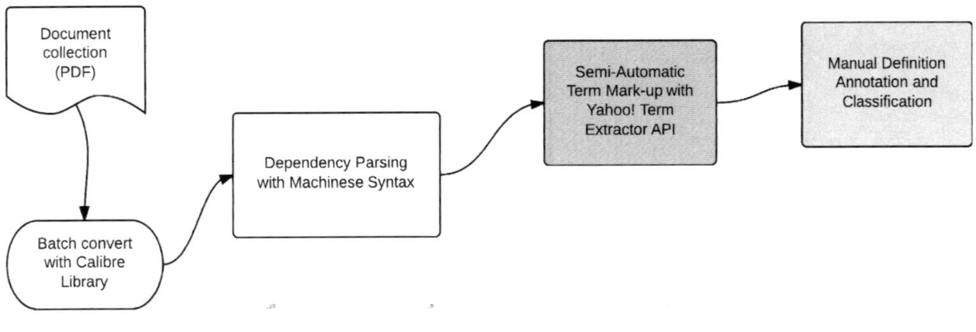

Figure 1: Summary of the steps involved in the compilation and annotation of the corpus.

a classification that looks at the patterns of the definitions alone, or at their information alone, might prove insufficient to capture the complexity of the way information is presented. Table 3 shows the 5 most frequent types of this two-dimensional classification, as well as their count and an example of each.

So far, the annotation process (summarized in Figure 1) has been examined, which consisted in automatic linguistic markup, semi-automatic terminology identification, and manual definition labelling and classification.

4 The Development of KESSI

Once the dataset is compiled and enriched, and can be used for training and testing purposes, we approach the DE task as (1) a binary classification task, where each sentence is labeled as *has_def* or *no_def*, and (2) a sequential labeling task, where each token is tagged according to whether it is *Inside*, *Outside*or at the *Beginning* of a definitional clause.

4.1 Binary Classification

Using the Weka workbench (Witten and Frank, 2005), we train a set of machine-learning algorithms in order to classify unseen sentences as containing or not containing a definition. However, a previous step seems necessary in order to handle properly the imbalanced dataset issue. According to Del Gaudio et al. (2013), few works have specifically addressed this issue through some kind of sampling. We take an approach similar to Degórski et al. (2008b), where a number of subsampled training datasets are used to increase the ratio of positive instances, specifically 1:1, 2:1 and 5:1. Moreover, simple linguistically motivated features were used. We extracted the 500 most frequent ngrams (`n = 1, 2, 3`), and used the linguistic information provided by the parser. This resulted in 1-3grams for surface forms, Part-Of-Speech and syntactic functions. In addition, we also added pattern-based features, like the presence or absence of the sequence "which is" or having a term followed by the verb "to be". Finally, the algorithms selected were Naïve Bayes, Decision Trees, SVM, Logistic Regression and Random Forests.

4.2 Sequential Labelling

Building up on the premise that both linguistic and structural features can be exploited for automatic DE, we propose a method to label each token in a sequence with `B_DefClause`, `I_DefClause` or `O_DefClause` tags (which correspond to whether a token is a the beginning, inside or outside a definition). For each sentence, each token has been manually annotated with these tags. Whenever a sequence of words that form a definition is found (what we refer as Definitional Clause), the tokens that are part of it are additionally labelled as Beginning, Inside or Outside for three more categories: Term, Definitional Verb and Definition. See Figure 2 for an illustrative example of this two-layered annotation schema.

4.2.1 Conditional Random Fields

Conditional Random Fields (Lafferty and McCallum, 2001) have been used extensively in NLP, e.g.

Type of Definition	Frequency	Example
Pattern type = is def Information type = intensional	135	Clicker's an electronic response device that's keyed to the instructors computer, so the instructor is getting an answer and can grade it.
Pattern type = verb def Information type = functional	111	Mice develop regulatory T- cells against non-inherited maternal alloantigens as a result of fetal exposure.
Pattern type = verb def Information type = extensional	52	Nano-ear is made from a microscopic particle of gold that is trapped by a laser beam.
Pattern type = is def Information type = functional	44	Iridium is not very common on Earth, but it is very common in asteroids.
Pattern type = punct def Information type = synonymic	32	(...) female determinant gene, S-ribonuclease gene.

Table 3: Most common types of definitions according to a Pattern/Information-based classification

Chinese Word Segmentation (Sun et al., 2013), Named Entity Recognition (Fersini and Messina, 2013), Sentiment Analysis (Jakob and Gurevych, 2010) or TimeML event recognition (Llorens et al., 2010). They are undirected graphical models where the dependencies among input variables x do no need to be explicitly represented. This allows to use richer and more global features of the input data, e.g. features like Part-of-Speech or ngram features of surrounding words.

4.2.2 Feature Selection

The definition of features is crucial for the architecture of the system (Llorens et al., 2010). We hypothesize that combining linguistic, statistic and structural information can contribute to the improvement of DE systems. For each token, these are the features extracted:

- **Term Frequency**: Raw count for the current token within the document.
- **Tf-idf**: Relative frequency score, which takes into account not only the token count within the current document, but its spread across the collection.
- **Token index**: The position of the token in the document.
- **Is_term**: Whether the token is a term or not.
- **Surface form**: The surface form of the token.
- **Lemma**: The token's lemma. In the case of extremely highly collocated multiword units, Machinese Syntax groups them together in one token. They are left as-is, regardless of potential capitalization.
- **Part-of-Speech**: Part-of-Speech of the token, including subtypes and number.
- **Syntactic Function**: Following a dependency grammar.
- **Who speaks**: Whether it is the interviewer, the interviewee, or a dangling token, in which case it is tagged as narrator.
- **BIO_term**: Regardless of the is_term label, we also investigate the token's position within a term BIO tagging scheme.
- **BIO_DefVerb**: Labels the connecting verb between a term and a definition.
- **BIO_Definition**: Labels the chunk that constitutes actual the definition.

Since CRF allow the encoding of long-distance relations, these features are combined in order to capture relevant combinations of features occurring before and after the current token (see Table 4).

5 Evaluation

The performance of KESSI was evaluated from two different perspectives. The reason for this being that it was necessary to account for the two approaches (binary classification and sequential labelling), on one hand, and the ultimate purpose of the system, on the other. Firstly, figures of Precision, Recall and F-Measure are provided and discussed for the classification approach, consider-

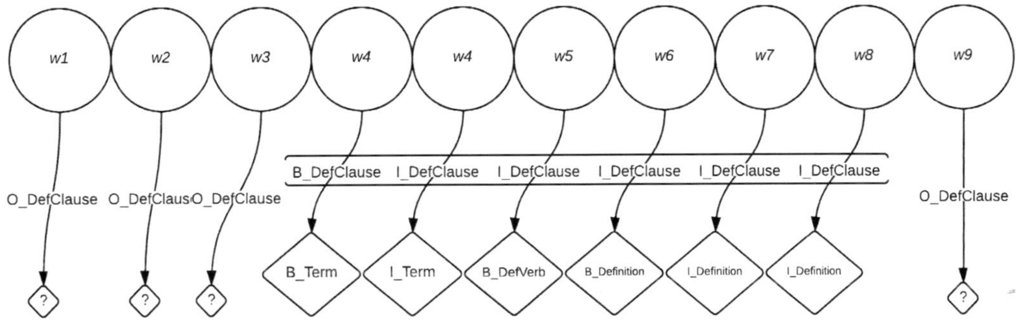

Figure 2: Visualization of the tagging schema.

Feature	Description
Pairs word-lemma	In a two-word window, we look at combinations surface form + lemma. In our example, this would be [it + ,], [it + lasts], [it + last], [last + essentially], and so on.
Pairs lemma + POS	In a two-word window, we would retrieve features like [it + V_PRES_SG3], [V_PRES_SG3 + essentially] or [essentially + ADV].
Who speaks	We focus on who mentions the current token. In our example, the interviewee.
Tf-Idf + surface form + lemma	In a two-word window, we would retrieve features like [3.32 + lasts + essentially] or [3.64 + essentially + forever]. Note that it it is possible to retrieve features from instances that are after the current token.

Table 4: Some of the features used for training the CRF model.

ing different resampling setups as well as different algorithms. Finally, Precision, Recall a nd F-Measure are reported on a high-granularity basis, in a hard evaluation, where only exact matching of a token was considered a true positive.

5.1 Classification Approach

Firstly, we examine results obtained with a simple ngram feature selection, where the 500 most frequent surface form uni, bi and trigrams are used as features for each sentence vector. Subsampling was carried out because we were more interested in correctly extracting positive instances, i.e. increasing Recall in is_def sentences. The highest F scores for positive instances were obtained under the following configurations:

1. Naïve Bayes - Original Dataset 10-fold Cross validation
2. Decision Trees - Subsample 2:1 - Test on original dataset

In setup (I), 207 positive instances out of 570 were correctly extracted, which yields a Recall of .36 for positive instances. However, by subsampling the training set to a 1:1 ratio (i.e. randomly removing negative instances until the remaining set contains the same number of positive and negative instances), it is possible to increase the desired results. As this approach cannot be tested by cross-validation, a supplied test set from the original dataset is used for testing. This test set did not overlap with the training set.

In (II), Recall increases to up to .6, as the system correctly extracts 66 out of 110 positive instances. Precision, however, remains low (P = .16). By incorporating more features where POS and syntactic functions are combined, we increase

	Original	S-1000	S-10000
All-S	P=0.97; R=0.89; F=0.93	P=0.03; R=0.98; F=0.07	P=0.08; R=0.48; F =0.15
1-S	P=0.97; R=0.90; F=0.93	P=0.03; R=0.99; F=0.06	P=0.47; R=0.95; F=0.63

Table 5: Results for the token-wise evaluation of KESSI

Recall in positive instances. For example, SVM trained with a 1:1 subsample training set shows an increase of up to .78. The effect this has on Precision is that it lowers it to .11. Finally, let us highlight the setup that obtained the highest recall for positive instances: Naïve Bayes algorithm trained with a subsampled 1:1 training set. Recall reaches .89, with the consequent drop in precision to .07.

We can conclude that combining surface form, Part-of-Speech and syntactic functions ngrams as features in a subsampled training set of 1:1 serves as the highest performing model. We consider a good model the one that correctly classifies the highest number of positive instances (i.e. those sentences that contain a definition), with the minimum loss with respect to negative instances.

5.2 CRF Evaluation

We propose a token-wise evaluation where each word is matched against the gold standard. If its `BIO_DefClause` tag does not match, it is considered incorrect. This has the advantage of knowing beforehand how many tokens we have, which is crucial for being able to compute Precision, Recall and F-Measure. It could be argued, however, that such approach is too restrictive, as it will consider as incorrect a `B_DefClause` token even if it is compared with an `I_DefClause` token, and this might not be always as accurate. In Table 5, the performance of KESSI is shown for three different sampling setups: Original train-set (Original), subsample of negative sentences down to 1000 (S-1000), and subsample of negative sentences down to 10000 (S-10000). For testing, a cut-off of the same size as in the Classification approach is used. Our test sets contain 20% of the overall positive instances, which in this case are either `B_DefClause` or `I_DefClause` tokens. This amounts to 111 definitions. Our test set consisted in, first, a dataset where all sentences are split according to their original format (All-S), and second, a dataset where all the instances are put together with no sentence boundary among them (1-S).

These results reveal that a radical resampling (leaving only 1000 negative instances), when using Conditional Random Fields, does not have a dramatic effect in performance. While Recall increases almost a 10% (from 0.89 to 0.98), Precision suffers from a strong decrease, in this case 94% (from 0.97 to 0.03). With scores nearing or above 90% in Precision, Recall and F-Measure, it seems safe to assume that using linguistic, statistic and structural features combined with CRF improve dramatically a DE system. In comparison with previous work in this field, where most datasets consisted in more structured text than interview transcripts, it also seems reasonable to claim that this method is better suited for more unstructured language.

6 Conclusions

Different stages involved in the design and development of a DE system have been presented. Once the criteria for the taxonomy were clear, an annotation task was carried out on 50 documents from The Science Magazine Podcast, where linguistic information, terminology and definitions were identified and classified. Then, the DE task was approached both as a classification problem and as a sequential labelling problem, and Precision, Recall and F-Measure results indicate that combining linguistic, structural and statistic features with Conditional Random Fields can lead to high performance. We propose the following directions for future work: Firstly, expanding the size and the dataset and incorporating additional features to the definition classification. Secondly, trying additional resampling techniques like the SMOTE algorithm in order to oversample the minority class. This algorithm has been applied successfully in this field (Del Gaudio et al., 2013). Thirdly, ensuring a more reliable annotation by incorporating additional annotators and computing some kind of agreement metric would seem advisable as in some cases a false positive might be due to the fact that the annotator missed a good definition. And finally, providing sentence-wise evaluation scores for the CRF approach, so that the two methods showcased could be evenly compared.

References

Claudia Borg. 2009. *Automatic Definition Extraction Using Evolutionary Algorithms*. MA Dissertation. University of Malta.

Lukasz Degórski, Lukasz Kobyliński and Adam Przepiórkowski. 2008. Definition extraction: improving balanced random forest. Proceedings of the International Multiconference on Computer Science and Information Technology, pp. 353-357

Lukasz Degórski, Michał Marcińczuk and Adam Przepiórkowski. 2008. Definition extraction using a sequential combination of baseline grammars and machine learning classifiers. Proceedings of the Sixth International Conference on Language Resources and Evaluation, LREC 2008.

Rosa Del Gaudio, Gustavo Batista and António Branco. 2013. Coping with highly imbalanced datasets: A case study with definition extraction in a multilingual setting. *Natural Language Engineering, pp. 1–33*

Luis Espinosa. *Forthcoming*. Classifying Different Definitional Styles for Different Users. Proceedings of CILC 2013, Alicante, 14-16 March 2013. Procedia Social and Behavioral Science. Elsevier ISSN: 1877-0428.

Ismail Fahmi and Gosse Bouma. 2006. Learning to identify definitions using syntactic features. Proceedings of the EACL 2006 workshop on Learning Structured Information in Natural Language Applications, pp. 64–71)

Elisabetta Fersini and Enza Messina. 2013. Named Entities in Judicial Transcriptions: Extended Conditional Random Fields. *Proceedings of the 14th international conference on Computational Linguistics and Intelligent Text Processing - Volume Part I* (CICLing'13), Alexander Gelbukh (Ed.), Vol. Part I. Springer-Verlag, Berlin, Heidelberg, (pp. 317–328).

Niklas Jakob and Iryna Gurevych. 2010. Extracting opinion targets in a single-and cross-domain setting with conditional random fields. In Proceedings of the 2010 Conference on Empirical Methods in Natural Language Processing (pp. 1035–1045). Association for Computational Linguistics.

John Lafferty and Andrew McCallum. 2001. Conditional random fields: Probabilistic models for segmenting and labeling sequence data. In Proceedings of the Eighteenth International Conference on Machine Learning (pp. 282-289).

Héctor Llorens, Elena Saquete and Borja Navarro-Colorado. 2010. TimeML events recognition and classification: learning CRF models with semantic roles. In Proceedings of the 23rd International Conference on Computational Linguistics (pp. 725–733). Association for Computational Linguistics.

Tony McEnery and Andrew Wilson. 2001. *Corpus Linguistics: An Introduction*. Edinburgh University Press.

Véronique Malaisé, Pierre Zweigenbaum and Bruno Bachimont. 2004. Detecting semantic relations between terms in definitions. In COLING (pp. 55–62).

Paola Monachesi and Eline Westerhout. 2008. What can NLP techniques do for eLearning?. In Proceedings of the International Conference on Informatics and Systems (INFOS08). Cairo. Egypt.

Smaranda Muresan and Judith Klavans. 2002. A method for automatically building and evaluating dictionary resources. In Proceedings of the Language Resources and Evaluation Conference (Vol. 1, No. 8, p. 30).

Roberto Navigli and Paola Velardi. 2010. Learning word-class lattices for definition and hypernym extraction. In Proceedings of the 48th Annual Meeting of the Association for Computational Linguistics (pp. 1318–1327). Association for Computational Linguistics.

Adam Przepiórkowski, Lukasz Degórski, Miroslav Spousta, Kiril Simov, Petya Oseneva, Lothar Lemnitzer, Vladislav Kuboň and Beata Wójtowicz. 2007. Towards the automatic extraction of definitions in Slavic. In Proceedings of the Workshop on Balto-Slavonic Natural Language Processing: Information Extraction and Enabling Technologies (pp. 43–50). Association for Computational Linguistics..

Josette Rebeyrolle and Ludovic Tanguy. 2000. *Repérage automatique de structures linguistiques en corpus: le cas des énoncés définitoires. Cahiers de grammaire*, 25:153–174.

Carlos Rodrguez. 2004. *Metalinguistic information extraction from specialized texts to enrich computational lexicons*. PhD Dissertation. Barceona: Universitat Pompeu Fabra.

Horacio Saggion and Robert Gaizauskas. 2004. Mining on-line sources for definition knowledge. In Proceedings of the 17th International FLAIRS Conference (pp. 45-52).

Alexy J. Sánchez and Melva J. Márquez R. 2005. Hacia un sistema de extracción de definiciones en textos jurídicos. Actas de la 1er Jornada Venezolana de Investigación en Lingüística e Informática. Venezuela..

Luiís Sarmento, Belinda Maia, Diana Santos, Ana Pinto and Luís Cabral. 2006. Corpógrafo V3 From Terminological Aid to Semi-automatic Knowledge Engineering. In Proceedings of the 5th International Conference on Language Resources and Evaluation (LREC 2006) (pp. 1502–1505).

Gerardo Sierra, Rodrigo Alarcón, César Aguilar and Alberto Barrón. 2006. Towards the building of a corpus of definitional contexts. In Proceedings of the 12th EURALEX International Congress, Torino, Italy (pp. 229–40).

Angelika Storrer and Sandra Wellinghoff. 2006. Automated detection and annotation of term definitions in German text corpora. In Proceedings of LREC (Vol. 2006).

Xu Sun, Yaozhong Zhang, Takuya Matsuzaki, Yoshimasa Tsuruoka and Jun'ichi Tsujii. 2013. Probabilistic Chinese word segmentation with non-local information and stochastic training. *Information Processing & Management, 49(3):pp. 626–636.*

Pasi Tapanainen and Timo Järvinen. 1997. A non-projective dependency parser. In Proceedings of the fifth conference on Applied natural language processing (pp. 64–71). Association for Computational Linguistics..

Eline Westerhout. 2009. Extraction of definitions using grammar-enhanced machine learning. In Proceedings of the 12th Conference of the European Chapter of the Association for Computational Linguistics: Student Research Workshop (pp. 88–96).

Eline Westerhout. 2010. *Definition extraction for glossary creation: a study on extracting definitions for semi-automatic glossary creation in Dutch.* PhD Dissertation. Utrecht University.

Eline Westerhout and Paola Mnachesi. 2007. Extraction of Dutch definitory contexts for elearning purposes. In Proceedings of the Computational Linguistics in the Netherlands (CLIN 2007), Nijmegen, Netherlands, (pp. 219–34).

Ian H. Witten and Eibe Frank. 2005. *ata Mining: Practical machine learning tools and techniques.* Morgan Kaufmann.

Chunxia Zhang and Peng Jiang. 2009. Automatic extraction of definitions. Computer Science and Information Technology, 2009. ICCSIT 2009. 2nd IEEE International Conference on (pp. 364–368). IEEE..

Event-Centered Simplification of News Stories

Goran Glavaš
Faculty of Electrical
Engineering and Computing
University of Zagreb, Croatia
goran.glavas@fer.hr

Sanja Štajner
Research Group in
Computational Linguistics
University of Wolverhampton, UK
sanjastajner@wlv.ac.uk

Abstract

Newswire text is often linguistically complex and stylistically decorated, hence very difficult to comprehend for people with reading disabilities. Acknowledging that events represent the most important information in news, we propose an event-centered approach to news simplification. Our method relies on robust extraction of factual events and elimination of surplus information which is not part of event mentions. Experimental results obtained by combining automated readability measures with human evaluation of correctness justify the proposed event-centered approach to text simplification.

1 Introduction

For non-native speakers, people with low literacy or intellectual disabilities, and language-impaired people (e.g., autistic, aphasic, congenitally deaf) newswire texts are difficult to comprehend (Carroll et al., 1999; Devlin, 1999; Feng, 2009; Štajner et al., 2012). Making news equally accessible to people with reading disabilities helps their integration into society (Freyhoff et al., 1998).

In news, syntactically complex and stylistically decorated sentences, combining several pieces of information of varying relevance, are frequent. For example, in *"Philippines and China diplomatically resolved a tense naval standoff, the most dangerous confrontation between the sides in recent years."* the "resolving of a standoff" is arguably a more relevant piece of information than the "standoff" being "the most dangerous confrontation in years". However, studies indicate that people with reading disabilities, especially people with intellectual disabilities, have difficulties discriminating relevant from irrelevant information (Pimperton and Nation, 2010), e.g., when sentences are particularly long and complex (Carretti et al., 2010; Feng, 2009). Thus, complex sentences need to be shortened and simplified, and any irrelevant content eliminated in order to reduce complexity of news stories and facilitate their comprehension.

News describes real-world events, i.e., events are dominant information concepts in news (Van Dijk, 1985; Pan and Kosicki, 1993). Although news is made up of event-oriented texts, the number of descriptive sentences and sentence parts relating to non-essential information is substantial (e.g., *"The South China Sea is home to a myriad of competing territorial claims"*). Such descriptions do not relate to any of the concrete events, but significantly contribute to the overall complexity of news.

Most existing approaches to text simplification address only lexical and syntactic complexity, i.e., they do not apply any content reduction (Carroll et al., 1998; Devlin and Unthank, 2006; Aluísio et al., 2008; Saggion et al., 2011). In this work we present a semantically-motivated, event-based simplification approach. We build upon state-of-the-art event extraction and discard text not belonging to extracted event mentions. We propose two event-based simplification schemes, allowing for different degrees of simplification. We evaluate event-centered simplification by combining automated measures of readability with human assessment of grammaticality and information relevance. Experimental results suggest that event-centered simplification is justified as it outperforms the syntactically-motivated baseline.

2 Related Work

Several projects dealt with automated text simplification for people with different reading difficulties:

people with alexia (Carroll et al., 1998; Devlin and Unthank, 2006), cognitive disabilities (Saggion et al., 2011), autism (Orasan et al., 2013), congenital deafness (Inui et al., 2003), and low literacy (Aluísio et al., 2008). Most of these approaches rely on rule-based lexical and syntactic simplification. Syntactic simplification is usually carried out by recursively applying a set of hand-crafted rules at a sentence level, not considering interactions across sentence boundaries. Lexical simplification usually substitutes difficult words with their simpler synonyms (Carroll et al., 1998; Lal and Ruger, 2002; Burstein et al., 2007).

Existing approaches dominantly rely on lexical and syntactic simplification, performing little content reduction, the exception being deletion of parenthetical expressions (Drndarevic et al., 2013). On the one hand, lack of content reduction has been recognized as one of the main shortcomings of automated systems (Drndarevic et al., 2013) which produce much worse simplification results compared to human. On the other hand, information extraction techniques help identify relevant content (e.g., named entities, events), but have not yet proven useful for text simplification. However, significant advances in event extraction (Ahn, 2006; Bethard, 2008; Llorens et al., 2010; Grover et al., 2010), achieved as the result of standardization efforts (Pustejovsky et al., 2003a; Pustejovsky et al., 2003b) and dedicated tasks (ACE, 2005; Verhagen et al., 2010), encourage event-oriented simplification attempts. To the best of our knowledge, the only reported work exploiting events for text simplification is that of Barlacchi and Tonelli (2013). They extract factual events from a set of Italian children's stories and eliminate non-mandatory event arguments. They evaluate simplified texts using only the automated score which can hardly account for grammaticality and information relevance of the output.

We follow the idea of exploiting factual events for text simplification, acknowledging, however, that newswire texts are significantly more complex than children's stories. Moreover, we complement automated readability measures with human assessment of grammaticality and information relevance. Furthermore, given that simplification systems often need to be tailored to the specific needs of a particular group (Orasan et al., 2013), and that people with different low literacy degrees need different levels of simplification (Scarton et al., 2010), we offer two different simplification schemes. To the best of our knowledge, this is the first work on event-based text simplification for English.

3 Event-Centered Simplification

The simplification schemes we propose exploit the structure of extracted event mentions. We employ robust event extraction that involves supervised extraction of factual event anchors (i.e., words that convey the core meaning of the event) and the rule-based extraction of event arguments of coarse semantic types. Although a thorough description of the event extraction system is outside the scope of this paper, we describe the aspects relevant to the proposed simplification schemes.

3.1 Event Extraction

Our event extraction system performs supervised extraction of event anchors and a rule-based extraction of event arguments.

Anchor extraction. We use two supervised models, one for identification of event anchors and the other for classification of event type. The first model identifies tokens being anchors of event mentions (e.g., *"resolved"* and *"standoff"* in *"Philippines and China resolved a tense naval standoff."*). The second model determines the TimeML event type (Pustejovsky et al., 2003a) for previously identified anchors. The models were trained with logistic regression using the following sets of features:

(1) *Lexical and PoS features* – word, lemma, stem, and PoS tag of the current token and the surrounding tokens (symmetric window of size 2);

(2) *Syntactic features* – the set of dependency relations and the chunk type (e.g., NP) of the current token. Additionally, we use features indicating whether the token governs nominal subject or direct object dependencies.

(3) *Modifier features* – modal modifiers (e.g., *might*), auxiliary verbs (e.g., *been*) and negations of the current token. These features help discriminate factual from non-factual events.

The supervised models were trained on the train portion of the EvExtra corpus[1], and tested on the separate test portion. The anchor identification model achieves precision of 83%, recall of 77%, and F-score performance of 80%. The model for event-type classification performs best for *Reporting* events, recognizing them with the F-score performance of 86%.

[1]http://takelab.fer.hr/data/grapheve/

Table 1: Some of the patterns for argument extraction

Name	Example	Dependency relations	Arg. type
Nominal subject	*"**China** confronted Philippines"*	*nsubj(confronted, China)*	Agent
Direct object	*"China disputes **the agreement**"*	dobj(disputes, agreement)	Target
Prepositional object	*"Philippines protested **on Saturday**"*; *"The confrontation **in South China Sea**"*; *"The protest **against China**"*	*prep(protested, on)* and *pobj(on, Saturday)*; *prep(confrontation, in)* and *pobj(in, Sea)*; *prep(protest, against)* and *pobj(against, China)*	Time Location Target
Participial modifier	*"The **vessel** carrying missiles"*; *"The **militant** killed in the attack"*	*partmod(vessel, carrying)*; *partmod(militant, killed)*	Agent Target
Noun compound	*"**Beijing** summit"*; *"**Monday** demonstrations"*; *"**UN** actions"*	*nn(summit, Beijing)*; *nn(demonstrations, Monday)*; *nn(actions, UN)*	Location Time Agent

Argument extraction. We implement a rule-based extraction of event arguments, using a rich set of unlexicalized syntactic patterns on dependency parses as proposed in (Glavaš and Šnajder, 2013). All extraction patterns are defined with respect to event anchor and identify head words of arguments. We focus on extracting arguments of four coarse-grained types – *agent*, *target*, *time*, and *location* – for which we believe are informationally most relevant for the event. In total, there are 13 different extraction patterns, and their representative subset is presented in Table 1 (in examples, the argument is shown in bold and the anchor is underlined).

Some extraction patterns perform argument detection and classification simultaneously (e.g., a *nominal subject* is always an *agent*). Other patterns identify argument candidates, but further semantic processing is required to determine the argument type (e.g., *prepositional objects* can be *temporals*, *locations*, or *targets*). To disambiguate the argument type in such cases, we use named entity recognition (Finkel et al., 2005), temporal expression extraction (Chang and Manning, 2012), and WordNet-based semantic similarity (Wu and Palmer, 1994). Patterns based on dependency parse identify only the argument heads words. The chunk of the argument head word is considered to be the full argument extent.

The argument extraction performance, evaluated on on a held-out set, is as follows (F-score): agent – 88.0%, target – 83.1%, time – 82.3%, location – 67.5%.

3.2 Simplification Schemes

We base our simplification schemes on extracted event mentions. The rationale is that the most relevant information in news is made up of factual events. Thus, omitting parts of text that are not events would (1) reduce text complexity by eliminating irrelevant information and (2) increase readability by shortening long sentences. We propose two different simplification schemes:

(1) *Sentence-wise simplification* eliminates all the tokens of the original sentence that do not belong to any of the extracted factual event mentions (event anchors or arguments). A single sentence of the original text maps to a single sentence of the simplified text, assuming that the original sentence contains at least one factual event mention. Sentences that do not contain any factual event mentions (e.g., *"What a shame!"*) are removed from the simplified text. Algorithm 1 summarizes the sentence-wise simplification scheme.

(2) *Event-wise simplification* transforms each factual event mention into a separate sentence of the output. Since a single phrase can be an argument of multiple event mentions, a single input token may constitute several output sentences (e.g., *"China sent in its fleet and provoked Philippines"* is transformed into *"China sent in its fleet. China provoked Philippines."*). We make three additional adjustments to retain the grammaticality of the output. Firstly, we ignore events of the *Reporting* type (e.g. *said*) as they frequently cannot constitute grammatically correct sentences on their own (e.g., *"Obama said."*). Secondly, we do not

Algorithm 1. Sentence-wise simplification

input: sentence s
input: set of event mentions $\mathcal{E}$

```
// simplified sentence (list of tokens)
S = {}
// list of original sentence tokens
T = tokenize(s)
foreach token t in T do
    foreach event mention e in E do
        // set of event tokens
        A = anchorAndArgumentTokens(e)
        // if the sentence token belongs to event
        if t in A do
            // include token in simplified sentence
            S = S ∪ t
            break
output: S
```

Algorithm 2. Event-wise simplification

input: sentence s
input: set of event mentions $\mathcal{E}$

```
// set of event-output sentence pairs
S = {}
// initialize output token set for each event
foreach e in E do
    S = S ∪ (e, {})
// list of original sentence tokens
T = tokenize(s)
foreach token t in T do
    foreach event mention e in E do
        // set of event tokens
        a = anchor(e)
        A = anchorAndArgumentTokens(e)
        // part of verbal, non-reporting event
        if t in A & PoS(a) ≠ N & type(t) ≠ Rep do
            // token is gerundive anchor
            if t = a & gerund(a)
                S[e] = S[e] ∪ pastSimple(a)
            else S[e] = S[e] ∪ t
output: S
```

transform events with nominal anchors into separate sentences, as such events tend to have very few arguments and are often arguments of verbal events. For example, in *"China and Philippines resolved a naval standoff"* mention *"standoff"* is a *target* of the mention *"resolved"*. Thirdly, we convert gerundive events that govern the clausal complement of the main sentence event into past simple for preserving grammaticality of the output. E.g., *"Philippines disputed China's territorial claims, triggering the naval confrontation"* is transformed into *"Philippines disputed China's territorial claims. Philippines triggered the naval confrontation."*, i.e., the gerundive anchor *"triggering"* is transformed into *"triggered"* since it governs the open clausal complement of the anchor *"disputed"*. Algorithm 2 summarizes the event-wise simplification scheme.

Table 2: Simplification example

Original *"Baset al-Megrahi, the Libyan intelligence officer who was convicted in the 1988 Lockerbie bombing has died at his home in Tripoli, nearly three years after he was released from a Scottish prison."*
Sentence-wise simplification *"Baset al-Megrahi was convicted in the 1988 Lockerbie bombing has died at his home after he was released from a Scottish prison."*
Event-wise simplification *"Baset al-Megrahi was convicted in the 1988 Lockerbie bombing. Baset al-Megrahi has died at his home. He was released from a Scottish prison."*
Event-wise with pron. anaphora resolution *"Baset al-Megrahi was convicted in the 1988 Lockerbie bombing. Baset al-Megrahi has died at his home. Baset al-Megrahi was released from a Scottish prison."*

It has been shown that anaphoric mentions cause difficulties for people with cognitive disabilities (Ehrlich et al., 1999; Shapiro and Milkes, 2004). To investigate this phenomenon, we additionally employ *pronominal anaphora resolution* on top of event-wise simplification scheme. To resolve reference of anaphoric pronouns, we use the coreference resolution tool from Stanford Core NLP (Lee et al., 2011). An example of the original text snippet accompanied by its (1) sentence-wise simplification, (2) event-wise simplification, and (3) event-wise simplification with anaphoric pronoun resolution is given in Table 2.

4 Evaluation

The text is well-simplified if its readability is increased, while its grammaticality (syntactic correctness), meaning, and information relevance (semantic correctness) are preserved.

We measure the readability of the simplified text automatically with two commonly used formulae. However, we rely on human assessment of grammaticality and relevance, given that these aspects are difficult to capture automatically (Wubben et al., 2012). We employ a syntactically motivated baseline that retains only the main clause of a sentence and discards all subordinate clauses. We used Stanford constituency parser (Klein and Manning, 2003) to identify the main and subordinate clauses.

Readability. We collected 100 news stories from EMM NewsBrief,[2] an online news clustering ser-

[2]http://emm.newsbrief.eu/NewsBrief/clusteredition/en/latest.html

Table 3: Readability evaluation

Original vs.	KFL	SMOG	SL	DL	NS
Baseline	-27.7% ± 12.5%	-14.0% ± 8.0%	-38.5% ± 12.1%	-38.5% ± 12.1%	0.0% ± 0.0%
Sentence-wise	-30.1% ± 13.9%	-16.3% ± 9.2%	-44.3% ± 11.1%	-49.8% ± 11.5%	-9.9% ± 8.7%
Event-wise	-50.3% ± 12.6%	-30.8% ± 10.5%	-65.5% ± 9.3%	-63.4% ± 12.6%	-10.0% ± 39.7%
Pronom. anaphora	-47.8% ± 13.9%	-29.4% ± 10.6%	-63.6% ± 10.3%	-61.2% ± 14.4%	-10.0% ± 39.7%

vice, and simplified them with the proposed simplification schemes. For each original story and its simplified versions, we compute two standard readability scores – Kincaid-Flesch Grade Level (KFL) (Kincaid et al., 1975) and SMOG Index (McLaughlin, 1969). We also compute common-sense indicators of readability: average sentence length (SL), average document length (DL), and number of sentences (NS). Readability scores, relative to the readability of the original text and averaged over 100 news stories, are given in Table 3.

Event-wise simplification significantly ($p < 0.01$)[3] increases the readability for all measures except NS. Large variance in NS for event-wise simplification is caused by large variance in number of factual events per news story. Descriptive news stories (e.g., political overviews) contain more sentences without any factual events, while sentences from factual stories (e.g., murders, protests) often contain several factual events, forming multiple sentences in the simplified text. Event-wise simplified texts are also significantly more readable than sentence-wise simplified texts ($p < 0.01$) for all measures except NS.

Human Evaluation. Readability scores provide no information about the content of the simplified text. In line with previous work on text simplification (Knight and Marcu, 2002; Woodsend and Lapata, 2011; Wubben et al., 2012; Drndarevic et al., 2013), we let human evaluators judge the grammaticality and content relevance of simplified text. Due to cognitive effort required for the annotation task we asked annotators to compare text snippets (consisting of a single sentence or two adjacent sentences) instead of whole news stories. For each simplification, evaluators were instructed to compare it with the respective original snippet and assign three different scores:

(1) *Grammaticality score* denotes the grammatical well-formedness of text on a 1-3 scale, where 1 denotes significant ungrammaticalities (e.g., missing subject or object as in *"Was prevented by the Chinese surveillance craft."*), 2 indicates smaller grammatical inconsistencies (e.g., missing conjunctions or prepositions, as in *"Vessels blocked the arrest Chinese fishermen in disputed waters"*), and 3 indicates grammatical correctness;

(2) *Meaning score* denotes the degree to which relevant information from the original text is preserved semantically unchanged in the simplified text on a 1-3 scale, where 1 indicates that the most relevant information has not been preserved in its original meaning (e.g., *"Russians are tiring of Putin"* → *"Russians are tiring Putin"*), 2 denotes that relevant information is partially missing from the simplified text (e.g., *"Their daughter has been murdered and another daughter seriously injured."* → *"Their daughter has been murdered."*), and 3 means that all relevant information has been preserved;

(3) *Simplicity score* indicates the degree to which irrelevant information has been eliminated from the simplified text on a 1-3 scale, where 1 means that a lot of irrelevant information has been retained in the simplified text (e.g., *"The president, acting as commander in chief, landed in Afghanistan on Tuesday afternoon for an unannounced visit to the war zone"*), 2 denotes that some of the irrelevant information has been eliminated, but not all of it (e.g., *"The president landed in Afghanistan on Tuesday afternoon for an unannounced visit"*), and 3 indicates that only the most relevant information has been retained in the simplified text (e.g., *"The president landed in Afghanistan on Tuesday"*).

Note that *Meaning* and *Simplicity* can, respectively, be interpreted as recall and precision of information relevance. The less relevant information is preserved (i.e., false negatives), the lower the *Meaning* score will be. Similarly, the more irrelevant information is preserved (i.e., false positives), the lower the *Simplicity* score will be. Considering that the well-performing simplification method should both preserve relevant and eliminate irrelevant information, for each simplified text we com-

[3] 2-tailed t-test if both samples are approx. normally distributed; Wilcoxon signed-rank test otherwise

Table 4: IAA for human evaluation

Aspect	weighted κ	Pearson	MAE
Grammaticality	0.68	0.77	0.18
Meaning	0.53	0.67	0.37
Simplicity	0.54	0.60	0.28

Table 5: Grammaticality and relevance

Scheme	Gramm. (1-3)	Relevance (1-3)
Baseline	2.57 ± 0.79	1.90 ± 0.64
Sentence-wise	1.98 ± 0.80	2.12 ± 0.61
Event-wise	2.70 ± 0.52	2.30 ± 0.54
Pronom. anaphora	2.68 ± 0.56	2.39 ± 0.57

pute *Relevance* score as the harmonic mean of its *Meaning* score and *Simplicity* score.

We compiled a dataset of 70 snippets of newspaper texts, each consisting of one or two sentences.[4] We simplified these 70 snippets using the two proposed simplification schemes (and additional pronominal anaphora resolution) and the baseline, obtaining that way four different simplifications per snippet, i.e., 280 pairs of original and simplified text altogether. Three evaluators independently annotated the same 40 pairs on which we measured the inter-annotator agreement (IAA). Since we observed fair agreement, the evaluators proceeded by annotating the remaining 240 pairs. Pairwise averaged IAA in terms of three complementary metrics – Weighted Cohen's Kappa (κ), Pearson correlation, and Mean Absolute Error (MAE) – is given in Table 4. As expected, IAA shows that grammaticality is less susceptible to individual interpretations than information (ir)relevance (i.e., *Meaning* and *Simplicity*). Nonetheless, we observe fair agreement for *Meaning* and *Simplicity* as well ($\kappa > 0.5$).

Finally, we evaluate the performance of the proposed simplification schemes on the 70 news snippets in terms of *Grammaticality* and *Relevance*. The results are shown in Table 5. All simplification schemes produce text which is significantly more relevant than the baseline simplification ($p < 0.05$ for sentence-wise scheme; $p < 0.01$ for the event-wise and pronominal anaphora schemes). However, sentence-wise simplification produces text which is significantly less grammatical than baseline simplification. This is because conjunctions and prepositions are often missing from sentence-wise simplifications as they do not form any event mention. The same issue does not arise in event-wise simplifications where each mention is converted into its own sentence, in which case eliminating conjunctions is grammatically desirable. Event-wise and pronominal anaphora schemes significantly outperform the sentence-wise simplification ($p < 0.01$) on both grammaticality and relevance. Most mistakes in event-wise simplifications originate from change of meaning caused by the incorrect extraction of event arguments (e.g., *"Nearly 3,000 soldiers have been killed in Afghanistan since the Talibans were ousted in 2001."* $\rightarrow$ *"Nearly 3,000 soldiers have been killed in Afghanistan in 2001."*).

Overall, the event-wise scheme increases readability and produces grammatical text, preserving at the same time relevant content and reducing irrelevant content. Combined, experimental results for readability, grammaticality, and information relevance suggest that the proposed event-wise scheme is very suitable for text simplification.

5 Conclusion

Acknowledging that news stories are difficult to comprehend for people with reading disabilities, as well as the fact that events represent the most relevant information in news, we presented an event-centered approach to simplification of news. We identify factual event mentions with the state-of-the-art event extraction system and discard text that is not part of any of the factual events. Our experiments show that the event-wise simplification, in which factual events are converted to separate sentences, increases readability and retains grammaticality of the text, while preserving relevant information and discarding irrelevant information.

In future work we will combine event-based schemes with methods for lexical simplification. We will also investigate the effects of temporal ordering of events on text simplification, as texts with linear timelines are easier to follow. We also intend to employ similar event-based strategies for text summarization, given the notable similarities between text simplification and summarization.

Acknowledgments. This work has been partially supported by the Ministry of Science, Education and Sports, Republic of Croatia under the Grant 036-1300646-1986. We thank the PhD students from the University of Wolverhampton for their annotation efforts. We also thank the reviewers for their constructive comments.

[4]The dataset is freely available at `http://takelab.fer.hr/evsimplify`

References

ACE. 2005. Evaluation of the detection and recognition of ACE: Entities, values, temporal expressions, relations, and events.

D. Ahn. 2006. The stages of event extraction. In *Proceedings of the COLING/ACL 2006 Workshop on Annotating and Reasoning about Time and Events*, pages 1–8.

S. M. Aluísio, L. Specia, T. A. S. Pardo, E. G. Maziero, and R. P. M. Fortes. 2008. Towards Brazilian Portuguese automatic text simplification systems. In *Proceedings of the eighth ACM symposium on Document engineering*, DocEng '08, pages 240–248, New York, NY, USA. ACM.

G. Barlacchi and S. Tonelli. 2013. ERNESTA: A sentence simplification tool for childrens stories in italian. In *Computational Linguistics and Intelligent Text Processing*, pages 476–487. Springer.

S. Bethard. 2008. *Finding Event, Temporal and Causal Structure in Text: A Machine Learning Approach*. Ph.D. thesis.

J. Burstein, J. Shore, J. Sabatini, Y.W. Lee, and M. Ventura. 2007. The automated text adaptation tool. In *Proceedings of Human Language Technologies: The Annual Conference of the North American Chapter of the Association for Computational Linguistics: Demonstrations*, NAACL-Demonstrations '07, pages 3–4, Stroudsburg, PA, USA. Association for Computational Linguistics.

B. Carretti, C. Belacchi, and C. Cornoldi. 2010. Difficulties in working memory updating in individuals with intellectual disability. *Journal of Intellectual Disability Research*, 54(4):337–345.

J. Carroll, G. Minnen, Y. Canning, S. Devlin, and J. Tait. 1998. Practical simplification of English newspaper text to assist aphasic readers. In *Proceedings of AAAI-98 Workshop on Integrating Artificial Intelligence and Assistive Technology (1998), pp. 7-10 Key: citeulike:8717999*, pages 7–10.

J. Carroll, G. Minnen, D. Pearce, Y. Canning, S. Devlin, and J. Tait. 1999. Simplifying text for language-impaired readers. In *Proceedings of the 9th Conference of the European Chapter of the ACL (EACL'99)*, pages 269–270.

A. X. Chang and C. D. Manning. 2012. SUTIME: A library for recognizing and normalizing time expressions. *Language Resources and Evaluation.*

S. Devlin and G. Unthank. 2006. Helping aphasic people process online information. In *Proceedings of the 8th international ACM SIGACCESS conference on Computers and accessibility*, Assets '06, pages 225–226, New York, NY, USA. ACM.

S. Devlin. 1999. *Simplifying Natural Language Text for Aphasic Readers*. Ph.D. thesis, University of Sunderland, UK.

B. Drndarevic, S. Štajner, S. Bott, S. Bautista, and H. Saggion. 2013. Automatic text simplication in Spanish: A comparative evaluation of complementing components. In *Proceedings of the 12th International Conference on Intelligent Text Processing and Computational Linguistics. Lecture Notes in Computer Science. Samos, Greece, 24-30 March, 2013.*, pages 488–500.

M. Ehrlich, M. Remond, and H. Tardieu. 1999. Processing of anaphoric devices in young skilled and less skilled comprehenders: Differences in metacognitive monitoring. *Reading and Writing*, 11(1):29–63.

L. Feng. 2009. Automatic readability assessment for people with intellectual disabilities. In *SIGACCESS Access. Comput.*, number 93, pages 84–91. ACM, New York, NY, USA, jan.

J. Finkel, T. Grenager, and C. Manning. 2005. Incorporating non-local information into information extraction systems by gibbs sampling. In *Proceedings of the 43rd Annual Meeting on Association for Computational Linguistics*, pages 363–370. Association for Computational Linguistics.

G. Freyhoff, G. Hess, L. Kerr, B. Tronbacke, and K. Van Der Veken, 1998. *Make it Simple, European Guidelines for the Production of Easy-to-Read Information for People with Learning Disability.* ILSMH European Association, Brussels.

Goran Glavaš and Jan Šnajder. 2013. Exploring coreference uncertainty of generically extracted event mentions. In *Proceedings of 14th International Conference on Intelligent Text Processing and Computational Linguistics*, pages 408–422. Springer.

C. Grover, R. Tobin, B. Alex, and K. Byrne. 2010. Edinburgh-LTG: TempEval-2 system description. In *Proceedings of the 5th International Workshop on Semantic Evaluation*, pages 333–336. Association for Computational Linguistics.

K. Inui, A. Fujita, T. Takahashi, R. Iida, and T. Iwakura. 2003. Text simplification for reading assistance: A project note. In *Proceedings of the second international workshop on Paraphrasing - Volume 16*, PARAPHRASE '03, pages 9–16, Stroudsburg, PA, USA. Association for Computational Linguistics.

J. P. Kincaid, R. P. Fishburne Jr, R. L. Rogers, and B. S. Chissom. 1975. Derivation of new readability formulas (automated readability index, fog count and flesch reading ease formula) for navy enlisted personnel. Technical report, DTIC Document.

D. Klein and C. D. Manning. 2003. Accurate unlexicalized parsing. In *Proceedings of the 41st Annual Meeting on Association for Computational Linguistics-Volume 1*, pages 423–430. Association for Computational Linguistics.

K. Knight and D. Marcu. 2002. Summarization beyond sentence extraction: A probabilistic approach to sentence compression. *Artificial Intelligence*, 139:91–107.

P. Lal and S. Ruger. 2002. Extract-based Summarization with Simplification. In *Proceedings of the ACL 2002 Automatic Summarization / DUC 2002 Workshop*.

H. Lee, Y. Peirsman, A. Chang, N. Chambers, M. Surdeanu, and D. Jurafsky. 2011. Stanford's multi-pass sieve coreference resolution system at the CoNLL-2011 shared task. In *Proceedings of the Fifteenth Conference on Computational Natural Language Learning: Shared Task*, pages 28–34. Association for Computational Linguistics.

H. Llorens, E. Saquete, and B. Navarro. 2010. Tipsem (english and spanish): Evaluating CRFs and semantic roles in TempEval-2. In *Proceedings of the 5th International Workshop on Semantic Evaluation*, pages 284–291. Association for Computational Linguistics.

G. H. McLaughlin. 1969. SMOG grading: A new readability formula. *Journal of reading*, 12(8):639–646.

C. Orasan, Evans. R., and I. Dornescu, 2013. *Towards Multilingual Europe 2020: A Romanian Perspective*, chapter Text Simplification for People with Autistic Spectrum Disorders, pages 287–312. Romanian Academy Publishing House, Bucharest.

Z. Pan and G. M. Kosicki. 1993. Framing analysis: An approach to news discourse. *Political communication*, 10(1):55–75.

H. Pimperton and K. Nation. 2010. Suppressing irrelevant information from working memory: Evidence for domain-specific deficits in poor comprehenders. *Journal of Memory and Language*, 62(4):380–391.

J. Pustejovsky, J. Castano, R. Ingria, R. Sauri, R. Gaizauskas, A. Setzer, G. Katz, and D. Radev. 2003a. TimeML: Robust specification of event and temporal expressions in text. *New Directions in Question Answering*, 2003:28–34.

J. Pustejovsky, P. Hanks, R. Sauri, A. See, R. Gaizauskas, A. Setzer, D. Radev, B. Sundheim, D. Day, L. Ferro, et al. 2003b. The TimeBank corpus. In *Corpus Linguistics*, volume 2003, page 40.

H. Saggion, E. Gómez Martínez, E. Etayo, A. Anula, and L. Bourg. 2011. Text simplification in Simplext: Making text more accessible. *Revista de la Sociedad Española para el Procesamiento del Lenguaje Natural*.

C. Scarton, M. de Oliveira, A. Candido, C. Gasperin, and S. M. Alusio. 2010. SIMPLIFICA: A tool for authoring simplified texts in Brazilian Portuguese guided by readability assessments. In *Proceedings of the NAACL HLT 2010: Demonstration Session*, pages 41–44.

A. Shapiro and A. Milkes. 2004. Skilled readers make better use of anaphora: A study of the repeated-name penalty on text comprehension. *Electronic Journal of Research in Educational Psychology*, 2(2):161–180.

T. A. Van Dijk. 1985. Structures of news in the press. *Discourse and communication: New approaches to the analysis of mass media discourse and communication*, 10:69.

M. Verhagen, R. Sauri, T. Caselli, and J. Pustejovsky. 2010. Semeval-2010 task 13: TempEval-2. In *Proceedings of the 5th International Workshop on Semantic Evaluation*, pages 57–62. Association for Computational Linguistics.

S. Štajner, R. Evans, C. Orasan, and R. Mitkov. 2012. What Can Readability Measures Really Tell Us About Text Complexity? In *Proceedings of the LREC'12 Workshop: Natural Language Processing for Improving Textual Accessibility (NLP4ITA)*, Istanbul, Turkey.

K. Woodsend and M. Lapata. 2011. Learning to simplify sentences with quasi-synchronous grammar and integer programming. In *Proceedings of the 2011 Conference on Empirical Methods in Natural Language Processing (EMNLP)*.

Z. Wu and M. Palmer. 1994. Verbs semantics and lexical selection. In *Proceedings of the 32nd Annual Meeting of the Association for Computational Linguistics*, pages 133–138. Association for Computational Linguistics.

S. Wubben, A. van den Bosch, and E. Krahmer. 2012. Sentence simplification by monolingual machine translation. In *Proceedings of the 50th Annual Meeting of the Association for Computational Linguistics: Long Papers - Volume 1*, ACL '12, pages 1015–1024, Stroudsburg, PA, USA. Association for Computational Linguistics.

Random Projection and Geometrization of String Distance Metrics

Daniel Devatman Hromada
Université Paris 8 – Laboratoire Cognition Humaine et Artificielle
Slovak University of Technology – Faculty of Electrical Engineering and Information Technology
hromi@giver.eu

Abstract

Edit distance is not the only approach how distance between two character sequences can be calculated. Strings can be also compared in somewhat subtler geometric ways. A procedure inspired by Random Indexing can attribute an D-dimensional geometric coordinate to any character N-gram present in the corpus and can subsequently represent the word as a sum of N-gram fragments which the string contains. Thus, any word can be described as a point in a dense N-dimensional space and the calculation of their distance can be realized by applying traditional Euclidean measures. Strong correlation exists, within the Keats Hyperion corpus, between such cosine measure and Levenshtein distance. Overlaps between the centroid of Levenshtein distance matrix space and centroids of vectors spaces generated by Random Projection were also observed. Contrary to standard non-random "sparse" method of measuring cosine distances between two strings, the method based on Random Projection tends to naturally promote not the shortest but rather longer strings. The geometric approach yields finer output range than Levenshtein distance and the retrieval of the nearest neighbor of text's centroid could have, due to limited dimensionality of Randomly Projected space, smaller complexity than other vector methods.

Mèδεις ageôμετρèτος eisitô μου tèή stegèή

1 Introduction

Transformation of qualities into still finer and finer quantities belongs among principal hallmarks of the scientific method. In the world where even "deep" entities like "word-meanings" are quantified and co-measured by ever-growing number of researchers in computational linguistics (Kanerva et al., 2000; Sahlgren, 2005) and cognitive sciences (Gärdenfors, 2004), it is of no surprise that "surface" entities like "character strings" can be also compared one with another according to certain metric.

Traditionally, the distance between two strings is most often evaluated in terms of edit distance (ED) which is defined as the minimum number of operations like insertion, deletion or substitution required to change one string-word into the other. A prototypical example of such an edit distance approach is a so-called Levenshtein distance (Levenshtein, 1966). While many variants of Levenshtein distance (LD) exist, some extended with other operations like that of "metathese" (Damerau, 1964), some exploiting probabilist weights (Jaro, 1995), some introducing dynamic programming (Wagner & Fischer, 1974), all these ED algorithms take as granted that notions of insertion, deletion etc. are crucial in order to operationalize similarity between two strings.

Within this article we shall argue that one can successfully calculate similarity between two strings without taking recourse to any edit operation whatsoever. Instead of discrete insert&delete operations, we shall focus the attention of the reader upon a purely positive notion, that of "occurence of a part within the whole" (Harte, 2002). Any string-to-be-compared shall be understood as such a whole and any continuous N-gram fragment observable within it shall be interpreted as its part.

2 Advantages of Random Projection

Random Projection is a method for projecting high-dimensional data into representations with less dimensions. In theoretical terms, it is founded on a Johnson-Lindenstrauss (Johnson & Lindenstrauss, 1984) lemma stating that *a small set of points in a high-dimensional space can be embedded into a space of much lower dimension in such a way that distances between the points are nearly preserved*. In practical terms, solutions based on Random Projection, or a closely related Random Indexing, tend to yield high performance when confronted with diverse NLP problems like synonym-finding (Sahlgren & Karlgren, 2002), text categorization (Sahlgren & Cöster, 2004), unsupervised bilingual lexicon extraction (Sahlgren & Karlgren, 2005), discovery of implicit inferential connections (Cohen et al., 2010) or automatic keyword attribution to scientific articles (El Ghali et al., 2012). RP distinguishes itself from other word space models in at least one of these aspects:

1. Incremental: RP allows to inject on-the-fly new data-points (words) or their ensembles (texts, corpora) into already constructed vector space. One is not obliged to execute heavy computations (like Singular Value Decomposition in case of Latent Semantic Analysis) every time new data is encountered.
2. Multifunctional: As other vector-space models, RP can be used in many diverse scenarios. In RI, for example, words are often considered to be the terms and sentences are understood as documents. In this article, words (or verses) shall be considered as documents and N-gram fragments which occur in them shall be treated like terms.
3. Generalizable: RP can be applied in any scenario where one needs to encode into vectorial form the set of relations between discrete entities observables at diverse levels of abstraction (words / documents, parts / wholes, features / objects, pixels/images etc.).
4. Absolute: N-grams and terms, words and sentences, sentences and documents – in RP all these entities are encoded in the **same** *randomly constructed yet absolute space* . Similarity measurements can be therefore realized even among entities which would be considered as incommensurable in more traditional approaches[1].

There is, of course, a price which is being paid for these advantages: Primo, RP involves stochastic aspects and its application thus does not guarantee replicability of results. Secundo, it involves two parameters D and S and choice of such parameters can significantly modify model's performance (in relation to corpus upon which it is applied). Tertio: since even the most minute "features" are initially encoded in the same way as more macroscopic units like words, documents or text, i.e. by a vector of length D "seeded" with D-S non-zero values, RP can be susceptible to certain limitations if ever applied on data discretisable into millions of distinct observable features.

3 Method

The method of geometrization of strings by means of Random Projection (RP) consists of four principal steps. Firstly, strings contained within corpus are "exploded" into fragments. Secondly, a random vector is assigned to every fragment according to RP's principles. Thirdly, the geometric representation of the string is obtained as a sum of fragment-vectors. Finally, the distance between two strings can be obtained by calculating the cosine of an angle between their respective geometric representations.

3.1 String Fragmentation

We define the fragment F of a word W having the length of N as any continuous[2] 1-, 2-, 3-...N-gram contained within W. Thus, a word of length 1 contains 1 fragment (the fragment is the word itself), words of length 2 contain 3 fragments, and, more generally, there exist N(N+1)/2 fragments for a word of length N. Pseudo-code of the fragmentation algorithm is as follows:

```
function fragmentator;
for frag_length (1..word_length) {
  for offset (0..(word_length - frag_length)) {
    frags[]=substr (word,offset,frag_length);
  }
}
```

where substr() is a function returning from the string *word* a fragment of length *frag_length* starting at specified *offset*.

[1] In traditional word space models, words are considered to be represented by the rows (vectors/points) of the word-document matrix and documents to be its columns (axes). In RP, both words (or word-fragments) and documents are represented by rows.

[2] Note that in this introductory article we exploit only continuous N-gram fragments. Interaction of RP with possibly other relevant patterns observable in the word – like N-grams with gaps or sequences of members of diverse equivalence classes [e.g. consonants/vowels] – shall be, we hope, addressed in our doctoral Thesis or other publications.

3.2 Stochastic fragment-vector generation

Once fragments are obtained, we transform them into geometric entities by following the fundamental precept of Random Projection:

To every fragment-feature F present in the corpus, let's assign a random vector of length containing D-S elements having zero values and S elements whose value is either -1 or 1.

The number of dimensions (D) and the seed (S) are the parameters of the model. It is recommended that S<<D. Table 1 illustrates how all fragments of the corpus containing only a word[3] "DOG" could be, given that S=2, randomly projected in a 5-dimensional space.

Fragment	Vector
D	0, 1, 0, 0, -1
O	1, 1, 0, 0, 0
G	0, 0, -1, 0, -1
DO	-1, 0, -1, 0, 0
OG	0, 1, 0, 1, 0
DOG	0, 0, 0, -1, -1

Table 1: Vectors possibly assigned to the fragments of the word "dog" by $RP_{5,2}$

3.3 String geometrization

Once random "init" vectors have been assigned to all word-fragments contained within the corpus, the geometrization of all word-strings is relatively straightforward by applying the following principle:

The vector representation of a word X can be calculated as a sum of vectors associated to fragments contained in the word X.

Thus, the vector representation of a word "dog" would be [0, 3, -2, 0, -3]. Note also that this vector for the word "dog" is different from randomly initialized fragment-vector referring to the fragment "dog". This is due to the fact that the vector space of "fragments" and "words" are two different spaces. One possible way how could one can collapse the fragment space with the string space is to convolute them by Reflected Random Indexing (Cohen et al., 2010) – such an approach, however, shall not be applied in a limited scope of this article.

3.4 String distance calculation

The string geometrization procedure calculates a vector for every string present in the corpus. Subsequently, the vectors can be compared with each other. While other measures like Jaccard index are sometimes also applied in relation to RI, the distance between words X and Y shall be calculated, in the following experiment, in the most traditional way. Id est, as a cosine of an angle between vectors V_X and V_Y.

[3] The role of fragment is analogical to the role of a "term" in Random Indexing. And the role of the "word" is identical to the role that "context" plays in RI.

4 Experiment(s)

Two sets of simulations were conducted to test our hypothesis. The first experiment looked for both correlations as well as divergences between three different word-couple similarity data-sets obtained by applying three different measures upon the content of the corpus. The second experiment focused more closely upon overlaps among the centroids of three diverse metric spaces under study.

4.1 Corpus and word extraction

ASCII-encoded version of the poem "The Fall of Hyperion" (Keats, 1819) was used as a corpus from which the list of words was extracted by

1. Splitting the poem into lines (verses).
2. Splitting every verse into words, considering the characters [:;,.?!()] as word separator tokens.
3. In order to mark the word boundaries, every word was prefixed with ^ sign and post-fixed with **$** sign.
4. All words were transformed into lowercase.

Corpus has size of 22812 bytes representing 529 lines which contain the total number of N_w=1545 distinct word types exploded into N_F=22340 distinct fragments.

4.2 "Word couple" experiment

Three datasets were created, all containing the list of all possible (i.e. $N_w * N_w$ = (1545 * 1545) / 2 =1193512) distinct word-couples. For every dataset, a string distance was calculated for every word couple. Within the first dataset, the distance was determined according to traditional Levenshtein distance metrics. For second dataset, an RPD distance has been calculated by measuring word couple's cosine distance within the vector space constructed by Random Projection of words fragments set up with parameters D=1000,S=5. The third dataset contains values obtained by measuring the cosine measure between two sparse non-random vector representations of two different words , whereby the features were obtained by means of the same fragmentation algorithm as in the case of RPD, but without Random Projection. In order to keep this scenario as pure as possible, no other processing (e.g. tf-idf etc.) was applied and the values which we shall label as „geometric distance“ (GD) denote simply the cosine between two vectors of a non-stochastically generated sparse fragment-word count matrix.

4.2.1 Results

Figure 1 shows relations between LD and RPD distances of all possible couples of all words contained in the Hyperion corpus. Both datasets seem to be strongly significantly corellated both according to Spearman‘s rho measure ($p < 2.2e-16$) as well as according to Pearson‘s product-moment correlation ($p < 2.2e-16$, cor = -0.2668235). While fifteen different LDs from the range of integers <0, 15> were observed among words of corpus, one could distinguish 252229 diverse real-numbered RPD values limited to interval <0, 1>.

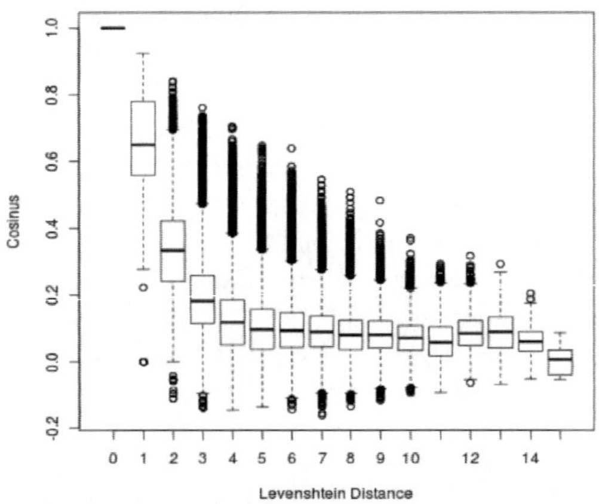

Figure 1: Scatter plot displaying relations between Levenshtein distances and cosine distances measured in the vector space constructed by $RI_{1000,5}$

String distance measured in the space constructed by $\mathbf{RP_{1000,5}}$ also strongly correlates (Pearson correlation coefficient = 0.992; Spearman rho = 0.679; minimal $p < 2.2e-16$ for both tests) with a GD cosine measure exploiting a non-deformed fragment-word matrix.

An important difference was observed, however, during a more „local“ & qualitative analysis of results produced by the two vectorial methods. More concretely: while non-stochastic „sparse“ cosine GD distance tends to promote as „closest“ the couples of **short** strings, *RPD yields the highest score for couples of* ***long*** *words*. This is indicated by the list of most similar word-couples generated by three methods present in Table 2.

GD	RPD
a ’	vessels vessel
it i	comfort comforts
i ’	sorrows sorrow
at a	’benign benign
o so	temples temple
o of	changing unchanging
as a	stream streams
o or	immortal’s immortal
’i i	breathe breath
an a	trance tranced

Table 2: Ten most similar world couples according to non-random “sparse” geometric distance (GD) and Randomly Projected Distance

4.3 The “centroid” experiment

Three types of concrete word-centroids were extracted from the corpus. A string having the smallest overall LD to all other strings in the corpus shall be labeled as the “Levenshtein centroid” (LC). A string having the maximal sum of cosines in relation to other words shall be labeled as the “Cosinal centroid” (CC). Contrary to LC and CC, for calculation of which one has to calculate distances with regard to all words in the corpus, the “Geometric Centroid” (GC) was determined as a word whose vector has the biggest cosine in regard to “Theoretical Centroid” (GC) obtained in a purely geometric way as a sum of all word-vectors. Stochastic CC_{RP} and GC_{RP} calculation simulations were repeated in 100 runs with D=1000, S=5.

4.3.1 Results

The word “**are**” was determined to be the LC of Hyperion corpus with average $LD_{ARE,X} = 4.764$ to all words of the corpus. The same word are was ranked, by a non-stochastic “sparse” geometric distance algorithm, as 3rd most central CC and 36th most closest term to GC . Table 3 shows ten terms with least overall LD to all other words of the corpus (LC), ten terms with biggest cosine in relation to all other terms of the corpus (CC_{GD})

and ten terms with biggest cosine in regard to hypothetical Theoretical Centroid (GC_{GD}) of a sparse non-projected space obtained from the Hyperion corpus.

Rank	LC	CC_{GD}	GC_{GD}
1	**are**	charm	**a**
2	**ore**	**red**	o
3	ate	arm	I
4	**ere**	**a**	'
5	one	**me**	he
6	toes	hard	to
7	sole	had	at
8	ease	reed	an
9	lone	domed	**me**
10	here	**are**	as

Table 3: Ten nearest neighbor words of three types of non-stochastic centroids

Shortest possible strings seem to be GC_{GD}'s nearest neighbors. This seems to be analogous to data presented on Table 2. In this sense does the GC_{GD} method seem to differ from the CC_{GD} approach which tends to promote longer strings.

Such a marked difference in behaviors between GC and CC approaches was not observed in case of spaces constructed by means of Random Projection. In 100 runs, both GC and CC centered approaches seemed to promote as central the strings of comparable content and length[4]. As is indicated by Table 4, the LC "are" turned out to be the closest (i.e. Rank 1, when comparing with Table 3) to all other terms in 6% of Random Projection runs. In 6% of runs the same term was labeled as the nearest neighbor to the geometrical centroid of the generated space. Other overlaps between all used methods are marked by bold writing in Tables 3 and 4.

Word	CC_{RPD}	GC_{RPD}
see	20	28
he	11	8
are	6	6
ore	5	6
ere	4	5
set	6	5
she	5	4
sea	4	4
a	9	4
red	1	3

Table 4: Central terms of Randomly Projected spaces and their frequency of occurence in 100 runs

Analogically to the observation described in the last paragraph of the section 4.2.1, it can be also observed that the strings characterized as "closest" to the Theoretical Centroid of vector spaces generated by Random Projection tend to be longer than "minimal" string nearest to GC_{GD} determined in the traditional non-stochastic feature-word vector space scenario.

5 Discussion

When it comes to CC_{RP}-calculation run lasted, in average, $CC_{RPD\text{-}detection}$ = 90 seconds, thus being almost twice as fast than the LC-calculation executed on the very same computer which lasted twice the time $LC_{detection}$= 157 s for the same corpus, indicating that the computational complexity of our PDL (Glazebrook et al., 1997) implementation of CC_{RP}-detection is lesser than the complexity of LC-detection based on PERL's Text::Levenshtein implementation of LD.

When it comes to the computational complexity of the GC-calculation, it is evident that GC is determined faster and by less complex process than LCs or CCs . This is so because in order to determine the GC_{RP} of N words there is no need to construct an N * N distance matrix. On the contrary, since every word is attributed coordinates in a randomly-generated yet *absolute* space, the detection of a hypothetic Geometric Centroid of all words is a very straightforward and cheap process, as well as the detection of GC's nearest word neighbor..

And since in RP, the length of GC-denoting vector is limited to a relatively reasonable low number of elements (i.e. D = 1000 in case of this paper), it is of no surprise that the string closest to GC shall be found more slowly by a traditional "sparse vector" scenario whenever the number of features (columns) > D. In our scenario with N_F=22340 of distinct features, it was almost 4 times faster to construct the vector space + find a nearest word to GC of the Randomly Projected space han to use a "sparse" fragment-term matrix optimized by storing only non-zero values ($GC_{RPD\text{-}NN\text{-}detection}$ ~ 6 sec ; $GC_{GD\text{-}NN\text{-}detection}$ ~ 22 sec).

Other thing worthy of interest could be that contrary to a "sparse" method which seems to give higher score to shorter strings, somewhat longer strings seem to behave as if they were naturally "pushed towards the centroid" in a dense space generated by RP. If such is, verily, the case, then we believe that the method presented hereby could be useful, for example, in domains of gene sequence analysis or other scenarios where pattern-to-be-discovered is "spread out" rather than centralized.

[4] In fact only in 22 runs did GC_{RPD} differ from CC_{RPD}

In practical terms, if ever the querying in RP space shall turn out to have lesser complexity than other vector models, our method could be useful within a hybrid system as a fast stochastic way to pre-select a limited set of "candidate" (possibly locally optimal) strings which could be subsequently confronted with more precise, yet costly, non-stochastic metrics ultimately leading to discovery of the global optimum.

Asides above-mentioned aspects, we believe that there exists at least one other theoretical reason for which the RP-based geometrization procedure could deem to be a worthy alternative to LD-like distance measures. That is: the cardinality of a real-valued <0, 1> range of a cosine function is much higher than a whole-numbered <0, max(length(word))> range possibly offered as an output of Levenshtein Distance. In other terms, outputs of string distance functions based on trigonometry of RP-based vector spaces are more subtler, more fine-grained, than those furnished by traditional LD. While this advantage does not hold for "weighted" LD measures we hope that this article could motivate future studies aiming to compare "weighted" LD and RPD metrics.

When it comes to the feature extracting "fragment explosion" approach, it could be possibly reproached to the method proposed hereby that 1) the fragmentation component which permutes blindly through all N-grams presented in the corpus yields too many "features"; that 2) that taking into account all of them during the calculation of the word's final vector is not necessary and could even turn to be computationally counter-productive; or that 3) bi-grams and tri-grams alone give better results than larger N (Manning et al., 2008). A primary answer to such an ensemble of reproaches could be, that by the very act of projecting data upon limited set of same non-orthogonal dimensions, the *noise could simply cancel itself out*[5]. Other possible answer to the argument could be that while the bi&tri-gram argument holds well for natural language structures, the method we aim to propose here has ambitions to be used beyond NLP (e.g. bio-informatics) or pre-NLP (e.g. early stages of language acquisition where the very notion of N-gram does not make sense because the very criterion of sequence segmentation & discretization was not yet established). At last but not least we could counter-argue by stating that often do the algorithms based on a sort of initial blind "computational explosion of number of features" perform better than those who do not perform such explosion, especially when coupled with subsequent feature selection algorithms. Such is the case, for example, of an approach proposed by Viola & Jones in (Viola & Jones, 2001) which caused the revolution in the computer vision by proposing that in order to detect an object, one should look for combinations of pixels instead of pixels.

In this paper, such combinations of "letter-pixels" were, *mutatis mutandi*, called "fragments". Our method departs from an idea that one can, and should, associate random vectors to such fragments. But the idea can go further. Instead of looking for occurrence of part in the whole, a more advanced RI-based approach shall replace the notion of "fragment occuring in the word" by a more general notion of "pattern which matches the sequence". Thus even the vector associated to pattern /d.g/ could be taken into account during the construction of a vector representing the word "dog".

Reminding that RP-based models perform very well when it comes to offering solutions to quite "deep" *signifiée*-oriented problems, we find it difficult to understand why could not be the same algorithmic machinery applied to the problems dealing with "surface", *signifiant*-oriented problems, notably given the fact that some sort of dimensionality reduction has to occur whenever the mind tries to map >4D-experiences upon neural substrate of the brain embedded in 3D physical space.

Given that all observed correlations and centroid overlaps indicate that the string distance calculation based on Random Projection could turn out to be a useful substitute for LD measure or even other more fine-grained methods. And given that RP would not be possible if the Johnson-Lindenstrauss's lemma was not valid, our results could be also interpreted as another empirical demonstration of the validity of the JL-lemma.

Acknowledgments

The author would like to thank Adil El-Ghali for introduction into Random Indexing as well as his comments concerning the present paper; to prof. Charles Tijus and doc. Ivan Sekaj for their support and to Aliancia Fair-Play for permission to execute some code on their servers.

[5] And this "noise canceling property" could be especially true for RP as defined in this paper where the rare non-zero values in the random "init" vectors can point in opposite directions (i.e. either -1 or 1).

References

Trevor Cohen, Roger Schvaneveldt & Dominic Widdows. 2010. Reflective Random Indexing and indirect inference: A scalable method for discovery of implicit connections. *Journal of Biomedical Informatics*, *43*(2), 240–256.

Fred J. Damerau. 1964. A technique for computer detection and correction of spelling errors. *Communications of the ACM*, *7*(3), 171–176.

Adil El Ghali, Daniel D. Hromada & Kaoutar El Ghali. 2012. Enrichir et raisonner sur des espaces sémantiques pour l'attribution de mots-clés. *JEP-TALN-RECITAL 2012*, 77.

Peter Gärdenfors. 2004. *Conceptual spaces: The geometry of thought*. MIT press.

Karl Glazebrook. Jarle Brinchmann, John Cerney, Craig DeForest, Doug Hunt, Tim Jenness & Tuomas Lukka. 1997. The Perl Data Language. *The Perl Journal*, *5*(5).

Verity Harte. 2002. *Plato on parts and wholes: The metaphysics of structure*. Clarendon Press Oxford.

Matthew A. Jaro. 1995. Probabilistic linkage of large public health data files. *Statistics in medicine*, *14*(5-7), 491–498.

William B. Johnson & Joram Lindenstrauss. 1984. Extensions of Lipschitz mappings into a Hilbert space. *Contemporary mathematics*, *26*(189-206), 1.

Pentti Kanerva, Jan Kristofersson & Anders Holst. 2000. Random indexing of text samples for latent semantic analysis. *Proceedings of the 22nd annual conference of the cognitive science society* (Vol. 1036).

John Keats. 1819. The Fall of Hyperion. A Dream. *John Keats. complete poems and selected letters*, 381–395.

Vladimir I. Levenshtein. 1966. Binary codes capable of correcting deletions, insertions and reversals. *Soviet physics doklady* (Vol. 10, p. 707).

Huma Lodhi, Craig Saunders, John Shawe-Taylor, Nello Cristianini & Chris Watkins. 2002. Text classification using string kernels. *The Journal of Machine Learning Research*, *2*, 419–444.

Christopher D. Manning, Prabhakar Raghavan & Hinrich Schütze. 2008. *Introduction to information retrieval*. Cambridge University Press.

Magnus Sahlgren. 2005. An introduction to random indexing. *Methods and Applications of Semantic Indexing Workshop at the 7th International Conference on Terminology and Knowledge Engineering, TKE* (Vol. 5).

Magnus Sahlgren & Rickard Cöster. 2004. Using bag-of-concepts to improve the performance of support vector machines in text categorization. *Proceedings of the 20th international conference on Computational Linguistics* (p. 487).

Magnus Sahlgren & Jussi Karlgren. 2002. Vector-based semantic analysis using random indexing for cross-lingual query expansion. *Evaluation of Cross-Language Information Retrieval Systems* (p. 169–176).

Magnus Sahlgren & Jussi Karlgren. 2005. Automatic bilingual lexicon acquisition using random indexing of parallel corpora. *Natural Language Engineering*, *11*(3), 327–341.

Alan M. Turing. 1936. On computable numbers, with an application to the Entscheidungsproblem. *Proceedings of the London mathematical society*, *42*(2), 230–265.

Paul Viola & Michal Jones. 2001. Rapid Object Detection using a Boosted Cascade of Simple. *Proc. IEEE CVPR 2001*.

Robert A. Wagner & Michael J. Fischer. 1974. The string-to-string correction problem. *Journal of the ACM (JACM)*, *21*(1), 168–173.

Improving Language Model Adaptation using Automatic Data Selection and Neural Network

Shahab Jalalvand
HLT research unit, FBK, 38123 Povo (TN), Italy
jalalvand@fbk.eu

Abstract

Since language model (LM) is very sensitive to domain mismatch between training and test data, using a group of techniques to adapt a big LM to specific domains is quite helpful. In this paper, we, benefit from salient performance of recurrent neural network to improve domain adapted LM. In this way, we first apply an automatic data selection procedure on a limited amount of in-domain data in order to enrich the training set. After that, we train a domain specific N-gram LM and improve it by using recurrent neural network language model trained on limited in-domain data. Experiments in the framework of EUBRIDGE [1] project on weather forecast dataset show that the automatic data selection procedure improves the word error rate around 2% and RNNLM makes additional improvement over 0.3%.

Keywords: Language model, automatic data selection, neural network language model, speech recognition

1 Introduction

Language models are widely used in different applications such as automatic speech recognition (ASR), machine translation; spell checking, handwriting detection etc. Basically, a language model tries to predict the next word in a sentence by considering a history of previous words. To provide this history, the language model needs to be trained on a large set of texts. Generally, the larger train set the better language model.

A main issue in language modeling arises from data sparseness in training set. It means that in a large training set, many of the n-grams[2] are very rare and, consequently, their probabilities are very small. Katz (1987) tried to overcome this problem by proposing back-off technique. In it, the probabilities of rare n-grams are estimated through linear interpolation of the probabilities of the lower order n-grams.

Discounting methods such as Witten-Bell estimate (Witten and Bell, 1991), absolute discounting (Ney and Essen, 1991), Kneser-Ney method (Kneser and Ney, 1995) and modified Kneser-Ney (Chen and Goodman, 1999) allow estimating back-off coefficients.

Recently, using neural network language model (NNLM) has been become of interest because it results more generalization in comparison to N-gram models. In NNLM, the words are represented in a continuous space. The idea of representing words in a continuous space for language modeling was started by Bengio (2003). It was followed by Schwenk (2007) who applied neural network for language modeling in large scale vocabulary speech recognition and obtained a noticeable improvement in word error rate. Mikolov (2010) pursued this way and used recurrent neural network for language modeling (RNNLM). The advantage of RNNLM on feed forward neural network, which was used by Bengio (2003) and Schwenk (2007) is that RNNLM can consider an arbitrary number of preceding words to estimate the probability of

[1] This work has been partially founded by the European project EUBRIDGE, under the contract FP7-287658

[2] Sequence of n words (usually 2, 3 or 4 words). By n-gram (with small "n") we refer to an n-word sequence and by N-gram (with capital "N") we refer to a language model based on n-grams

next word, while, feed forward NNLM can only see a fixed number of preceding words. Thanks to positive performance of RNNLM toolbox developed by Mikolov (2011), we use this, in our specific task which is weather forecast transcription in the framework of EUBRIDGE project.

In addition to data sparseness, the performance of language model is affected by mismatch between training and test data. This leads to reduction of language model accuracy. The problem is that it is not always easy to collect sufficient amount of related data in order to train a specific-domain LM. Therefore, research on LM domain adaptation, as well as automatic selection of auxiliary text data is still of large interest.

There are methods which try to adapt a big language model to a limited amount of in-domain data such as Latent Semantic Analysis (Bellegarda, 1988), Mixture (Foster, 2007), Minimum Discrimination information (Federico, 1999) and Lazy MDI (Ruiz, 2012). Another group of methods try to automatically retrieve auxiliary documents from text resources such as Internet. Among them, we are interested in the ones reported in (Maskey, 2009) and (Falavigna, 2012) which are based on information retrieval measures such as LM perplexity and Term Frequency Inverse Document Frequency (TF-IDF).

This paper aims at transcribing a weather forecast speech corpus consisting of audio recordings that are divided into development and test sets. In addition, a small text corpus of weather forecast has been given within EUBRIDGE project. We use this corpus as in-domain data. In this way, we first utilize an automatic data selection procedure to collect more an auxiliary data set. Then, we train an N-gram language model on the selected data and decode the test audio recording. For each audio, an n-best list is produced which is then processed and re-ranked by means of a neural network language model. We show the N-gram which is trained on the automatically selected data is around 2% (in terms of word error rate) better than the original one and neural network language model improves it up to 0.3%.

In Section 2 and 3, we briefly describe Neural Network Language Model (NNLM) and Recurrent NNLM, respectively. Then, in section 4 we describe the process of preparing data and also the experiments which are confirmed by perplexity and WER results. Finally, Section 5 concludes the paper.

2 Neural Network Language Model (NNLM)

In NNLM, a word is represented by a $|V|$-dimensional vector of 0s and 1s. $|V|$ is the size of vocabulary. In $vector_{wi}$ that represents i^{th} word in the vocabulary, all the elements are zero except i^{th} element which is 1 (see Figure 1). For a 4-gram NNLM, three vectors are concatenated and given to the input layer. Thus, the input vector would be $3x|V|$-dimensional and the input layer has the same number of neurons.

Usually there is a projection layer with linear activation function which reduces the dimension of input vectors and maps them into a continuous space. The output of the projection layer is given to a hidden layer with nonlinear activation function (sigmoid, hyperbolic tangent etc). The output of hidden layer is then given to the output layer which has $|V|$ neurons for $|V|$ candidate words. j^{th} neuron in this layer computes the probability of observing j^{th} word after three previous words (in 4-gram NNLM). The activation function that is used in this layer is a softmax function which guarantees that the sum of all probabilities is 1 and each probability is between zero and 1 (Schwenk, 2007).

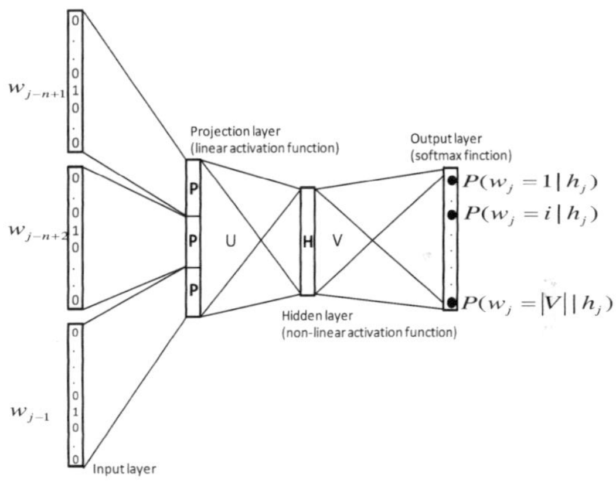

Figure 1: Neural network LM

The computations that are needed for each layer are as follows:

$$d_j = \tanh\left(\sum_l c_l . U_{jl} + b_j\right) \quad \forall j = 1,...,H, \quad (1)$$

$$o_i = \sum_j d_j . V_{ij} + k_i \quad \forall i = 1,...,N, \quad (2)$$

$$p_i = \frac{e^{o_i}}{\sum_{l=1}^{N} e^{o_l}} \quad \forall i = 1,...,N, \quad (3)$$

d_j is the output of jth neuron in projection layer. U and V are the weight matrices from projection to hidden and from hidden to output layers, respectively. b and k are the bias vectors of hidden and output layers, respectively. o_i shows the output of ith output neuron. The training procedure is done using a back-propagation algorithm (Schwenk, 2007).

3 Recurrent Neural Network Language Model (RNNLM)

Instead of projection layer, in RNNLM, there are recursive arcs in hidden layer which connect the outputs of hidden neurons to their input and work as a cache memory for neural network.

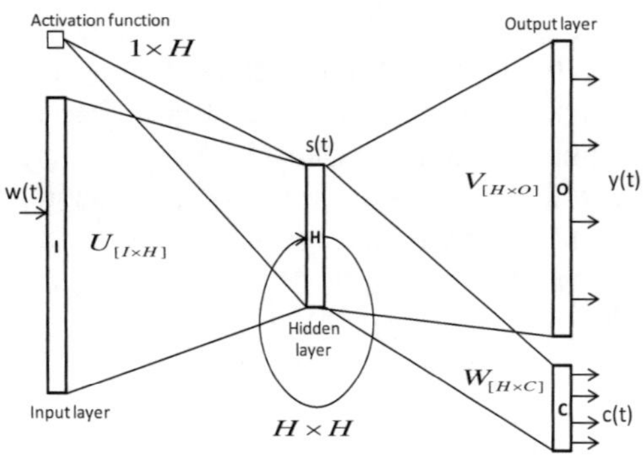

Figure 2: Recurrent Neural Network LM

For a training set with I unique words, an input layer with I neurons is needed. If the size of hidden layer is $|H|$, then the weight matrix between input and hidden layers (U) will be $I\times|H|$-dimensional. Since the hidden neurons are fully connected by the recursive arcs, there are $|H|\times|H|$ additional weighted connections. Furthermore, we need a $1\times|H|$-dimensional vector to store the activation function of each hidden neuron.

In a class based language model, there are two types of output: probability of classes and probability of words. To implement a class-based RNNLM, two sets of neurons in the output layer are needed: one for computing the probabilities of words and the other for the probabilities of classes. From hidden neurons to word output neurons there are $|H|\times|O|$ connections, which are shown in matrix V and from hidden neurons to class output neurons there are $|H|\times|C|$ connections which are shown in matrix W (the number of classes is equal to $|C|$).

Considering this architecture for neural network language model, the formulation of each layer should be changed as follows:

$$x(t) = \left[w(t)^T \; s(t-1)^T\right]^T \qquad (4)$$

$x(t)$, that is the input vector of hidden layer is a $|V|+|H|$-dimensional vector; $w(t)$ is the vector of observed word at time t; $s(t-1)$ is the output of hidden layer at time $t-1$ ($s(0)$ can be initialized by 0.1). The output of the hidden layer is computed by:

$$s_j(t) = \tanh\left(\sum_i x_i(t).U_{ji}\right) \quad \forall j = 1,\dots,H \qquad (5)$$

In which, $s_j(t)$ is the output of jth hidden neuron. $x_i(t)$ is i^{th} element of input vector and U_{ji} indicates the weight of the connection between neuron i and neuron j from input to hidden layer, respectively. The probability over the classes is computed by:

$$c_l(t) = SOFTMAX\left(\sum_j s_j(t).W_{lj}\right) \qquad (7)$$

In which $c_l(t)$ is the output of lth output neuron which shows the probability of class l for the word which has been observed at time t. w_{lj} is the weight of the connection between j^{th} neuron of hidden layer and l^{th} neuron of output layer. Using a similar equation just by replacing matrix W by matrix V, we can compute the probability of each word over the classes.

$$y_c(t) = SOFTMAX\left(\sum_j s_j(t).V_{cj}\right) \qquad (8)$$

Therefore, the overall probability of a word is computed by:

$$p(w_i \mid history) = p(c_i \mid s(t))P(w_i \mid c_i, s(t)) \qquad (9)$$

where i varies from 1 to the number of vocabulary size. c_i is the class that w_i belongs to that.

Because of the complexity of this model, it is quite hard to use it for huge text corpora. This is why, researchers usually use this model on small training sets or sometimes they partition a huge training set into several small sets and build an RNNLM on each partition and make an interpolation between them.

In the next experiments we train an RNNLM on the small in-domain data and use it to re-score the output of the speech decoder. We show that this approach improves the WER of the decoder up to 0.3%.

4 Experiments

As previously mentioned, we are given a quite small set of in-domain data, consisting of weather forecast texts (around 1 Million words) and a large, out-domain corpus, called GoogleNews that includes around 1.6G words. There are two major challenges:

- First, training a language model on a large domain-independent set is very costly in time and computation and also the resulted model cannot be very efficient in our specific task which is weather forecast transcription.
- Second, the available domain-specific data is to some extent small and the model which is trained on it is not general enough.

Two possible solutions are:

- We can use the available in-domain set to select similar sentences from the huge out-domain set in order to enrich our in-domain training set.
- Or, we can cluster the domain-independent set using word similarity measures. It is expected that the sentences from the same cluster belong to the same domain. Then, we can train a specific language model for each cluster.

We focus on the first solution and utilize it in our experiments. This idea is already proposed by Maskey (2009) for re-sampling an auxiliary data set for language model adaptation in a machine translation task. We use a similar approach to collect in-domain sentences from GoogleNews.

4.1 Text Corpora and Language Models

The source used for generating the documents for training a domain-independent LM is Google-news. Google-news is an aggregator of news provided and operated by Google, that collects news from many different sources, in different languages, and each group of articles consists of similar contents. We download daily news from this site, filter-out useless tags and collect texts. Google-news data is grouped into 7 broad domains (such as economy, sports, science, technology, etc). After cleaning, removing double lines and application of a text normalization procedure, the corpus results into about 5.7M of documents, or a total of about 1.6G of words. The average number of words per document is 272 (refer to (Girardi, 2007) for details about the web document retrieval process applied in this work).

On this data we trained a 4-gram back-off LM using the modified shift beta smoothing method as supplied by the IRSTLM toolkit (Federico, 2008). The LM results into about 1.6M unigrams, 73M bigrams, 120M 3-grams and 195M 4-grams. The LM is used to compile a static Finite State Network (FSN) which includes LM probabilities and lexicon for two ASR decoding passes. In the following we will refer to this LM as GN4gr-ALL.

Within the EUBRIDGE project we were also given a set of in-domain text data, specifically around 1M words related to weather reports published on the BBC web site, that was first used to train a corresponding 4-gram LM (in the following we will call it IN4gr-1MW).Then, with the latter LM we automatically select, using perplexity as similarity measure, from the whole Google-news database an auxiliary corpus of about 100M words. On this corpus we trained a corresponding 4-gram LM and we adapted it to the weather domain using the 1MW in-domain corpus (as adaptation data) and LM-mixture (as adaptation method). The resulting adapted LM contains about 278K unigrams, 9.4M bigrams, 7.9M 3-grams and 9.5M 4-grams. In the following we will refer to it as IN4gr-100MW.

Using the last language model (IN4gr-100MW) and a pre-trained acoustic model which is described in the next subsection we extract the 1000-best list from the decoder and re-score this list using a recurrent neural network language model (RNNLM).

Before that, we need to investigate different types of RNNLM with different configuration in order to find the best one for our specific task. In this way, we trained RNNLMs with 250, 300, 350, 400, 450, 500 hidden neurons and 200, 300, 500, 600, 1000 and 8000 classes on the 1MW in-domain data. Figure 4 compares the perplexity of these models on a development set consisting of 12K words which is completely isolated from the test set.

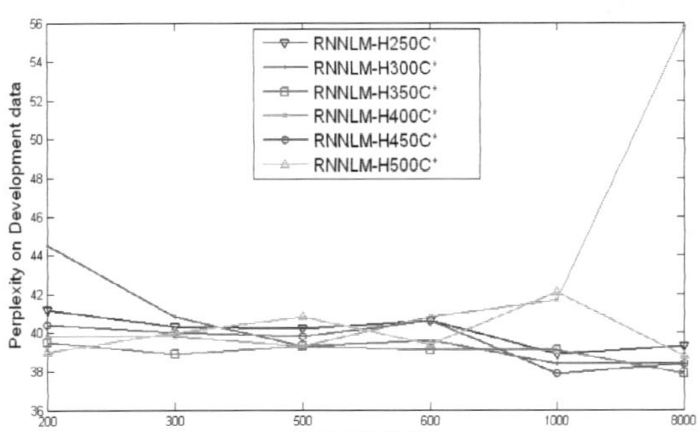

Figure 3. Perplexity of different RNNLMs on development data

As it can be seen from Figure 4, by increasing the number of classes the performance of RNNLM improves. For example, the best three RNNLMs are the ones with: H350C8000,

H450C1000 and H300C1000 (exp. rnnlmH300C1000 is an RNNLM with 300 hidden neurons and 1000 classes).

In accordance with Mikolov (2011), RNNLM works better when it is interpolated with an N-gram. Thus, we train a 4-gram language model based on Kneser-Ney smoothing method using SRI toolkit (Stolcke, 2002) and interpolate it with the best RNNLMs by different weights (lambda). Figure 5 shows the result of these interpolations.

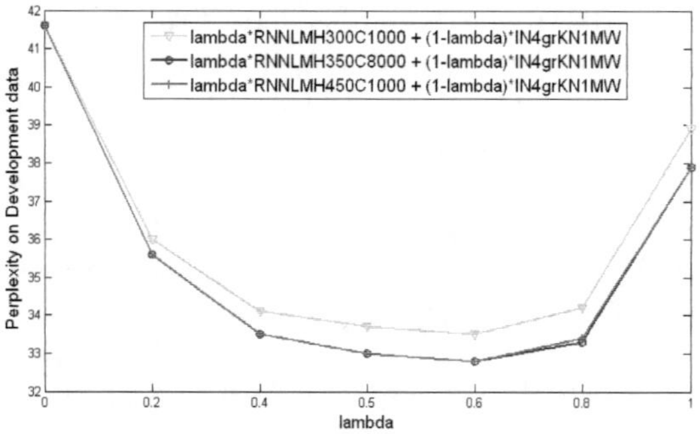

Figure 4. Interpolation of RNNLM scores and 4-gram scores

When lambda is zero, just N-gram score has been considered and when lambda is 1, just the score of RNNLM is used. It is seen that interpolation of N-gram and RNNLM improves the performance of the system. Correspondingly, we see that rnnlmH350C8000 and rnnlmH450C1000 show the highest performance in interpolation with IN4grKN-1MW. In following, we will use the latter to re-score the n-best list obtained from decoder.

4.2 Generation of N-best Lists

As previously mentioned we used the RNNLM, trained on 1MW in-domain set of data, to re-score n-best lists produced during ASR decoding. Details on both acoustic model training and ASR decoding process can be found in (Falavigna, 2012). In short for this work, speech segments to transcribe have been manually detected and labeled in terms of speaker names (i.e. no automatic speech segmentation and speaker diarization procedures have been applied).

In both first and second decoding passes the system uses continuous density Hidden Markov Models (HMMs) and a static network embedding the probabilities of the baseline LM. A frame synchronous Viterbi beam-search is used to find the most likely word sequence corresponding to each speech segment. In addition, in the second decoding pass the system generates a word graph for each speech segment. To do this, all of the word hypotheses that survive inside the trellis during Viterbi beam search are saved in a word lattice containing the following information: initial word state in the trellis, final word state in the trellis, related time instants and word log-likelihood. From this data structure and given the LM used in the recognition steps, WGs are built with separate acoustic likelihood and LM probabilities associated to word transitions. To increase the recombination of paths inside the trellis and consequently the densities of the WGs, the so called word pair approximation is applied. In this way the resulting graph error rate was estimated to be around 1/3 of the corresponding WER.

The best word sequences generated in the second decoding pass are used to evaluate the baseline performance. Instead, the corresponding word graphs are used to generate lists of 1000 sentences each. To do this a stack decoding algorithm is employed (Hart, 1972), where the score of each partial theory is given by summing the forward score of the theory itself with the total backward score in the final state of the same theory (i.e. the look-ahead function used in the algorithm is the total backward probability associated to the final state of the given theory). Finally, each 1000-best list is re-scored using the RNNLM trained on 1MW in-domain text data set. Note that in this latter decoding step, acoustic probabilities remain unchanged, i.e. the latter decoding step implements a pure linguistic rescoring.

4.3 Speech Recognition Results

An overview of the experiments has been given in Figure 5. The first set of results is obtained by using GN4gr-ALL language model which is trained on whole Google-news data. Then, a small N-gram (IN4gr-100MW) is trained on the in-domain data that is used in the procedure of automatic data selection (see section 4.1). Utilizing the resulted data set, a bigger model (IN4gr-100MW) is trained and adapted to the in-domain data.

Thus, the second and third set of results is obtained by using IN4gr-1MW and IN4gr-100MW along with the decoder. In order to improve the final results, we use rnnlmH450C1000 which is trained on in-domain data to re-score the 1000-best list extracted from previous decoding phase.

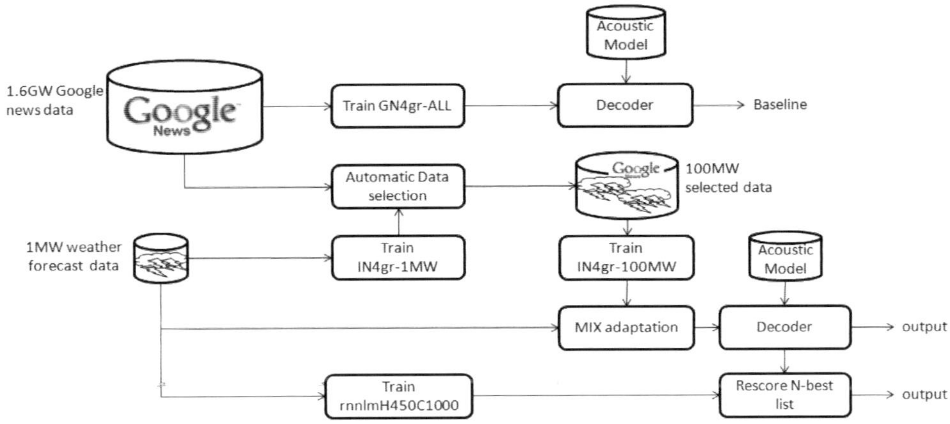

Figure 5. An overview of the speech recognition system

Table 1. compares the WER resulted from using these language models in the decoding phase. It can be seen that the in-domain language model which is trained on the small set of in-domain text is dramatically better than the huge out-domain model. By applying automatic data selection approach and collecting the most useful texts from Google-news we obtained 0.3% improvement and by utilizing RNNLM for rescoring the n-best lists we reach another 0.3% improvement in word error rate.

Table 1. %WER with different language models (Oracle Error Rate is 9.7%)

Language model	Development set	Test set
GN4gr-ALL	16.2	15.1
IN4gr-1MW	14.3	12.8
IN4gr-100MW	14.0	12.6
0.5*IN4gr-100MW + 0.5*rnnlmH450C1000	**13.7**	**12.3**

Although it's not a salient improvement from the third to fourth row of the table, we should notice that the RNNLM model has re-scored an N-best list, which in the best conditions, it gives 9.7% WER. That is, if we ideally select the best sentences from these n-best lists we cannot reach better result than 9.7%.

5 Conclusion

Given a small set of in-domain data and a huge out-domain corpus, we proposed a thorough system which applies an automatic data selection approach to train a general in-domain language model. In addition, we used a continuous space language model to improve the generality of the model and consequently to improve the accuracy of ASR.

In future, we will benefit from RNNLM in the procedure of data selection. That is, instead of evaluation of candidate sentences using N-gram, we will rank them using RNNLM.

Moreover, it would be worthwhile to explore the performance of a group of small RNNLM on the selected data rather than a single N-gram LM.

Acknowledgments

I would like to express my special thanks of gratitude to my supervisor, Daniele Falavigna, who kindly helped me to do the experiments and write this paper.

References

Andreas Stolcke. 2002. *SRILM - An Extensible Language Modeling Toolkit*. In Proceedings of the International Conference on Statistical Language Processing, Denver, Colorado.

Christian Girardi. 2007. *Htmcleaner: Extracting Relevant Text from Web. 3rd Web as Corpus workshop (WAC3)*, Presses Universitaires de Louvain, pp. 141-143.

Daniele Falavigna, Roberto Gretter, Fabio Brugnara, and Diego Giuliani. 2012. *Fbk @ iwslt 2012 - ASR Track*. in Proc. of the International Workshop on Spoken Language Translation, Hong Kong, HK.

George Foster and Roland Kuhn. 2007. *Mixture Model Adaptation for SMT*. In Proceedings of the Second Workshop on Statistical Machine Translation, StatMT '07, pages 128–135, Stroudsburg, PA, USA. association for Computational Linguistics.

Hermann Ney, Ute Essen. 1991. *On Smoothing Techniques for Bigram-based Natural Language Modelling*. Proceedings of the IEEE International Conference on Acoustics, Speech and Signal Processing '91, volume 2, pp. 825–829.

Holger Schwenk. 2007. *Continuous Space Language Models*. in Computer Speech and Language, volume 21, pp. 492-518.

Ian H. Witten and Timothy C. Bell. 1991. *The Zero-frequency Problem: Estimating the Probabilities of Novel Events in Adaptive Text Compression*. IEEE Transactions on Information Theory, 37, pp. 1085–1094.

Jerome R. Bellegarda. 1998. *A Multispan Language Modeling Frame-work for Large Vocabulary Speech Recognition*. IEEE Transactions on Speech and Audio Processing, vol. 6, no. 5, pp. 456–467.

Marcello Federico, Nicola Bertoldi, and Mauro Cettolo. 2008. *IRSTLM: an Open Source Toolkit for Handling Large Scale Language Model*. in Proc. Of INTERSPEECH, Brisbane, Australia, pp. 1618–1621

Marcello Federico. 1999. *Efficient Language Model Adaptation Through MDI Estimation*. In Proceedings of the 6th European Conference on Speech Communication and Technology, vol. 4, Budapest, Hungary, pp. 1583–1586.

Nick Ruiz and Marcello Federico. 2012. *MDI Adaptation for the Lazy: Avoiding Normalization in LM Adaptation for Lecture Translation*. In Proceedings of the International Workshop on Spoken Language Translation, Hong Kong, China.

Peter E. Hart. Nils J. Nilsson. Bertram Raphael. 1972. *Correction to A Formal Basis for the Heuristic Determination of Minimum Cost Paths*. SIGART Newsletter 37: 28–29

Sameer Maskey, Abhinav Sethy. 2009. *Resampling Auxiliary Data for Language Model Adaptation in Machine Translation for Speech*. in ICASSP 2009, Taiwan

Stanley F. Chen and Jushua Goodman. 1999. *An Empirical Study of Smoothing Techniques for Language Modeling*. Computer Science and Language, 4(13), pp. 359-393.

Tomas Mikolov, Anoop Deoras, Stefan Kombrink, Lukas Burget, Jan Cernocky. 2011. *Empirical Evaluation and Combination of Advanced Language Modeling Techniques*. In: Proceedings of the 12th Annual Conference of the International Speech Communication Association (INTERSPEECH 2011). Florence, IT.

Tomas Mikolov, Martin Karafiat, Lukas Burget, Jan Honza Cernocky, Sanjeev Khudanpur. 2010. *Recurrent Neural Network Based Language Model*. In Proc. INTERSPEECH2010. pp. 1045–1048

Yoshua Bengio, Réjean Ducharme, Pascal Vincent, and Christian Jauvin. 2003. *A Neural Probabilistic Language Model*. In journal of machine learning research 3, pp. 1137-1155.

Unsupervised Learning of A-Morphous Inflection with Graph Clustering

Maciej Janicki
University of Leipzig, Master's Programme in Computer Science
macjan@o2.pl

Abstract

This paper presents a new approach to unsupervised learning of inflection. The problem is defined as two clusterings of the input wordlist: into lexemes and into forms. Word-Based Morphology is used to describe inflectional relations between words, which are discovered using string edit distance. A graph of morphological relations is built and clustering algorithms are used to identify lexemes. Paradigms, understood as sets of word formation rules, are extracted from lexemes and words belonging to similar paradigms are assumed to have the same inflectional form. Evaluation was performed for German, Polish and Turkish and the results were compared to conventional morphological analyzers.

1 Introduction

Inflection is the part of morphology concerned with systematic variation of word forms in different syntactic contexts. Because this variation is expressed with patterns that appear over many words, it can be discovered using as little data as a plain wordlist. In the following sections, I will present a general, language-independent approach for the unsupervised learning of inflection, which makes use of simple algorithms, like string edit distance and graph clustering, along with Word-Based Morphology, a morphological theory that rejects the notion of morpheme.

It seems plausible to distinguish inflection from other morphological phenomena (derivation, compounding). Inflection examines the correspondence between items of the lexicon and their surface realizations, while derivation and compounding operate inside lexicon (Stump, 1998). The purpose of morphological annotation of texts, for example for Information Retrieval or Part-of-Speech tagging, is mostly to determine, for a given word, which lexical item (*lexeme*) in which syntactic context (*form*) it realizes. We are less interested in how this lexical item was created. For example, we would like to know that the words *gives* and *give* express the same meaning, while *giver* and *forgive* mean something different. Therefore, what we need is an *inflectional*, rather than a full *morphological* analysis. In the task of unsupervised learning of morphology, distinguishing inflection from derivation is a major challenge. Despite its usefulness, it has not been approached in state-of-the-art systems.

2 Related Work

The task of unsupervised learning of morphology has an over fifty years long history, which is exhaustively presented by Hammarström and Borin (2011). The most popular formulation of this problem is learning segmentation of words into morphemes. State-of-the-art systems for learning morpheme segmentation include Morfessor (Creutz et al., 2005) and Linguistica (Goldsmith, 2006). Both rely on optimization-based learning techniques, such as Minimum Description Length, or Maximum A-Posteriori estimate.

Some other authors use the approach that is called *group and abstract* by Hammarström and Borin (2011). First, they group the words according to some similarity measure, which is supposed to give high values for morphologically related words. Then, they abstract morphological rules from the obtained groups. Yarowsky and Wicentowski (2000) use a combination of four different similarity functions: string edit distance, contextual similarity, frequency similarity and transformation probabilities. Kirschenbaum et al. (2012) use contextual similarity.

The learning of morphology has already been formulated as a clustering problem by Janicki

(2012), which uses mutual information to identify inflectional paradigms, a method that is also employed here. However, the algorithm presented there handles only suffix morphologies and only clustering into lexemes is performed. Word-based morphology has been previously used for the unsupervised learning task by Neuvel and Fulop (2002), but for the purpose of generating unseen words, rather than inducing inflectional analysis.

3 Morphology without Morphemes

Traditional morphological theory uses the notion of *morpheme*: the smallest meaningful part of a word. Morphological analysis of a word is typically understood as splitting it into morphemes and labeling each morpheme with semantic or functional information. However, morphological operations often include phenomena that are not plausibly described by the notion of morpheme. That is why alternative theories were proposed, in which variations between word forms are described with rules operating on phonological representations of whole words, without isolating morphemes or setting boundaries.

The term *Word-Based Morphology* can be traced back to Aronoff (1976). In his analysis of derivational morphology, he shows that the minimal meaningful elements of a language are words, rather than morphemes. He formulates the hypothesis that new words are formed by *Word-Formation Rules*, which always operate on a whole existing word.

Aronoff's ideas motivate the theory developed by Anderson (1992), which presents a complete, a-morphous description of morphology, while maintaining the distinction between inflection, derivation and compounding. In Anderson's theory, the lexicon is a set of *lexical stems*, where lexical stem is defined as "word minus its inflectional material". Turning stems to surface words is done by word-formation rules, which are triggered by particular syntactic contexts. The inflectional system of the language is the set of word-formation rules, along with their applicability conditions. Derivation is performed by word-formation rules of a different type, which operate on stems to form other stems, rather than surface words.

Finally, Ford et al. (1997) present an entirely word-based morphological theory, which radically criticizes all kinds of abstract notions of morphological analysis (like stem or morpheme). It claims that there is only one kind of rule, which is used to describe systematic patterns between surface words, and which can be represented in the following form:

$$/\mathrm{X}/_{\alpha} \leftrightarrow /\mathrm{X}'/_{\beta}$$

where X and X′ are words and α and β morphological categories. No distinction is made between inflection and derivation.

Since in the task of unsupervised learning of inflection the only available data are surface words, the last theory seems especially plausible. A candidate morphological rule can be extracted from virtually any pair of words. The "real" rules can be distinguished from pairs of unrelated words basing on their frequency and co-occurrence or interaction with other rules. However, the application of Ford et al.'s theory will here be restricted to inflection, with the purpose of finding *lexemes* – clusters of words connected by inflectional rules. The lexemes provide enough information to derive stems and word-formation rules in the sense of Anderson's theory, which can be further used for learning derivation and compounding, since, in my opinion, the latter are better described as relations between lexemes, rather than surface words.

4 What to Learn?

Conventional inflectional analyzers, like for example Morfeusz[1] (Woliński, 2006) for Polish, provide two pieces of information for each word: the *lexeme*, to which this word belongs, and the *tag*, describing the inflectional form of it. For example, for the German[2] word *Häusern* (dative plural of the noun *Haus* 'house'), the correct analysis consists of the lexeme HAUS and the tag 'Dative Plural'.

Our task is to train an analyzer, which will provide similar analysis, using only a plain list of words. We certainly cannot achieve exactly the same, because we do not have access to lemmas and labels for grammatical forms. However, we can identify a lexeme by listing all words that belong to it, like HAUS $=\{Haus, Hauses, Häuser, Häusern\}$. Similarly, we will identify an inflectional form by listing all

[1]See `http://sgjp.pl/demo/morfeusz` for an online demo.

[2]German is used as source of examples, because English inflection is often too simple to illustrate the discussed issues.

words that have this form. For example, the German 'Dative Plural' will be defined as: DAT.PL = $\{$*Bäumen*, *Feldern*, *Häusern*, *Menschen*, ...$\}$.

In this way, inflectional analysis can be seen as two clustering problems: grouping words into *lexemes* and into *forms*. If an unsupervised analyzer is able to produce those two clusterings, then the results could be converted into a 'proper' inflectional dictionary with a minimal human effort: annotating each cluster with a label (lemma or stem for lexemes and inflectional tag for forms) which cannot be extracted automatically.

In my opinion, formulating inflectional analysis as a clustering problem has certain advantages over, for instance, learning morpheme segmentation. The clustering approach provides similar information as conventional inflectional analyzers, and can be directly used in many typical applications, like lexeme assignment (equivalent to stemming/lemmatization) in Information Retrieval, or grammatical form labeling, for example for the purpose of Part-of-Speech Tagging. It also gets rid of the notions of morpheme and segmentation, which depend on the morphological theory used, and can be problematic.[3] Finally, well-established clustering evaluation measures can be used for evaluation.

5 The Algorithm

5.1 Building the Morphology Graph

At first, for each word in the data, we find similar words wrt. string edit distance. An optimized algorithm, similar to the one presented by Bocek et al. (2007), is used to quickly find pairs of similar words. For each word, we generate substrings through deletions. We restrict the number of substrings by restricting the number of deletions to five characters at the beginning of the word, five at the end and five in a single slot inside the word, whereas the total number must not exceed half of the word's length. This is enough to capture almost all inflectional operations. Then, we sort the substrings and words that share a substring are considered similar.

The systematic variation between similar words is described in terms of Word-Based Morphology: for each pair (w_1, w_2), we extract the operation needed to turn w_1 into w_2. We formulate it in terms of adding/substracting a prefix, performing a certain internal modification (insertion, substitution, deletion) and adding/substracting a suffix. For example, the operation extracted from the pair (*senden*, *gesandt*) would be *-:ge-/e:a/-en:-t*, while the operation extracted from the pair (*absagen*, *sagten*) would be *ab-:-/-:t/-:-* (substract the prefix *ab-*, insert *-t-*, no suffixes).

I believe that the notion of *operation*, understood as in the above definition, is general enough to cover almost all inflectional phenomena and does not have a bias towards a specific type of inflection. In particular, prefixes are treated exactly the same way as suffixes. The locus and context of internal modification is not recorded, so the pairs *sing:sang*, *drink:drank* and *begin:began* are described with the same operation. This is important, because the algorithm involves computing frequency of the operations. Note that this also means that operations cannot be used for deriving one word from another unambigously, but this is not needed in the algorithm presented here.

From the above data, we build the *morphology graph*, in which the vertices are the words, and the edges are operations between words. Because every operation is reversible, the graph is undirected. We assign a weight to every edge, which is the natural logarithm of the frequency of the corresponding operation: frequent operations are likely to be inflectional rules, while the infrequent are mostly random similarities between words. We set a minimal frequency needed to include an operation in the graph on 1/2000 of the size of the input wordlist.

5.2 Clustering Edges

Inflectional rules tend to occur in groups, called *paradigms*. For example, if a German noun uses the *-er* suffix to form nominative plural, it also uses *-ern* for dative plural and probably *-es* for genitive singular. This property can be expressed by means of mutual information, which has been described by Janicki (2012): inflectional rules that belong to the same paradigm tend to have high mutual information values, measured over the probability of occurring with a random word.

The morphology graph stores for each word the information, which operations can be applied to it. These operations can be inflectional rules, as well as derivational rules and random similarities. By clustering the operations according to mutual in-

[3] See for example the discussion of evaluation problems in (Goldsmith, 2006).

formation, we identify groups of operations which show strong interdependence, which means that they are likely to be paradigms or fragments of those. Derivational rules and random similarities show mostly no interdependence, so they form singleton clusters.

We use the complete-linkage clustering with a fixed threshold value. It is much faster than the hierarchical clustering applied by Janicki (2012) and produces similar results. The threshold value does not have much influence on the final results: it should not be too high, so that real paradigms are split. If it is too low and some non-inflectional operations are mixed together with inflectional paradigms, it can still be fixed in the next step. I used the threshold value 0.001 in all my experiments and it performed well, regardless of language and corpus.

5.3 Clustering the Graph into Lexemes

The previous steps provide already some clues about which words can belong to the same lexeme. Operations are assigned weights according to their frequency, and interdependent operations are grouped together. Now we can apply a graph clustering algorithm, which will split our graph into lexemes, using the above information.

We use the Chinese Whispers clustering algorithm (Biemann, 2006). It is very simple and efficient and it does not require any thresholds or parameters. At the beginning, it assigns a different label to every vertex. Then it iterates over the vertices in random order and each vertex receives labels passed from its neighbours, from which it chooses the most "promoted" label, according to the sum of weights of the edges, through which this label is passed. The procedure is repeated as long as anything changes. The algorithm has already been succesfully used for many NLP problems, but, to my knowledge, not for unsupervised learning of morphology.

A slight modification is made to the Chinese Whispers algorithm to take advantage of the edge clustering performed in the previous step. Every word is split into multiple vertices: one for each edges cluster. During the clustering, they are treated as completely different vertices. It ensures us that we will not pick non-inflectional operations together with inflectional ones or merge two distinct paradigms. After the clustering however, we again leave only one vertex per word: the one whose label has the biggest score understood the same way as in Chinese Whispers algorithm. Finally, by grouping words together according to their label, we obtain the clustering into lexemes.

5.4 Extracting Paradigms and Forms

Given the lexemes, we can easily compute the *paradigm* for each word, understood as the set of operations that generates this word's whole lexeme. Paradigms will be used to derive clustering into forms. We observe that if two words have the same paradigm, they almost certainly share the grammatical form, which is illustrated in table 1. Unfortunately, the reverse is not true: words that share the form do not necessarily share the paradigm. Firstly, in every corpus there are many missing word forms. Continuing the example from table 1, let's assume that the words *Mannes* and *Bändern* are missing. Then, the words {*Haus*, *Mann*, *Band*} would all have different, although similar, paradigms. The second reason is that one form may be created in different ways, depending on the inflection class of the lexeme. The operation *:/a:ä/:er* is only one of many ways of forming nominative plural in German.

A quick solution to the above problems is clustering paradigms according to cosine similarity. For each paradigm P, we define a corresponding vector of operation frequencies:

$$\vec{v}[op] = \begin{cases} ln(freq(op)) & \text{if } op \in P \\ 0 & \text{if } op \notin P \end{cases}$$

where op is a morphological operation and $freq(op)$ its number of occurences. The similarity between two paradigms is defined as 0 if they share less then a half of their operations, and as the cosine of the angle between their vectors otherwise. We use the Chinese Whispers algorithm again for clustering paradigms. Finally, we group the words into forms using the assumption that two words have the same form, if their paradigms belong to the same cluster.

6 Evaluation

For the evaluation of the clusterings, I used the extended BCubed measure (Amigó et al., 2009). Contrary to other popular clustering evaluation measures (e.g. cluster purity), it penalizes all possible kinds of errors and no cheat strategy exists for it. For example, it is sensitive to splitting a correct cluster into parts. It also allows overlapping clusters and classes, which can be the case in

Word	Form	Paradigm
Haus, Mann, Band	NOM.SG	:/:/:es, :/a:ä/:er, :/a:ä/:ern
Hauses, Mannes, Bandes	GEN.SG	:/:/es:, :/a:ä/s:r, :/a:ä/s:rn
Häuser, Männer, Bänder	NOM.PL	:/ä:a/er:, :/ä:a/r:s, :/:/:n
Häusern, Männern, Bändern	DAT.PL	:/ä:a/ern:, :/ä:a/rn:s, :/:/n:

Table 1: The correspondence between form and paradigm. Same paradigm implies same form.

inflectional analysis, as some surface words may be realizations of multiple lexemes. The results are given in the usual terms of Precision, Recall and F-measure.

I used corpora from Leipzig Corpora Collection[4] to build input wordlists of approximately 200,000 words for German, Polish and Turkish. The golden standard clusterings were constructed by analyzing the input data with conventional morphological analyzers: Morfeusz (Woliński, 2006) for Polish, Morphisto (Zielinski and Simon, 2009) for German and TRmorph (Çöltekin, 2010) for Turkish. Words that have the same lemma, according to the morphological analyzer used, were grouped into golden standard lexemes, and words that share all their inflectional tags – into golden standard form clusters. Words that were unknown to the analyzer, were not included in results calculation.

The evaluation results for lexeme clustering are given in table 2. All datasets achieve good precision, around 90 %. The recall for Polish and German is also high. In addition to performing well on suffix-based inflectional operations, the algorithm also succeeded in finding many German plural forms that involve vowel alternation (umlaut). Problematic is the significantly lower recall score for Turkish. The reason is the Turkish agglutinative morphology, with very large paradigms, especially for verbs. Complex forms are often treated as derivations and large verb lexemes are split into parts.

[4] http://corpora.uni-leipzig.de

Testing set	Precision	Recall	F-measure
German	87.8 %	79.8 %	83.5 %
Polish	89.0 %	80.1 %	84.3 %
Turkish	92.9 %	41.4 %	57.3 %

Table 2: Lexeme evaluation.

Testing set	Precision	Recall	F-measure
German	64.1 %	12.8 %	21.4 %
Polish	61.5 %	34.8 %	44.4 %
Turkish	45.6 %	10.8 %	17.5 %

Table 3: Form evaluation.

In general, the algorithm performs well in distinguishing inflection from derivation, as long as lexemes have enough inflected forms. The Chinese Whispers algorithm identifies strongly interconnected sets and inflection usually involves more forms and more frequent operations than derivation. A problem emerges for rare lexemes, which are only represented by one or two words in the corpus, and which take part in many common derivations, like the German prefixing. It can happen that derivational operations connect them stronger than inflectional ones, which results in clusterings according to derivational prefixes. For example, we obtain {*abdrehen*, *aufdrehen*, ...} in one cluster and {*abgedreht*, *aufgedreht*, ...} in another. This is one of the most common mistakes in the German dataset and it should be addressed in further work.

Table 3 shows the results for clustering into forms. They are considerably lower than in lexeme clustering. The main reason for low precision is that there are some distinctions in morphosyntactical information that are not visible in the surface form, like gender in German. The second reason are small paradigms that are induced for words, for which only a few forms appear in the corpus. Small paradigms do not provide enough grammatical information and lead to clustering distinct forms of rare words together. Recall scores are even lower than precision, which is caused by the issues discussed in section 5.4. Clustering paradigms according to cosine similarity is by far not enough to solve these problems.

Comparing my algorithm to other authors' work is difficult, because, to my knowledge, no other approach is designed for the definition of the problem presented here – clustering words into lexemes and forms. Comparing it to morpheme segmentation algorithms would need converting morpheme segmentation to lexemes and forms, which is not a trivial task.

7 Conclusion

I have shown that a full inflectional analysis can be defined as two clusterings of the input wordlist: into *lexemes* and *forms*. My opinion is that for the purpose of unsupervised learning of inflection, such output is more useful and easier to evaluate, than morpheme segmentation. From a theoretical view, my approach can be seen as a minimalist description of inflection, which uses only words as data and describes the desired information (lexeme and form) in terms of word sets, while getting rid of any abstract units of linguistic analysis, like morpheme or stem.

Further, I have provided an algorithm, which learns inflection through graph clustering, based on the Word-Based theory of morphology. I have compared it to the output of state-of-the-art hand-crafted morphological analyzers. The algorithm performs especially well in the task of clustering into lexemes for inflectional morphologies and is capable of discovering non-concatenative operations. Many errors are due to missing word forms in the corpus. The output can be applied directly or used to minimize human effort while constructing an inflectional analyzer.

The presented algorithm will be subject to further work. The results of lexeme clustering could probably be improved with a more careful scoring of operations, rather than just simple frequency. Other possibly useful features should be examined, perhaps making use of the information available in unannotated corpora (like word frequencies or context similarity). A better algorithm for clustering into forms is also needed, because cosine similarity does not give satisfactory results. Finally, I will try to approach derivation and compounding with methods similar to the one presented here.

References

Enrique Amigó, Julio Gonzalo, Javier Artiles, and Felisa Verdejo. 2009. A comparison of extrinsic clustering evaluation metrics based on formal constraints. *Inf. Retr.*, 12(4):461–486.

Stephen R. Anderson. 1992. *A-Morphous morphology*. Cambridge University Press.

Mark Aronoff. 1976. *Word formation in generative grammar*. Linguistic inquiry. Monographs. MIT Press.

Chris Biemann. 2006. Chinese whispers - an efficient graph clustering algorithm and its application to natural language processing problems. In *Proceedings of TextGraphs: the Second Workshop on Graph Based Methods for Natural Language Processing*, pages 73–80.

Thomas Bocek, Ela Hunt, and Burkhard Stiller. 2007. Fast Similarity Search in Large Dictionaries. Technical Report ifi-2007.02, Department of Informatics, University of Zurich, April. http://fastss.csg.uzh.ch/.

Çağrı Çöltekin. 2010. A Freely Available Morphological Analyzer for Turkish. In Nicoletta Calzolari (Conference Chair), Khalid Choukri, Bente Maegaard, Joseph Mariani, Jan Odijk, Stelios Piperidis, Mike Rosner, and Daniel Tapias, editors, *Proceedings of the Seventh International Conference on Language Resources and Evaluation (LREC'10)*, Valletta, Malta, may. European Language Resources Association (ELRA).

Mathias Creutz, Krista Lagus, and Sami Virpioja. 2005. Unsupervised morphology induction using morfessor. In Anssi Yli-Jyrä, Lauri Karttunen, and Juhani Karhumäki, editors, *Finite-State Methods and Natural Language Processing, 5th International Workshop*, volume 4002 of *Lecture Notes in Computer Science*, pages 300–301. Springer.

Alan Ford, Rajendra Singh, and Gita Martohardjono. 1997. *Pace Pāṇini: Towards a word-based theory of morphology*. American University Studies. Series XIII, Linguistics, Vol. 34. Peter Lang Publishing, Incorporated.

John Goldsmith. 2006. An algorithm for the unsupervised learning of morphology. *Nat. Lang. Eng.*, 12(4):353–371.

Harald Hammarström and Lars Borin. 2011. Unsupervised learning of morphology. *Computational Linguistics*, 37(2):309–350.

Maciej Janicki. 2012. A Lexeme-Clustering Algorithm for Unsupervised Learning of Morphology. In Johannes Schmidt, Thomas Riechert, and Sören Auer, editors, *SKIL 2012 - Dritte Studentenkonferenz Informatik Leipzig*, volume 34 of *Leipziger Beiträge zur Informatik*, pages 37–47. LIV, Leipzig.

Amit Kirschenbaum, Peter Wittenburg, and Gerhard Heyer. 2012. Unsupervised morphological analysis of small corpora: First experiments with kilivila. In Frank Seifart, Geoffrey Haig, Nikolaus P. Himmelmann, Dagmar Jung, Anna Margetts, and Paul Trilsbeek, editors, *Potentials of Language Documentation: Methods, Analyses, and Utilization. Language Documentation & Conservation Special Publication*, pages 25–31. Manoa: University of Hawaii Press.

Sylvain Neuvel and Sean A. Fulop. 2002. Unsupervised learning of morphology without morphemes. In *Proceedings of the ACL-02 workshop on Morphological and phonological learning - Volume 6*, MPL '02, pages 31–40, Stroudsburg, PA, USA. Association for Computational Linguistics.

Gregory T. Stump. 1998. Inflection. In Andrew Spencer and Arnold M. Zwicky, editors, *The Handbook of Morphology*, pages 13–43. Blackwell Publishing.

Marcin Woliński. 2006. Morfeusz a Practical Tool for the Morphological Analysis of Polish. In Mieczysław A. Kłopotek, Sławomir T. Wierzchoń, and Krzysztof Trojanowski, editors, *Intelligent Information Processing and Web Mining*, Advances in Soft Computing, pages 503–512. Springer-Verlag, Berlin.

David Yarowsky and Richard Wicentowski. 2000. Minimally supervised morphological analysis by multimodal alignment. In *Proceedings of the 38th Annual Meeting on Association for Computational Linguistics*, ACL '00, pages 207–216.

Andrea Zielinski and Christian Simon. 2009. Morphisto – an open source morphological analyzer for german. In *Proceedings of the 2009 conference on Finite-State Methods and Natural Language Processing: Post-proceedings of the 7th International Workshop FSMNLP 2008*, pages 224–231, Amsterdam, The Netherlands. IOS Press.

Statistical-based System for Morphological Annotation of Arabic Texts

Nabil Khoufi
ANLP Research Group
MIRACL Laboratory
University of Sfax
nabil.khoufi@fsegs.rnu.tn

Manel Boudokhane
ANLP Research Group
MIRACL Laboratory
University of Sfax
manel.boudokhane@gmail.com

Abstract

In this paper, we propose a corpus-based method for the annotation of Arabic texts with morphological information. The proposed method proceeds in two stages: the segmentation stage and the morphological analysis stage. The morphological analysis stage is based on a statistical method using an annotated corpus. In order to evaluate our method, we conducted a comparative analysis between the results generated by our system AMAS (Arabic Morphological Annotation System) and those carried out by a human expert. As input, the system accepts an Arabic text and generates as a result an annotated text with morphological information in XML format.

1 Introduction

In the linguistic field, morphology is the study of the word's internal structure. It consists in identifying, analysing and describing the structure of morphemes and other units of meaning in a language.

Morphological annotation in Natural Language Processing (NLP) is considered as a preliminary step during any automatic language processing approach. It consists in attributing labels for each word in a text such as the part of speech (POS) (name, verb, adjective, etc.) the gender (feminine, masculine), the number (singular, dual, plural), etc. Such data are useful in the most of applications of NLP such as text analysis, error correction, parsing, machine translation, automatic summarization, etc. Therefore, developing a robust morphological annotation system is needed.

In this paper, we present a brief description of related Arabic morphological ambiguity. Then, we give an overview of the state-of-the-art. The description of the proposed method for annotation of the Arabic text is thereafter introduced. The following section describes our morphological analysis. An example of analysis is then presented with a brief description of AMAS interface. Finally, we provide the evaluation of our system and a discussion of the obtained results.

2 Arabic Morphological Ambiguity

Like all Semitic languages, Arabic is characterised by a complex morphology and a rich vocabulary. Arabic is a derivational, flexional and agglutinative language. In fact, an Arabic word is the result of a combination of a trilateral or quadrilateral root with a specific schema. Moreover, there are many verbal and nominal lemmas that can be derived from an Arabic root. Furthermore, from a verbal or nominal lemma, many flexions are possibly indicating variations in tense (for verbs), in case (for nouns), in gender (for both), etc. Agglutination in Arabic is another specific phenomenon. In fact, in Arabic, articles, prepositions, pronouns, etc. can be affixed to adjectives, nouns, verbs and particles to which they are related. Derivational, flexional and agglutinative aspects of the Arabic language yield significant challenges in NLP. Thus, many morphological ambiguities have to be solved when dealing with Arabic language. In fact, many Arabic words are homographic: they have the same orthographic form, though the pronunciation is different (Attia, 2006). In most cases, these homographs are due to the non vocalization of words. This means that a full vocalization of words can solve these ambiguities, but most of the Arabic texts like books, web pages, news, etc are not vocalized.

We present, in the following, some of these homographs:

Unvocalized word	فرح		
Vocalized forms	فَرُحْ	فَرْحٌ	فَرِحَ
Meaning	so, go	Marriage	Was happy
International Phonetic Alphabet	farho	farhU	fariħa

Table 1 Homographs due to absence of short vowels

In Arabic some conjugated verbs or inflected nouns can have the same orthographic form. Adding short vowels to those words makes differences between them.

Unvocalized word	يهرب	
Vocalized forms	يُهَرِّبُ	يَهْرِبُ
Meaning	He smuggles	He escapes
International Phonetic Alphabet	i:har ~ibu	i:hribu

Table 2: Homographs due to the absence of the character chadda "ّ"

The presence of chadda inside a particular word changes its meaning.

3 State-of-the-art

The annotation task is an important step in NLP. In fact its accuracy strongly influences the results of the following modules in an NLP process such as parsing. Annotation is also used to create a knowledge base such as annotated corpora, which are helpful for the conception of effective NLP software, especially those based on machine learning techniques. Regarding Arabic text annotation, we identify several methods that can be used. All these methods use the same information to annotate a particular word in a given text: its context and its morphology. What differs is the way to represent these elements and prioritise information. In this section, we focus on morphological analysis which is the main task in a morphological annotation system. The overview of the state of the art of Arabic computational morphology shows that there are two main approaches: the knowledge-based approach and the statistical-based approach (Saoudi et al. 2007).

The knowledge-based approach uses symbolic rules and linguistic information. The designer handles all the labelling rules and the linguistic information (such as Root-base, Lexeme-base, Stem-base…) to perform morphological analysis. Some morphological analysers using knowledge-based methods for Arabic have been developed such as Xerox two-level morphology system (Beesley, 2001) ; Sebawai system (Darwish, 2002) for shallow parsing ; Araparse system (Ouersighni, 2002) ; Buckwalter Arabic morphological analyser (Buckwalter, 2004) ; Attia morphological analyser (Attia, 2006) ; ElixirFM analyser(Smrz, 2007) and Abouenour morphological analyser (Abouenour, 2008).

Statistical-based methods utilize machine learning techniques to extract linguistic knowledge from natural language data directly. In fact, the aim of these methods is to learn how to balance between alternative solutions and how to predict useful information for unknown entities through rigorous statistical analysis of the data. Statistical-based analysers can be grouped in two main families: unsupervised learning analysers and supervised learning analysers. Unsupervised learning analysers learn from a raw corpus without any additional information; they use a distributional analysis to automatically group words into classes or groups of words (grammatical categories). This learning method is not being frequently used (Clark, 2003). On the other hand, supervised learning analysers learn from a prelabelled corpus, which allows the preparation of all the necessary data for annotation. These data are created from dictionaries in order to assign to each word of the corpus a set of information: category, lemma, average frequency of occurrence, etc. To the best of our knowledge, among the systems using supervised learning we can mention the morphological analyser developed by Boudlal (Boudlal et al., 2008) ;TBL Analyser (AlGahtani et al., 2007); MADA morphological analyser (Habash et al., 2009) ;(Mansour et al., 2009) analyser, which is an adaptation of MorphTagger to Arabic language, and Diab analyser (Diab, 2010) which is a part of the AMIRA tool kit for Arabic processing.

As far as we know, statistical-based methods remain largely untapped for Arabic language. Furthermore, the comparison of the results of existing analysers shows that a statistical-based analyser gives better results than a knowledge based analyser (see table 3). These good results depend on the use of large amounts of annotated corpora. Since we have access to the Penn Arabic Treebank (ATB) corpus and assume that the statistical analysers provide better results, we opted for a statistical method to build our annotation system of Arabic texts.

Approach	System	accuracy
Statistical based	Diab	**95.49**
	Habash	**97.5**
	Mansour	**96.12**
	AlGahtani	**96.9**
Knowledge based	Ouersigni	76
	Abouenour	82.14

Table 3: Comparison of evaluation results

4 Proposed Method

Our method for morphological annotation of Arabic texts is based on the machine learning approach. Our method consists of two stages: during the first one, the text is segmented into sentences, which are then segmented into words by using punctuation marks and spaces. Then, the obtained words which are the objects of agglutination are also segmented using a stem database to identify the prefixes, suffixes and clitics of each word. The second stage consists of the morphological analysis of the segmented units by referring to the learning corpus; we apply statistical rules to identify the label having the highest probability and supposed to be the most probable one.
A detailed description of these stages will be given in the following section.

4.1 Principle of The Word's Segmentation

This task is harder for Arabic text than for English or French due to the special features of Arabic as shown in section 2. The main issue of the segmentation is to separate the minimal units such as clitics, prefixes and suffixes from the words.

The principle of our method of segmentation is effective. First of all, we begin by segmenting the text into sentences, then into tokens by using spaces and punctuation marks. We obtain a set of tokens which are compared with the stem database elements to try to identify the lexical minimal units. If the word is recognized in the stem database, it is saved in the segmentation file. Some tokens remain unrecognized in the stem-database. To identify them, we create a pruning process which proceeds as follows:

- Identification of the prefixes, suffixes and clitics in the unrecognized token by referring to the pre- and post-base list.
- Deleting prefixes, suffixes and clitics.
- Comparison of the pruned word with the stem database elements. If the word is found, it is saved as a lexical minimal unit; if not, it is saved as an unknown word.

Figure 1 illustrates the steps of our segmentation stage.

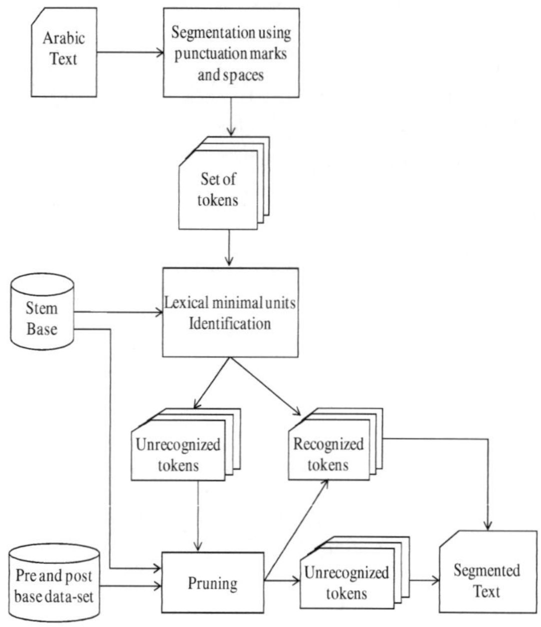

Figure 1: The segmentation stage.

4.2 Principle of The Morphological Analysis

The morphological annotation of a given language consists in assigning the POS (adjective, verb, name ...) and the morphological features (gender, number, person, tense, etc.) to recognized word in the segmented text.
During the morphological analysis, we use an annotated corpus as a knowledge base to predict the morphological category of each word of the input text. This process receives the segmented text (output of the segmentation stage) as an input and generates an annotated text as an output (see figure 2). In this section we begin by presenting the used corpus then we detail the principle of our morphological analysis.

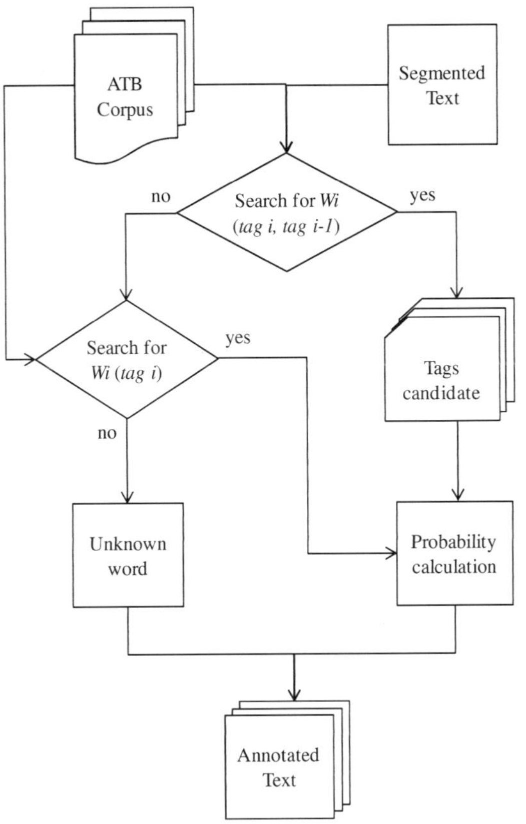

Figure 2: The morphological analysis stage.

Our learning corpus, the Penn Arabic Treebank (ATB), was developed by the LDC at the University of Pennsylvania (Maamouri et al., 2004). It consists of data from linguistic sources written in modern standard Arabic. The corpus consists of 599 unvowelled texts of different stories from a Lebanese news agency publication.

To achieve the morphological annotation of Arabic text, we adopt a statistical method. We use the ATB annotated corpus to extract all possible annotations for a word then we choose the most probable one using the N-gram model, more precisely the first and second order known as unigram and bi-gram. Indeed, (Mustafa and Al-Radaideh, 2004) found that a bi-gram method offers higher overall effectiveness values than the tri-gram method for text processing.

The principle of this model states that the calculation of the probability of occurrence for a given label depends on the label that precedes it. The frequency of the words and the labels will be calculated from the annotated corpus ATB. Probabilities are generated by the conditional probability formula:

$$P(t\_i/t\_i\text{-}1)=P(t\_i\text{-}1,t\_i))\,/\,P(t\_i\text{-}1)$$

Where *t_i* is the tag of the word *i* and *t_i-1* is the tag of the previous word *i-1*. *P(t_i-1, t_i)* is the sequence frequency of the two words tag *i* and *i-1* . *P (t_i-1)* is the frequency of the tag *t_i-1*.

The analysis process is as follows: We perform a search in the learning corpus for occurrences of the word i (Wi in figure 2). We then extract all the morphological tags of this word from the ATB. Probabilities are then distributed to these tags according to the conditional probability formula. The tag that have the highest probability will be used as the annotation of the word i. There is an exception in the use of the formula for the first word of each sentence and also for each word preceded by an unknown word. If the word is not found in the training corpus, the user has the option to manually annotate the unfound word or to keep it as an unknown word. This process occurs in a sequential mode until the annotation of the whole text. We use the same tag set used in the ATB.

We apply our method to a sentence to show the different results.

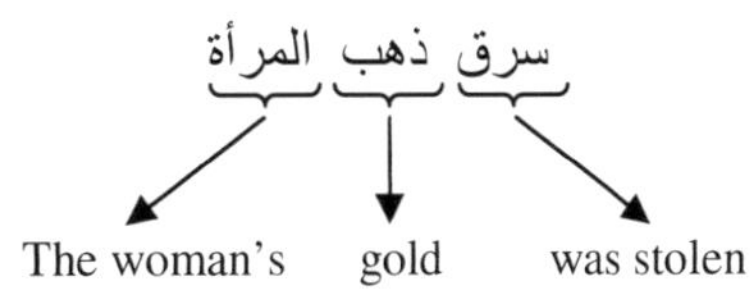

In this sentence we have three words; the word سرق is a verb; this annotation is obtained using the frequency calculation (Case of the first word in a sentence). The ambiguity lies in the word ذهب which has two possibilities to be annotated: verb or noun according to our learning corpus. To choose the right annotation, we take into consideration the annotation of the previous word (i.e verb). Probabilities are then calculated and we obtain P (verb/verb) =0.2 and P (noun/verb) =0.8. So ذهب as noun is selected because it has the highest probability. The word المرأة is annotated as a noun because it's the only annotation found in the learning corpus. The sentence will be annotated as follows:

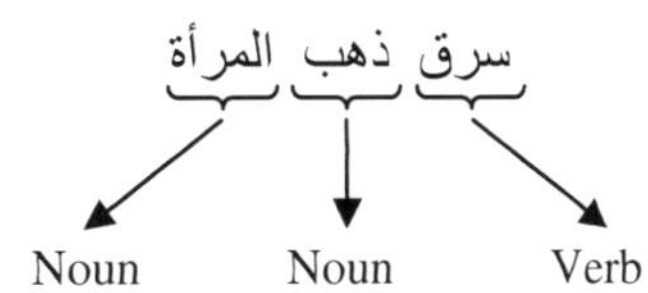

5 The AMAS System

The method that we proposed for the morphological annotation of Arabic texts has been implemented through the AMAS (Arabic Morphological Annotation System) system. In this section, we present the implementation details. The implementation of this method has been done using the Java programming language.

5.1 Used Linguistic Data

The stem database: During the segmentation phase, we used the stem base of the morphological analyser AraMorph[1], which is the Java port of the homonym product developed in Perl by Tim Buckwalter. This stem database contains a large number of stems with a lot of other information such as possible vocalized forms, labels, etc. The entire database is written with the Tim Buckwalter transliteration. We made some changes to its structure, which consists in:

- First, removing unhelpful data such as English translation, syntactic tags and keeping only the stems,
- And second, transliterating the stems from Buckwalter form to the Modern Standard Arabic form.

Pre- and post-base lists: In order to segment agglutinated tokens, a pre- and post-base list is necessary to identify them. The creation of this list was inspired from Abbes's (Abbes, 2004) works. These lists were adapted to our segmentation process. Indeed only pre- and post-bases used in the training corpus were considered in the segmentation process.

5.2 AMAS Interface

As input, the system accepts an Arabic text. Then, the user can segment the text via the segmentation menu. The system then displays the results in a text area as shown in the screen-shot presented in figure 3. The user has the possibility to modify the results if it is necessary to correct some mistakes.

Once the text is segmented and saved in a text file, we proceed to the annotation step using the annotation menu. The user must specify if the analysis should be fully automatic or semi-automatic. If the user chooses the semi automatic option, he must indicate the right annotation to unknown words. The system will be updated with the user annotations. This information can be taken into consideration through the annotation process for the rest of the text. Otherwise, there is no need for the user's contribution and the process will be conducted automatically.
The result is presented in the form of a well-structered XML file. Each Arabic word is presented with its original form, its Buckwalter transliteration, its most probable morphological annotation and its probability (see figure 4).

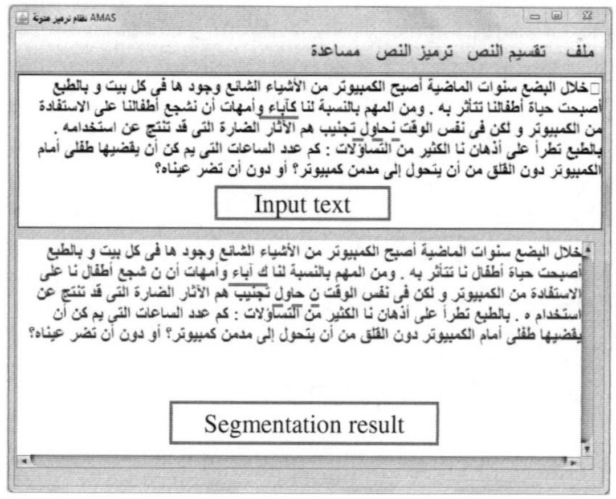

Figure 3: AMAS's segmentation interface.

6 Obtained Results

In order to evaluate our system, we used the EASC corpus (The Essex Summaries Arabic Corpus) proposed by (El-Hdj et al., 2010). It contains 153 texts covering different areas such as art, health, politics, tourism, etc. we performed the evaluation on 22 texts containing 10148 segmented words. We then conducted a comparative study between the results generated by our system (automatic annotation process) and those presented by a linguist.
The evaluation operation consists in calculating the recall and precision measures for each domain in the corpus. The average of those measures is then calculated. The average measures for Precision, Recall and F-score are respectively 89.01%, 80.24% and 84.37%.
These results are encouraging and represent a good start for the application of statistical approach for annotation of Arabic texts. Our results are better than Ouersigni and Abouenour systems results which confirm our hypothesis. The difference in performance between our system and state of the art statistical systems is due to the following:

1 http://www.nongnu.org/aramorph/english/index.html, free software licensed under GPL.

- The propagation of segmentation errors to the morphological analysis involves annotation errors. For example, there is a problem in the segmentation of the agglutination of the article "ال" and the preposition "ل"(e.g التنقل + ل ←للتنقل).
- Unknown words annotation during the morphological analysis, which is likely to influence the annotation of the following word and may decrease the accuracy of the system,
- The way to choose annotation for the first word of a sentence is not precise enough.

Another reason for these results is that the ATB doesn't contain all words. Some words like "الأشرعة" or "الكمبيوتر" do not exist in the ATB. There is also a difference between the word's spelling in the ATB and the test corpus. For example, the same word is written "إستخدام" in the test corpus and "آستخدام" in the ATB. These two words have the same meaning and same morphological annotation but "آستخدام" is annotated as unknown word by our system.

Neverthless, our annotation system produces good results and annotate the majority of the words.


```
<?xml version="1.0" encoding="UTF-8"?>
- <Texte>
  - <Mot MotBuckwalter="xlAl" MotArabe="خلال">
      <Annotation>NOUN+a/CASE_DEF_ACC</Annotation>
      <Probabilite-associée>0.6165413</Probabilite-associée>
    </Mot>
  - <Mot MotBuckwalter="AlbDE" MotArabe="البضع">
      <Annotation>Unknown</Annotation>
      <Probabilite-associée/>
    </Mot>
  - <Mot MotBuckwalter="snwAt" MotArabe="سنوات">
      <Annotation>NOUN+At/NSUFF_FEM_PL+K/CASE_INDEF_GEN</Annotation>
      <Probabilite-associée>0.9027778</Probabilite-associée>
    </Mot>
  - <Mot MotBuckwalter="AlmADyp" MotArabe="الماضية">
      <Annotation>DET+mADiy/ADJ+ap/NSUFF_FEM_SG+i/CASE_DEF_GEN</Annotation>
      <Probabilite-associée>0.8055556</Probabilite-associée>
    </Mot>
  - <Mot MotBuckwalter=">SbH" MotArabe="أصبح">
      <Annotation>PV+a/PVSUFF_SUBJ:3MS</Annotation>
      <Probabilite-associée>0.974359</Probabilite-associée>
    </Mot>
```


Figure 4: Annotation results.

7 Conclusion and Perspectives

In this paper, we outlined some problems of computational Arabic morphology. Then, we proposed our method for morphological annotation of Arabic texts. We also presented our Arabic morphological annotation system AMAS based on the proposed method. AMAS is implemented using the Java programming language and has been evaluated using EASC corpus. The obtained results are very encouraging (i.e. precision = 89.01% ; recall = 80.24% ; F-measure = 84.37%). As a perspective, we intend to add a stem database to reduce the number of unknown words in the morphological analysis. In addition, we plan to expand n-gram model from 2 to 4. Indeed, It is shown (McNamee and Mayfield, 2004) that the use of n-grams of length 4 is most effective and stable for European languages.

Acknowledgments

The authors would like to thank Mr. Chafik Aloulou and Mrs. Lamia Hadrich Belguith for their valuable comments and participation in the progress of this work within the ANLP-MIRACL laboratory.

References

Ramzi Abbes. 2004. *La conception et la réalisation d'un concordancier électronique pour l'arabe*, Ph.D thesis, ENSSIB/INSA, Lyon, France.

Lahsen Abouenour, Said El Hassani, Tawfiq Yazidy, Karim Bouzouba and Abdelfattah Hamdani. 2008. Building an Arabic Morphological Analyzer as part of an Open Arabic NLP Platform. In *Workshop on HLT and NLP within the Arabic world: Arabic Language and local languages processing Status Updates and Prospects At the 6th Language Resources and Evaluation Conference (LREC'08)*, Marrakech, Morocco.

Shabib AlGahtani, William Black, and John McNaught. 2009. Arabic part-of-speech-tagging using transformation-based learning. In *Proceeedings of the 2nd International Conference on Arabic Language Resources and Tools*, Cairo, Egypt.

Mohammed Attia. 2006. An Ambiguity controlled Morphological Analyzer for Modern Standard Arabic Modelling Finite State Networks. *In The challenge of Arabic for NLP/MT conference, the British Computer Society Conference*, pages 48-67, London.

Kenneth Beesley. 2001. Finite-State Morphological Analysis and Generation of Arabic at Xerox Research: Status and Plans in 2001. In *Proceedings of the Arabic Language Processing: Status and Prospect-39th Annual Meeting of the Association for Computational Linguistics*, Toulouse, France.

Abderrahim Boudlal, Rachid Belahbib, Abdelhak Lakhouaja, Azzeddine Mazroui, Abdelouafi Meziane and Mohamed Ould Abdallahi Ould Bebah. 2008. A Markovian Approach for Arabic Root Extraction. In *The International Arab Conference on Information Technology*, Hammamet, Tunisia.

Tim Buckwalter. 2004. Issues in Arabic Orthography and Morphology Analysis. In *The Workshop on Computational Approaches to Arabic Script-based Languages*, COLING, Geneva.

Alexander Clark. 2003. Combining Distributional and Morphological Information for Part of Speech Induction. In *Proceedings of the tenth Annual Meeting of the European Association for Computational Linguistics EACL 2003*, pages 59-66.

Kareem Darwish. 2002. Building a Shallow Arabic Morphological Analyzer in One Day. In *Proceedings of the ACL-02 workshop on Computational approaches to semitic languages*, Stroudsburg, PA, USA.

Mona Diab. 2009. Second Generation Tools (AMIRA 2.0): Fast and Robust Tokenization, POS tagging, and Base Phrase Chunking, *MEDAR 2nd International Conference on Arabic Language Resources and Tools*, Cairo, Egypt.

Mahmoud El-Haj, Udo Kruschwitz, and Chris Fox. 2010. Using Mechanical Turk to Create a Corpus of Arabic Summaries. In *the Language Resources and Human Language Technologies for Semitic Languages workshop held in conjunction with the 7th International Language Resources and Evaluation Conference*, pages 36-39, Valletta, Malta.

Nizar Habash, Owen Rambow and Ryan Roth. 2009. MADA+TOKAN: A Toolkit for Arabic Tokenization, Diacritization, Morphological Disambiguation, POS Tagging, Stemming and Lemmatization. In *Proceedings of the 2nd International Conference on Arabic Language Resources and Tools (MEDAR)*, Cairo, Egypt.

Mohamed Maamouri, Ann Bies, Tim Buckwalter, and Wigdan Mekki. 2004. The Penn Arabic Treebank: Building a Large-Scale Annotated Arabic Corpus. In *NEMLAR International Conference on Arabic Language Resources and Tools.*

Saib Mansour, Khalil Sima'an and Yoad Winter. 2007. Smoothing a Lexicon-based POS tagger for Arabic and Hebrew. In *proceedings of ACL 2007 Workshop on Computational Approaches to Semitic Languages: Common Issues and Resources.* Prague, Czech Republic.

Paul McNamee, James Mayfield. 2004. Character N-Gram Tokenization for European Language Text Retrieval. *In Journal Information Retrieval,* volume 7, issue 1-2, pages 73 – 97.

Suleiman H. Mustafa and Qacem A. Al-Radaideh. 2004. Using N-grams for Arabic text searching. In *Journal of the American Society for Information Science and Technology archive*, Volume 55, Issue 11, Pages 1002-1007 John Wiley & Sons, Inc. New York, USA.

Riadh Ouersighni. 2002. *La conception et la réalisation d'un système d'analyse morpho-syntaxique robuste pour l'arabe : utilisation pour la détection et le diagnostic des fautes d'accord.* Ph.D. thesis, Lumiere-Lyon2 university, France.

Abdelhadi Soudi, Gunter Neumann and Antal Van den Bosch. 2007. Arabic Computational Morphology: Knowledge-based and Empirical Methods. In *Arabic Computational Morphology*, pages 3-14, Springer.

Otakar Smrz. 2007. ElixirFM — Implementation of Functional Arabic Morphology. In *Proceedings of the 2007 Workshop on Computational Approaches to Semitic Languages: Common Issues and Resources,* pages 1-8, Prague, Czech Republic.

A System for Generating Cloze Test Items from Russian-Language Text

Andrey Kurtasov
Vologda State Technical University
Russia
akurtasov@gmail.com

Abstract

This paper studies the problem of automated educational test generation. We describe a procedure for generating cloze test items from Russian-language text, which consists of three steps: sentence splitting, sentence filtering, and question generation. The sentence filtering issue is discussed as an application of automatic summarization techniques. We describe a simple experimental system which implements cloze question generation and takes into account grammatical features of the Russian language such as gender and number.

1 Introduction

In recent years, e-learning has become a widely used form of post-secondary education in Russia. Highly-developed Learning Management Systems (LMS), such as Moodle[1], have been broadly accepted by Russian colleges and universities. These systems provide rich opportunities for delivering, tracking and managing education, and significantly help to reduce a teacher's workload as well as to establish distance learning. One of the most noticeable functions provided by the LMSs is assessment, which is implemented through automated tests. However, the task of preparing questions for the tests is not yet automated. The teacher has to compose all the test items manually, and this is a time-consuming task.

Moodle allows using different types of test items for student assessment, including calculated questions, multiple-choice questions, matching questions, and questions with embedded answers, also known as *cloze* questions or *fill-in-the-blank* questions.

We are considering the opportunity for automated test generation based on extracting sentences from electronic documents. We find this approach promising, because electronic textbooks are widely used, and many texts with potential educational value are available through the Internet. As a starting point, we aim to study methods for generating cloze questions, because they are obviously the easiest to be produced from sentences. To produce a cloze question, one takes a sentence and replaces some of the words in the sentence with blanks.

Once we have studied how to extract useful sentences from the text and how to select words to blank out, we will continue our research in order to develop methods for generating more complicated types of test items, such as multiple-choice.

2 Related Work

The idea of automating the composition of test items is not new.

For instance, several Russian authors, including Sergushitcheva and Shvetcov (2003) and Kruchinin (2003), suggest using formal grammars (FG) to generate test questions with variable parts. Although the development of FG-based templates is performed manually, this approach allows generating multiple various tests of different types (including multiple-choice) and eliminates students' cheating.

The approach of generating test items by extracting sentences from electronic documents has received significant attention in English-language literature. Several authors have considered different kinds of test items in terms of automation. For instance, cloze questions were studied

[1] Available from: https://moodle.org/

by Mostow et al. (2004) for the purpose of reading comprehension assessment. Mitkov et al. (2006) implemented an environment that allows producing multiple-choice questions with distractors. Heilman (2011) developed a system for generating wh-questions that require an answer to be typed in.

However, only a few authors have considered this approach for Russian. Voronets et al. (2003) published one of the first papers on the topic, in which they proposed applying this approach to instructional texts used in cosmonaut training. Sergushitcheva and Shvetcov (2006) considered using this approach in combination with the FG-based one.

3 Workflow for Computer-Assisted Test Generation

Our idea is to establish a system that delivers computer-assisted test authoring and leverages Natural Language Processing (NLP) techniques to provide the teacher with test items, which are generated automatically from electronic textbooks or similar texts. After the generation the test can be passed to the Moodle LMS and used for student assessment.

Fig. 1 shows the basic workflow of the system, which could be considered as a computer-assisted procedure. The system takes a text as an input and produces test items as the output. The test items are then presented to teachers, who select and edit the ones that they consider useful.

4 Text Processing

The approach is based on sequential application of linguistic processors that perform the following tasks on the text:

- Sentence splitting – to acquire sentences from which the system will produce questions for test items
- Sentence filtering – to filter the set of sentences so that it contains the most salient sentences
- Question generation – to convert the sentences into questions

4.1 Sentence Splitting

At first sight, a sentence is a sequence of characters that ends with ".", "!" or "?". In practice we should keep in mind that these characters can also be used inside one sentence (Grefenstette and Tapanainen, 1994). To address this issue, we initially used a simple tokenization algorithm that had been developed for educational purposes. It took into account abbreviations, proper name initials and other special cases. For instance, the algorithm recognized commonly used Russian abbreviations containing periods, such as "г." (year), "гг." (years), "и т. д." (etc.), "т. е." (i.e.), "т. н." (so called), "напр." (e.g.) and so on.

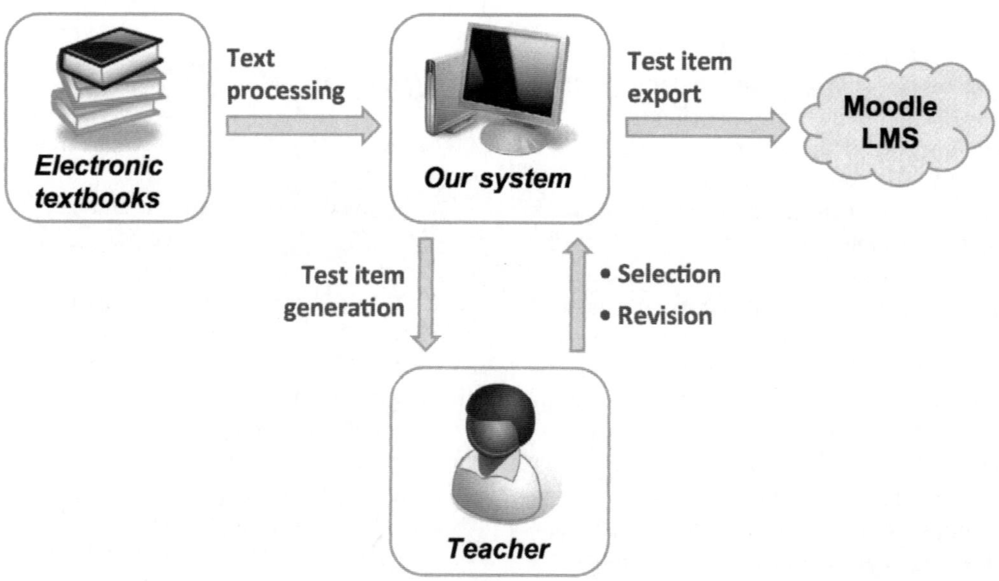

Figure 1: Workflow

In the current system, we use a tokenization module provided by the AOT toolkit[2]. It takes into account more text features including bulleted lists, sentences enclosed in quote marks or parentheses, URLs and mail addresses. In practice, it performs sentence splitting with fairly high precision, therefore this step of text processing does not introduce a significant number of errors in the resulting test items.

4.2 Sentence Filtering

It is obvious that not every sentence acquired from a text is appropriate for question generation. Therefore, we suppose that the sentence set could be filtered in order to provide better results. Reducing a text document in order to retain its most important portions is known as document summarization.

The NLP field studies different techniques for automatic text summarization, with two general approaches: extraction and abstraction. Extractive summaries (extracts) are produced by concatenating several sentences taken exactly as they appear in the materials being summarized. Abstractive summaries (abstracts), are written to convey the main information in the input and may reuse phrases or clauses from it, but the summaries are overall expressed in the words of the summary author (Nenkova and McKeown, 2011). It means that abstracts may contain words not explicitly present in the original.

In our task, the main goal is removing unimportant sentences, therefore we can use extraction-based summarization. Generally, we need to assign an importance score to each sentence and include the highest-scoring sentences in the resulting set. Since 1950s, different methods for scoring sentences have been studied, and they are now usually applied in combination. For example, Hynek and Jezek (2003) listed the following methods: sentence length cut-off (short sentences are excluded), use of cue phrases (inclusion of sentences containing phrases such as "in conclusion", "as a result" etc.), sentence position in a document / paragraph, occurrence of frequent terms (based on TF-IDF term weighting), relative position of frequent terms within a sentence, use of uppercase words, and occurrence of title words.

To date, we have not completed our research in this direction, and we use an unfiltered set of sentences in the current system. However, at the question generation stage we apply some rules that allow selecting sentences of a particular structure, e.g. those containing definitions or acronyms.

4.3 Question Generation

Our current approach uses different algorithms to generate questions for a cloze test. We also take into account the category of the blanked-out word and add a hint into the question, explaining what kind of answer is expected. The algorithms can be divided into two groups depending on how deeply the sentence is analyzed.

The algorithms of the first group simply read the sentence as a sequence of characters looking for acronyms, numbers or definitions. Definitions are recognized based on the common words used to define a term in Russian, such as "является" (is), "представляет собой" (represents) or the combination of a dash and the word "это" (a Russian particle commonly used in definitions; usually preceded by a dash). Below is an example sentence followed by a generated question:

```
Source: Сеть — это группа из двух
или более компьютеров, которые
предоставляют совместный доступ к
своим аппаратным или программным
ресурсам.

Result: .... (определение) — это
группа из двух или более
компьютеров, которые предоставляют
совместный доступ к своим
аппаратным или программным
ресурсам.
```

Or, in English:

```
Source: A network is a group of two
or more computers that provide
shared access to their hardware or
software resources.

Result: ..... (definition) is a
group of two or more computers that
provide shared access to their
hardware or software resources.
```

The system recognized a sentence containing a definition and replaced the term "Сеть" (network) with a blank. After the blank, it inserted a hint in parentheses: "определение" (definition).

The next example shows how the system can process numbers:

```
Source: Как известно, классическая
концепция экспертных систем
сложилась в 1980-х гг.
```

[2] Available from: http://aot.ru/

```
Result: Как известно, классическая
концепция экспертных систем
сложилась в ....... (число)-х гг.
```

Or, in English:

```
Source: As is well known, the
classical conception of expert
systems has developed in 1980s.

Result: As is well known, the
classical conception of expert
systems has developed in .......
(number)s.
```

The system recognized a sentence containing a number (1980) and replaced it with a blank. After the blank, it inserted a hint in parentheses: "число" (number). The teacher can edit this question by removing the cue phrase ("Как известно" — "As is well known") and moving the hint to a better position.

The algorithms of the first group are fairly easy to implement and perform relatively fast.

The algorithms of the second group generate questions based on morpho-syntactic analysis of a sentence. They allow producing questions to the sentence's subject ("что?" — "what?"; "кто?" — "who?"), adverbial of place or time ("где?" — "where?"; "когда?" — "when?"), or to adjectives contained in the sentence ("какой?" — "what?"). To perform the morpho-syntactic analysis, we use the AOT toolkit. It helps to define proper hints for the questions, considering the gender and number of the blanked-out word. For example:

```
Source: В отличие от перцептронов
рефлекторный алгоритм напрямую
рассчитывает адекватную входным
воздействиям реакцию
интеллектуальной системы.

Result: В отличие от перцептронов
......... (какой?) алгоритм
напрямую рассчитывает адекватную
входным воздействиям реакцию
интеллектуальной системы.
```

Or, in English:

```
Source: In contrast to perceptrons,
the reflective algorithm directly
calculates the reaction of the
intelligent system with respect to
input actions.

Result: In contrast to perceptrons,
the ......... (what?) algorithm
directly calculates the reaction of
the intelligent system with respect
to input actions.
```

The system recognized an adjective ("рефлекторный" — "reflective") and replaced it with a blank. After the blank, it inserted a hint in parentheses: "какой?" ("what?").

These algorithms are more complicated than those of the first group and perform slower.

One of the issues, which arise at the question generation stage, is that the current system does not attempt to determine whether blanking out a particular word produces a useful question, which results in a number of superfluous questions that the teacher has to reject manually.

5 Preliminary Experiments

Even though sentence filtering is not yet implemented, our preliminary experiments show that the system may produce relatively fair results with certain text documents. For initial assessment of the system, we tried generating questions for a Russian-language textbook on intelligent information systems. A human judge was asked to classify the resulting questions into 3 categories: *ready to use*, *correctable*, and *useless*.

About 40% of the questions generated with the algorithms of the second group were *ready to use* in a test without modification. It means a teacher would not have to edit the questions by removing superfluous words, replacing pronouns with corresponding nouns etc. About 23% of the questions were *correctable*, i.e. they could be used in a test after some manual correction.

The algorithms of the first group were not as effective (about 15% of generated questions were either *ready to use* or *correctable*), but we expect them to be more effective with texts that contain many explicit definitions (e.g. glossaries) or numbers (e.g. books with history dates).

We also tested the running time of the algorithms on different hardware configurations (from a netbook to a powerful state-of-the-art workstation). The second group algorithms, due to their relative complexity, performed significantly slower than those of the first group, even with short texts. However, it never took more than three minutes to generate questions for an average size textbook (about 250 pages) using any of the algorithms (including sentence splitting time).

6 Conclusions and Future Work

We have done preliminary research regarding two methods for generating test items from electronic documents. We have developed a simple experimental system that allows a teacher to generate questions for a cloze test. Test authoring in the system is presented as a computer-assisted procedure. The system proposes the generated test items to the teacher who selects and edits the ones that are appropriate for use in the test, and then the test is passed to the Moodle LMS. An advantage of the system is that it is specifically developed for the Russian language and it processes texts with respect to morpho-syntactic features of the language, e.g. it can recognize a sentence's subject.

According to initial experiments, the current system performs fairly well in particular cases. However, we have discovered a number of complex problems that should be assessed and addressed in the near future:

1. It may be difficult for the teacher to select useful items. There are at least two ways to address this issue:
    a. If we implement text summarization, the system will be able to produce test items from the most salient sentences of the text.
    b. We should develop a method for selecting the appropriate words to blank out. One idea is to apply a glossary of domain-specific terms to identify such terms in each sentence. We assume that it is more useful to blank out special terms than common words.
2. In order to reduce the need in manual post-editing of the questions, we should consider the following:
    a. Processed sentences may contain anaphora. If the current system uses such a sentence to generate a test item, the teacher has to resolve the anaphora manually (e.g. to replace pronouns with corresponding nouns). Therefore we should study ways of automatic anaphora resolution, which could be implemented in the system.
    b. It might be useful to remove common cue phrases while performing sentence splitting.
3. Fill-in-the-blank is a trivial style of test. Using this kind of exercise in Moodle may be ineffective, because Moodle will only recognize answers that exactly match the blanked-out word. Therefore, we should consider ways to generate distractors in order to establish multiple choice testing.
4. Comprehensive experiments should be conducted:
    a. We should use a representative selection of text sources to substantially evaluate the portion of useful test items that the system is able to produce.
    b. We should assess how the approach compares against people identifying test items without the system, with respect to consumed time and difficulty of the test items. Our suggestion is to involve a group of human judges to annotate questions as useful or not.

These problems define the main directions for future work.

Acknowledgments

The author thanks his advisor, Prof. Dr.sc. Anatolii N. Shvetcov, for his guidance and support, and the anonymous reviewers for their insightful remarks. This research is still at the preliminary stage, therefore any feedback or advice is much appreciated.

References

Gregory Grefenstette, Pasi Tapanainen. 1994. What is a Word, what is a Sentence? Problems of Tokenisation. *Proceedings of 3rd conference on Computational Lexicography and Text Research*, Budapest, Hungary.

Michael Heilman. 2011. *Automatic Factual Question Generation from Text*. Ph.D. Dissertation, Carnegie Mellon University.

Jiri Hynek, Karel Jezek. 2003. A practical approach to automatic text summarization. *Proceedings of the ELPUB 2003 conference*, Guimaraes, Portugal.

Vladimir V. Kruchinin. 2003. *Generators in Programs for Computer-based Training.* Izdatelstvo Tomskogo Universiteta, Tomsk, Russia (В. В. Кручинин. 2003. *Генераторы в компьютерных учебных программах.* Издательство Томского университета, Томск, Россия) [in Russian].

Ruslan Mitkov, Le An Ha, Nikiforos Karamanis. 2006. A computer-aided environment for generating multiple-choice test items. *Natural Language Engineering*, 12(2): 1–18.

Jack Mostow, Joseph Beck, Juliet Bey, Andrew Cuneo, June Sison, Brian Tobin and Joseph Valeri. 2004. Using automated questions to assess reading comprehension, vocabulary, and effects of tutorial interventions. *Technology, Instruction, Cognition and Learning* (2): 97–134.

Ani Nenkova and Kathleen McKeown. 2011. Automatic Summarization. *Foundations and Trends in Information Retrieval*, 5(2–3): 103–233.

Anna P. Sergushitcheva, Anatolii N. Shvetcov. 2003. Synthesis of Intelligence Tests by means of a Formal Production System. *Mathematics, Computer, Education: Conference Proceedings*, vol. 10 (1): 310–320. R&C Dynamics, Moscow – Izhevsk, Russia (А. П. Сергушичева, А. Н. Швецов. 2003. Синтез интеллектуальных тестов средствами формальной продукционной системы. *Математика, Компьютер, Образование. Сборник научных трудов*, выпуск 10 (1): 310–320. R&C Dynamics, Москва – Ижевск, Россия) [in Russian].

Anna P. Sergushitcheva, Anatolii N. Shvetcov. 2006. The Hybrid Approach to Synthesis of Test Tasks in Testing Systems. *Mathematics, Computer, Education: Conference Proceedings*, vol. 13 (1): 215–228. R&C Dynamics, Moscow – Izhevsk, Russia (А. П. Сергушичева, А. Н. Швецов. 2006. Гибридный подход к синтезу тестовых заданий в тестирующих системах. *Математика, Компьютер, Образование. Сборник научных трудов*, выпуск 13 (1): 215–228. R&C Dynamics, Москва – Ижевск, Россия) [in Russian].

I. V. Voronets, Anatolii N. Shvetcov, Viktor S. Alyoshin. 2003. A Universal Automated System for Knowledge Assessment and Self-teaching based on Analysis of Natural-language Texts of Textbooks. *Proceedings of the 5th International Scientific and Practical Conference "Manned Spaceflight"*, Star City, Moscow Region, Russia (И. В. Воронец, А. Н. Швецов, В. С. Алешин. 2003. Универсальная автоматизированная система тестирования знаний и самообразования, основанная на анализе естественно-языковых текстов учебных пособий. *Сб. докл. Пятой международной научно-практической конференции "Пилотируемые полеты в космос"*, Звездный Городок, Москва, Россия) [in Russian].

Korean Word-Sense Disambiguation Using Parallel Corpus as Additional Resource

Chungen Li
Pohang University of Science and Technology
jiafei427@gmail.com

Abstract

Most previous research on Korean Word-Sense Disambiguation (WSD) were focusing on unsupervised corpus-based or knowledge-based approach because they suffered from lack of sense-tagged Korean corpora.Recently, along with great effort of constructing sense-tagged Korean corpus by government and researchers, finding appropriate features for supervised learning approach and improving its prediction accuracy became an issue. To achieve higher word-sense prediction accuracy, this paper aimed to find most appropriate features for Korean WSD based on Conditional Random Field (CRF) approach. Also, we utilized Korean-Japanese parallel corpus to enlarge size of sense-tagged corpus, and improved prediction accuracy with it. Experimental result reveals that our method can achieve 95.67% of prediction accuracy.

1 Introduction

In computational linguistic, lexical ambiguity is one of the first problems that people faced with in Natural Language Processing (NLP) area (Ide and Véronis, 1998).

Resolving semantic ambiguity - Word-Sense Disambiguation (WSD) is the computational process of identifying an ambiguous word's semantic sense according to its usage in a particular context from a set of predefined senses. E.g. For two Korean sentences:

- "**사과**를 먹는 그녀는 참 사랑스러웠다."(The girl who's eating **apple** was so adorable.)
- "**사과**를 하는 그의 진지한 모습에 용서했다."(I accepted the **apology** by his sincerity.)

Then WSD system will disambiguate senses for the Korean word "사과/sakwa" in the first sentence as sense "Apple" and the later as "Apology".

WSD has characteristic of variationoun because it's ubiquitous across all languages. It is also known as one of central challenges in various NLP research because many of them can take WSD's advantage to improve their performances such as Machine Translation (MT) (Carpuat and Wu, 2007), Automatic Speech Recognition (ASR), Information Extraction (IE), and Information Retrieval (IR) (Zhong and Ng, 2012).

According to what kinds of resources are used, WSD can be classified into knowledge-based approach, corpus-based approach, and hybrid approach: Knowledge-based approach relies on knowledge-resources like Machine Readable Dictionary (MRD), WordNet, and Thesaurus; Corpus-based approach trains a probabilistic or statistical model using sense-tagged or raw corpora; Hybrid approach is combining aspects of both of the knowledge and corpus based methodologies, using the interaction of multiple resources to approach WSD.

However, most WSD research on Korean were focusing on unsupervised approach and knowledge-based because lack of sense-tagged Korean corpora (Yoon et al., 2006; Min-Ho Kim, 2011; Yong-Min Park, 2012; Jung Heo, 2006). With effort and collaboration of researchers and government, there are several Korean corpora available (Kang and Kim, 2004). Also it has been proved that supervised learning algorithm can lead a WSD system to the best result.

In this research, we tried to find most appropriate feature set for WSD system based on Conditional Random Field (CRF) approach, and also we constructed sense-tagged Korean corpus via Korean-Japanese parallel corpus to enlarge training examples and achieve better sense prediction accuracy.

This paper is organized as follows: Section two represented the over-all architecture of our method, corpora that used in our research, and explained the method of constructing sense-tagged Korean corpus, Section three showed evaluation result of our WSD method and compared it with other different systems, Section four made a conclusion for this research and experiments.

2 Construct Sense-Tagged Corpus & Enlarge Training Data

In this research, we used two types of different sense-tagged Korean corpora. First one is from 21st Century Sejong Corpora (Kang and Kim, 2004) which is constructed by Korean researchers and funded by government, and the other is automatically constructed sense-tagged Korean corpus by utilizing Korean-Japanese parallel corpus. In this chapter we will introduce Sejong corpora briefly and present proposed method that construct sense-tagged Korean corpus and convert it to the format in Sejong corpora to enlarge the training examples.

2.1 Overall Architecture

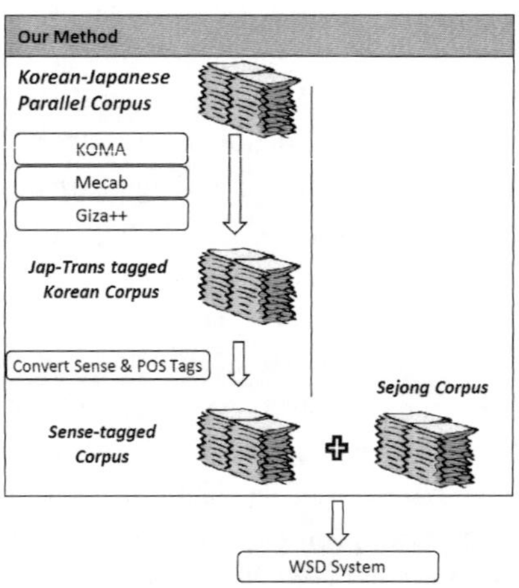

Figure 1: Overall Architecture of Constructing Sense-tagged Corpus

From the overall architecture(Figure 1) we can see mainly it has three important stages: First, we will construct Japanese-translation tagged corpus using Korean-Japanese parallel corpus. Then, we will convert that Japanese-translation tags to sense-id from the original sense-tagged Sejong corpus, and we also need transformation for the Part-Of-Speech tags to match the format of the sense-tagged corpus. Finally, we will then merge that constructed Sense-tagged corpus with Sejong sense-tagged corpus, and use that as training data for the WSD system.

2.2 21st Century Sejong Corpora

The 21st Century Sejong Corpora (Kang and Kim, 2004) are one part of the 21st Century Sejong Project that aimed to build Korean national corpora to provide Korean language resources for academia, education and industry. Among the different corpora, we chose semantically tagged Korean corpora which is consists of around 150 million eojeol[1] and tagged word-senses by using 'Standard Korean Dictionary'.

2.3 Construct Sense-Tagged Korean Corpus via Korean-Japanese Parallel Corpora

For constructing sense-tagged Korean corpus using parallel text, we went through with these four steps:

(1) Align Korean-Japanese parallel corpus in word-level.

(2) Tag ambiguous Korean words by Japanese-translations in the sentence.

(3) For each Korean target words, cluster synonymous Japanese-translations, and map the groups to the sense inventory id in the 'Standard Korean Dictionary'.

(4) Change POS-tags to the Sejong's POS-tags.

With theses four steps, then we will be able to obtain a sense-tagged Korean corpus with same format as Sejong sense-tagged corpora.

2.3.1 Align Korean-Japanese Parallel Corpus in Word-Level

In this step, we need to use alignment algorithm to make sentence aligned Korean-Japanese parallel corpus aligned in word-level.

There are many alignment algorithms (Melamed, 1998; Och and Ney, 2000) available and used by much research already.

First of all, to align parallel corpora in word-level, we need to tokenize Korean and Japanese sentences using morphological analyzer respectively.

For Korean, we used in-house Korean morphological analyzer-KOMA to tokenize and obtain the Part-Of-Speech (POS) tags for each sentence in

[1]In Korean, an eojeol is a sequence of morphemes, it consists of more than one umjeol, and each eojeol is separated with spaces.

Korean, and we used MeCab (Kudo, 2005) to analyze Japanese side.

After morphological analysis of Korean and Japanese sentences, tokenized sentences for both side will be input to the GIZA++ (Och and Ney, 2000) for word alignment procedure.

From the output of GIZA++, then we will be able to acquire the word-level aligned parallel corpus which means each Korean word token are aligned with Japanese word token.

2.3.2 Tag Ambiguous Korean Words by Japanese-Translations

In this step, we filtered and selected Japanese translations which will be served as the "sense-tags" for the corresponding Korean words.

We tagged ambiguous Korean words by Japanese translation from output result of the previous step, so that these Korean words can be regarded to have been disambiguated by different Japanese translations.

From Japanese translation tagged corpus, we observed many ambiguous words are tagged by erroneous and inefficient Japanese translations by error propagation of morphological analyzer and word alignment algorithm.

To reduce this error, we decided filter and eliminate those sentences with incorrect Japanese translation tags by two strategies.

First, we obtained the Japanese translation group for each ambiguous Korean word from the parallel text to apply these two following rules for filtering. (1) From the group of the Japanese translations which have been aligned to ambiguous Korean words, we chose Japanese translations with frequencies above the threshold. Because most of the Japanese translations aligned to the corresponding Korean target word with low occurrence counts are erroneous by morphological analyzer and word alignment of GIZA++.
(2) The one-length Japanese translations which don't belong to Kanji are excluded because Hiragana or other Romaji, Numbers, Punctuations etc. with one length would not be useful for representing senses for ambiguous Korean target words.

2.3.3 Cluster Synonymous Japanese Translations & Map to Sense Id

In this step, we transformed "sense-tags" represented by Japanese-translations to the sense-id in the Sejong Corpus.

From the previous stage, we could get a set of Japanese translations for the corresponding Korean target word. Mapping each Japanese-translations to sense-id in Sejong may need lots of time which will be very inefficient. So we decided to cluster the Japanese-translations with similar meaning which may create several groups for Japanese-translations then map each group which represents different sense to type of sense-id in Sejong corpus.

With following three processes, we made different Japanese-translation groups for each corresponding Korean target word by utilizing Mecab and Japanese-WordNet (Isahara et al., 2010) as resources.

(1) First of all, we checked pronunciations for each Japanese translation token with Mecab to cluster the same words with different forms because even for the same word, some of them are showed up in full-Kanji, some are full-Hiragana, and some are mixture form of Kanji and Hiragana in the corpus (e.g. 油-しょうゆ-しょう油). Mecab could give pronunciation for each Japanese word, then we used this information to check whether two Japanese words' pronunciations are same or not. If two Japanese words' are having same pronunciations, they will be recognized as same word and be grouped as one.

(2) Secondly, we used partial matching method to check If two words are representing same meaning by our pattern. Because Japanese Kanji is originally from Chinese characters, so each of words can represent specific meaning, and also there are several different forms in Japanese to show some respect such as adding a Japanese Hiragana character - 'お' in front of a noun. So, if two Japanese translations are exactly matched without first or last character of one word, they will be considered as same meaning (e.g. 祈り – お祈り, 船-船舶).

(3) Finally, we used Japanese WordNet and Wu & Palmer's algorithms (Wu and Palmer, 1994) to calculate the similarity score between Japanese translations.

Japanese WordNet is developed by the National Institute of Information and Communications Technology (NICT) since 2006 to support for Natural Language Processing research in Japan. This research was inspired by the Princeton WordNet and the Global WordNet Grid, and aimed to create a large scale, freely available, semantic dictionary of Japanese, just like other languages such as English WordNet or Chinese WordNet.

The Wu & Palmer measure calculates relatedness by considering the depths of the two synsets in the WordNet taxonomies, so with this calculated similarity score we could know how much two Japanese words are related to the other. Two Japanese words are clustered to same group if the similarity score for that two words is higher than the threshold.

With these three processes above, we will be able to have different groups of Japanese-translations with different meaning (or sense). We used Sejong's sense definition table from 'Standard Korean Dictionary' to create the matching table from the sense-id in Sejong to the our Japanese-translation groups for each corresponding Korean target word. After that, each ambiguous Korean target word will have different senses represented by Sejong's sense-id which is mapped to the different groups of Japanese-translations.

Then the Japanese-translation tag for each Korean target word in our constructed corpus will be changed to the corresponding Sejong sense-id by the matching table.

2.3.4 Combine Sejong and Constructed Corpora

From the previous stage, we could have a sense-tagged corpus which has exactly same sense-id with Sejong, but here we also have to change the POS tags since our constructed sense-tagged corpus is analyzed and tokenized by our in-house (KOMA) morphological analyzer.

To combine Sejong sense-tagged corpora and automatically constructed corpora, we needed to have not only the same format of sense-id, but also for the same format of POS tagset.

By the careful observation, we found the Sejong have 44 different types of POS tags while our in-house analyzer have 62 different types.

So we mapped the POS tags s from our in-house morphological analyzer which is more fine-grained to Sejong's POS tags, and rewrite the tags in the constructed corpora automatically using that POS tag mapping table.

At the end, we constructed the sense-tagged corpus which have same form of sense-id and POS tags which could be used as enlarging the training data from Sejong sense-tagged corpora.

3 Experimental Result

3.1 Accuracy of Sense-Tagged Corpora

We checked the accuracy for grouping for synonymous Japanese translations manually to evaluate the automatically constructed sense-tagged corpora.

To construct sense-tagged Korean corpora, we used Korean-Japanese parallel text that consists of 608,692 sentences, and extracted 40,622 sentences of sense-tagged corpora targeting 200 of ambiguous Korean nouns.

Evaluation result shows that we clustered 606 Japanese words correctly into same groups among 686 words, which give us 88.34% (606/686) of accuracy. However, when we check the frequencies of those incorrectly grouped Japanese translations that appeared in the parallel corpora for the corresponding Korean WSD target word, it showed only 2.65% (1,410/53,264) error rate which is quite low.

Also when we tried to evaluate those groups of Japanese-translations by how many of them can be actually map to the sense-id in the Sejong's "Standard Korean Dictionary". Result showed that among 515 different Japanese-translation groups, 480 of them can be mapped to Sejong's sense-id, so the mapping accuracy would be then 93.204% from this observation.

3.2 Finding Appropriate Window Size

As previously mentioned, to use content words as feature, we need to find most appropriate window size for it. We tried to compare several different window sizes with two different features – Y. K. Lee* and our own feature set by training the WSD model using constructed Korean WSD corpus without merging it into the Sejong Corpus. In this experiment, we used 5-fold cross-validation to calculate the prediction accuracy (Table 3.2) .

From the observation for result of the comparison experiment, we found window size 2 had best performance with our feature set (Table 3.2). So we decided to extract content words by window size 2 as the feature for our CRF approach.

3.3 WSD Prediction Accuracy

For the evaluation of WSD system, we made three different types of training data to compare three different systems.

Window Size	Prediction Accuracy (%)		
	Y. K. Lee*	ours	Comparison
2	**88.87**	**90.88**	**+2.01**
4	88.65	90.47	+1.82
6	88.02	90.14	+2.12
8	87.73	89.90	+2.17
10	87.50	89.79	+2.29

Table 1: Classifier Accuracy Comparison using 5-fold Cross Validation

	ours	Y. K. Lee*	Base-Line
Sejong	95.57	94.88	76.19
Sejong+	95.67	94.96	76.19
CK	78.33	72.32	76.19

Table 2: The Comparison of Different WSD Systems

3.4 Training and Test Data

First of all, we randomly chose 90% (256,304 sentences) of corpora for the training data , and 10% (28,627 sentences) for test data from Sejong corpora.

Second, we used constructed sense-tagged corpus by our method as training corpus to check its credibility.

Also, we combined training data from Sejong and our constructed sense-tagged corpus to see how does it affect the WSD system.

3.5 Comparison of WSD Systems with Different Features

We compared three different WSD systems: The base-line system which is choosing the Most Frequent Sense (MFS) only; The WSD system using features from Lee (Lee and Ng, 2002); and The WSD system with our own feature set.

From the result we observed that our WSD system outperformed the baseline system (MFS) around 13.6% of prediction accuracy, and it also proved that system with our feature was able to reach higher prediction accuracy by 0.57% of improvement compare to system used features from Y. K. Lee*. Meanwhile, adding the sense-tagged corpora to Sejong resulted 0.1% improvement of prediction accuracy.

4 Comparison with Related Works

We compared our result to two most recent Korean WSD systems (Table. 4), Kim (Min-Ho Kim, 2011) utilized Korean WordNet and raw corpus to disambiguate word sense, Park (Yong-Min Park, 2012) built word vectors from Sejong sense-tagged corpus to resolve word senses. Among three different types of WSD approaches, our method showed best performance. Although Park (Yong-Min Park, 2012) was targeting 583 words which is triple size of our target word, they used only 200 sentences for evaluation which is quite small compare to our test size (28,627 Sentences).

Author	Target	Test	Accuracy
Kim et al. 2011	10	574	86.2
Park et al. 2012	583	200	94.02
Our Method	200	28,627	95.67

Table 3: The Comparison With Previous Work

Conclusion

In this research, we mainly targeting two things: First, construct sense-tagged corpus using Korean-Japanese parallel corpus. Second, find appropriate feature set for the Korean WSD system.

To construct sense-tagged corpus using parallel text, we represented a way to cluster synonymous Japanese words using several heuristic rules combining the Japanese WordNet.

Using this constructed sense-tagged corpus, the WSD system outperformed 2.14% than the baseline system which choosing most frequent sense only, and also the WSD system using enlarged training data with this corpus have achieved best performance with 95.67% of prediction accuracy.

This research also had focused on finding most appropriate feature template by comparing several different features. Feature set created our own with enlarged training corpus, we achieved better prediction accuracy compared to the previous best Korean WSD work using same Sejong sense-tagged corpus.

References

Marine Carpuat and Dekai Wu. 2007. Improving statistical machine translation using word sense disambiguation. In *Proceedings of the 2007 Joint Conference on Empirical Methods in Natural Language Processing and Computational Natural Language Learning (EMNLP-CoNLL)*, pages 61–72.

Nancy Ide and Jean Véronis. 1998. Introduction to the special issue on word sense disambiguation: the state of the art. *Computational Linguistics*, 24(1):2–40.

Hitoshi Isahara, Francis Bond, Kiyotaka Uchimoto, Masao Utiyama, and Kyoko Kanzaki. 2010. Development of the japanese wordnet.

Huychel Seo Jung Heo, Myengkil Cang. 2006. Homonym disambiguation based on mutual information and sense-tagged compound noun dictionary. *Proceedings of Korea Computer Congress*, 33:1073–1089.

BM Kang and Hunggyu Kim. 2004. Sejong korean corpora in the making. In *Proceedings of LREC*, pages 1747–1750.

Taku Kudo. 2005. Mecab: Yet another part-of-speech and morphological analyzer. *http://mecab. sourceforge. net/.*

Yoong Keok Lee and Hwee Tou Ng. 2002. An empirical evaluation of knowledge sources and learning algorithms for word sense disambiguation. In *Proceedings of the ACL-02 conference on Empirical methods in natural language processing-Volume 10*, pages 41–48. Association for Computational Linguistics.

Ilya Dan Melamed. 1998. Empirical methods for exploiting parallel texts.

Hyuk-Chul Kwon Min-Ho Kim. 2011. Word sense disambiguation using semantic relations in korean wordnet. *Proceedings of Korea Computer Congress*, 38.

Franz Josef Och and Hermann Ney. 2000. Improved statistical alignment models. In *Proceedings of the 38th Annual Meeting on Association for Computational Linguistics*, pages 440–447. Association for Computational Linguistics.

Zhibiao Wu and Martha Palmer. 1994. Verbs semantics and lexical selection. In *Proceedings of the 32nd annual meeting on Association for Computational Linguistics*, pages 133–138. Association for Computational Linguistics.

Jae-Sung Lee Yong-Min Park. 2012. Word sense disambiguation using korean word space model. *Journal of Korea Contents Association.*

Yeohoon Yoon, Choong-Nyoung Seon, Songwook Lee, and Jungyun Seo. 2006. Unsupervised word sense disambiguation for korean through the acyclic weighted digraph using corpus and dictionary. *Information processing & management*, 42(3):710–722.

Zhi Zhong and Hwee Tou Ng. 2012. Word sense disambiguation improves information retrieval. In *Proceedings of the 50th Annual Meeting of the Association for Computational Linguistics: Long Papers-Volume 1*, pages 273–282. Association for Computational Linguistics.

Towards Basque Oral Poetry Analysis: A Machine Learning Approach

Mikel Osinalde, Aitzol Astigarraga, Igor Rodriguez and **Manex Agirrezabal**
Computer Science and Artificial Intelligence Department,
University of the Basque Country (UPV/EHU), 20018 Donostia
teagenes@hotmail.com
aitzol.astigarraga@ehu.es
igor.rodriguez@ehu.es
manex.agirrezabal@ehu.es

Abstract

This work aims to study the narrative structure of Basque greeting verses from a text classification approach. We propose a set of thematic categories for the correct classification of verses, and then, use those categories to analyse the verses based on Machine Learning techniques. Classification methods such as Naive Bayes, k-NN, Support Vector Machines and Decision Tree Learner have been selected. Dimensionality reduction techniques have been applied in order to reduce the term space. The results shown by the experiments give an indication of the suitability of the proposed approach for the task at hands.

1 Introduction

Automated text categorization, the assignment of text documents to one or more predefined categories according to their content, is an important application and research topic due to the amount of text documents that we have to deal with every day. The predominant approach to this problem is based on Machine Learning (ML) methods, where classifiers learn automatically the characteristics of the categories from a set of previously classified texts (Sebastiani, 2002).

The task of constructing a document classifier does not differ so much from other ML tasks, and a number of approaches have been proposed in the literature. According to Cardoso-Cachopo and Oliveira (2003) , they mainly differ on how documents are represented and how each document is assigned to the correct categories. Thus, both steps, document representation and selection of the classification method are crucial for the overall success. A particular approach can be more suitable for a particular task, with a specific data, while another one can be better in a different scenario (Zelaia et al., 2005; Kim et al., 2002; Joachims, 1998).

In this paper we analyse the categorization of traditional Basque impromptu greeting verses. The goal of our research is twofold: on the one hand, we want to extract the narrative structure of an improvised Basque verse; and, on the other hand, we want to study to what extent such an analysis can be addressed through learning algorithms.

The work presented in this article is organized as follows: first we introduce Basque language and *Bertsolaritza*, Basque improvised context poetry, for a better insight of the task at hand. Next, we give a general review of computational pragmatics and text classification domains, examining discourse pattern, document representation, feature reduction and classification algorithms. Afterwards, the experimental set-up is introduced in detail; and, in the next section, experimental results are shown and discussed. Finally, we present some conclusions and guidelines for future work.

2 Some Words about Basque Language and *Bertsolaritza*

Basque, *euskara*, is the language of the inhabitants of the Basque Country. It has a speech community of about 700,000 people, around 25% of the total population. Seven provinces compose the territory, four of them inside the Spanish state and three inside the French state.

Bertsolaritza, Basque improvised contest poetry, is one of the manifestations of traditional Basque culture that is still very much alive. Events and competitions in which improvised verses, *bertso*-s, are composed are very common. In such performances, one or more verse-makers, named *bertsolaris*, produce impromptu compositions about topics or prompts which are given to them by a theme-prompter. Then, the verse-maker takes a few seconds, usually less than a minute, to compose a poem along the pattern of a prescribed verse-form that also involves a rhyme scheme. Melodies are chosen from among hundreds of tunes.

Figure 1: *Bertsolari Txapelketa Nagusia*, the national championship of the Basque improvised contest poetry, held in 2009

When constructing an improvised verse strict constraints of meter and rhyme must be followed. For example, in the case of a metric structure of verses known as *Zortziko Txikia* (small of eight), the poem must have eight lines. The union of each odd line with the next even line, form a strophe. And each strophe, in turn, must rhyme with the others. But the true quality of the *bertso* does not only depend on those demanding technical requirements. The real value of the *bertso* resides on its dialectical, rhetorical and poetical value. Thus, a *bertsolari* must be able to express a variety of ideas and thoughts in an original way while dealing with the mentioned technical constraints.

The most demanding performance of Basque oral poetry, is the *Bertsolari Txapelketa*, the national championship of *bertsolaritza*, celebrated every four years (see Fig.1). The championship is composed by several tasks or contests of different nature that need to be fulfilled by the participants. It always begins with extemporaneous improvisations of greetings, a first verse called *Agurra*. This verse is the only one in which the poet can express directly what she/he wants. For the rest of the contest, the theme-prompter will prescribe a topic which serves as a prompt for the *bertso*, and also the verse metric and the number of iterations. For that reason, we thought the *Agurra* was of particular interest to analyse ways verse-makers use to structure their narration.

3 Related Work

3.1 Computational Pragmatics

As stated in the introduction, the aim of this paper is to notice if there is any discourse pattern in greeting verses. In other words, we are searching certain defined ways verse-improvisers in general use to structure their discourse.

If the study of the meaning is made taking into account the context, we will have more options for getting information of the factors surrounding improvisation (references, inferences, what improvisers are saying, thinking, self-state, context). The field that studies the ways in which context contributes to meaning is called pragmatics. From a general perspective, Pragmatics refers to the speaker and the environment (Searle, 1969; Austin, 1975; Vidal, 2004).

The study of extra-linguistic information searched by pragmatics is essential for a complete understanding of an improvised verse. In fact, the understanding of the text of each paragraph does not give us the key for the overall meaning of the verse. There is also a particular world's vision and a frame of reference shared with the public; and, indeed, we have been looking for those keys. We believe that the verse texts are not linear sequences of sentences, they are placed regarding a criterion and the research presented here aims to detect this intent.

Therefore, searching for the discourse facts in greeting verses led us to study their references.

3.2 Text Categorization

The goal of text categorization methods is to associate one or more of a predefined set of categories to a given document. An excellent review of text classification domain can be found in (Sebastiani, 2002).

It is widely accepted that how documents are represented influences the overall quality of the classification results (Leopold and Kindermann, 2002). Usually, each document is represented by an array of words. The set of all words of the training documents is called vocabulary, or dictionary. Thus, each document can be represented as a vector with one component corresponding to each term in the vocabulary, along with the number that represents how many times the word appears in the document (zero value if the term does not occur). This document representation is called the bag-of-words model. The major drawback of this text representation model is that the number of features in the corpus can be considerable, and thus, intractable for some learning algorithms.

Therefore, methods for dimension reduction are required. There exists two different ways to carry out this reduction: data can be pre-processed, i.e., some filters can be applied to control the size of the system's vocabulary. And, on the other hand, dimensionality reduction techniques can be applied.

3.2.1 Pre-processing the Data

We represented the documents based on the aforementioned bag-of-word model. But not all the words that appear in a document are significant for text classification task. Normally, a pre-processing step is required to reduce the dimensionality of the corpus and, also, to unify the data in a way it improves performance.

In this work, we applied the following pre-processing filters:

- **Stemming**: remove words with the same stem, keeping the most common among them. Due to its inflectional morphology, in Basque language a given word lemma makes many different word forms. A brief morphological description of Basque can be found in (Alegria et al., 1996). For example, the lemma *etxe* (house) forms the inflections *etxea* (the house), *etxeak* (houses or the houses), *etxeari* (to the house), etc. This means that if we use the exact given word to calculate term weighting, we will loose the similarities between all the inflections of that word. Therefore, we use a stemmer, which is based on the morphological description of Basque to find and use the lemmas of the given words in the term dictionary (Ezeiza et al., 1998).

- **Stopwords**: eliminate non-relevant words, such as articles, conjunctions and auxiliary verbs. A list containing the most frecuent words used in Basque poetry has been used to create the stopword list.

3.2.2 Dimensionality Reduction

Dimensionality reduction is a usual step in many text classification problems, that involves transforming the actual set of attributes into a shorter, and hopefully, more predictive one. There exists two ways to reduce dimensionality:

- **Feature selection** is used to reduce the dimensionality of the corpus removing features that are considered non-relevant for the classification task (Forman, 2003). The most well-known methods include: Information Gain, Chi-square and Gain Ratio (Zipitria et al., 2012).

- **Feature transformation** maps the original list of attributes onto a new, more compact one. Two well-known methods for feature transformation are: Principal Component Analysis (PCA) (Wold et al., 1987) and Latent Semantic Analysis (LSA) (Deerwester et al., 1990; Hofmann, 2001).

The major difference between both approaches is that feature selection selects a subset from the original set of attributes, and feature transformation transforms them into new ones. The latter can affect our ability to understand the results, as transformed attributes can show good performance but little meaningful information.

3.2.3 Learning Algorithms

Once the text is properly represented, ML algorithms can be applied. Many text classifiers have been proposed and tested in literature using ML techniques (Sebastiani, 2002), but text categorization is still an active area of research, mainly because there is not a general faultless approach.

For the work presented here, we used the following algorithms: Nearest Neighbour Classifier (IBk) (Dasarathy, 1991), Nave Bayes Classifier (NB) (Minsky, 1961), J48 Decision Tree Learner (Hall et al., 2009) and SMO Support Vector Machine (Joachims, 1998).

All the experiments were performed using the Weka open-source implementation (Hall et al., 2009). Weka is written in Java and is freely available from its website [1].

In Fig.2, the graphical representation of the overall Text Classification process is shown.

4 Experimental Setup

The aim of this section is to describe the document collection used in our experiments and to give an account of the stemming, stopword deletion and dimensionality reduction techniques we have applied.

[1] http://www.cs.waikato.ac.nz/ml/weka/

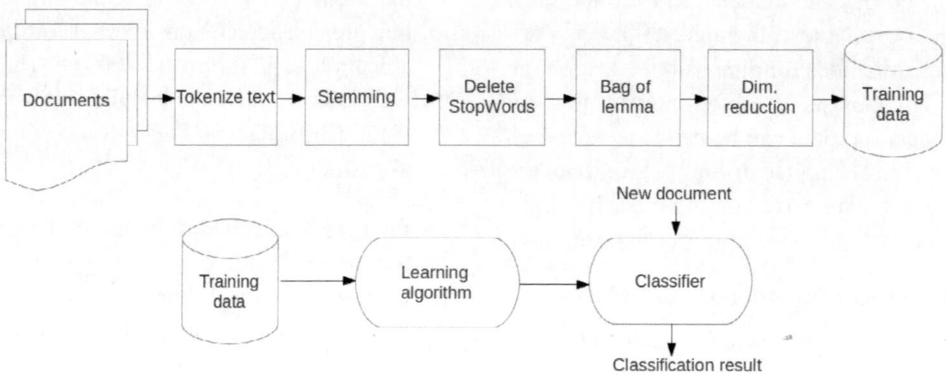

Figure 2: The overall process of text categorization

4.1 Categorization

To make a correct categorization of the verses, before anything else the unit to be studied needs to be decided. We could take as a unit of study the word, the strophes or the entire verses. Considering that we want to extract the structure that would provide information about the decisions made by the improviser and the discourse organization, we decided that the strophe[2] was the most appropriate unit to observe those ideas. Therefore, the first job was to divide the verses in strophes. After that, we began to identify the contents and features in them. The goal was to make the widest possible characterization and, at the same time, select the most accurate list of attributes that would make the strophes as much distinguishable as possible.

We sampled some strophes from the verse corpus described in section 4.2 and analysed them one by one. We had two options when categorizing the strophes: first, analyse and group all the perceived topics, allowing us to propose a realistic classification of the strophes from any verse. And second, make a hypothesis and adjust the obtained data to the hypothesis. We decided to take both paths.

After analysing each of the strophes and extracting their topics, we made the final list, sorted by the relevance of the categories. We obtained a very large list of contents and we arranged it by the importance and by the number of appearance. But that thick list did not help us in our mission as we wanted. So we agreed to try to define and limit the collection of attributes. And we decided to use the second option. Therefore, we studied the foundations of discourse analysis (Roberts and Ross, 2010; Gumperz, 1982), and the classifications proposed by critics of the improvisation field (Egaña et al., 2004; Diaz Pimienta, 2001); and then, we compared them with our predicted one. Merging both approaches we tried to build a strong set of categories.

Combining inductive and deductive paths we formed a list of six categories. So the initial big list that we gathered was filtered to a more selective classification. Therewith, we found possible to label the majority of the strophes in the analysed verses, and also get a significant level of accuracy.

Thus, these are the categories to be considered in the verse classification step:

1. Message: the main idea
2. Location: references to the event site
3. Public: messages and references relating to the audience
4. Event: messages and references relating to the performance itself
5. Oneself aim or Oneself state
6. Miscellaneous: padding, junk. Sentences with no specific meaning or intend.

As well as the five categories closely linked to the communication situation, there is another that we called Miscellaneous (padding, filling). Due to

[2] a pair of stanzas of alternating form on which the structure of a given poem is based

the demanding nature of the improvisation performances, they usually are sentences not very full of content and intent.

We have decided to consider each one of them as a separate goal, and hence six classifiers were to be obtained, one for each category. Thus, each categorization task was addressed as a binary classification problem, in which each document must be classified as being part of $category_i$ or not (for example, Location vs. no Location).

4.2 Document Collection

For the task in hands, we decided to limit our essay to greeting verses from tournaments. We selected 40 verses of a corpus of 2002 verses and divided them into strophes (212 in total). But when we began assigning categories (1-6) to each strophe, we realized we were in blurred fields. It was pretty difficult to perform that task accurately and we thought it was necessary to ask some expert for help. Mikel Aizpurua[3] and Karlos Aizpurua[4] (a well-known judge the former and verse improviser and Basque poetry researcher the latter) agreed to participate in our research, and they manually labelled one by one the 212 strophes.

In that study, we considered each binary class decision as a distinct classification task, where each document was tested as belonging or not to each category. Thus, the same sentence could effectively belong to more than one categories (1 to 6 category labels could be assigned to the same sentence).

As an example, let us have a look to an initial greeting verse composed by Anjel Larrañaga, a famous verse-maker (see Fig.3).

There we can see that each strophe (composed of two lines), was labelled in one, two or even tree different categories.

- (1) (3): Message, Public
- (5): Oneself aim
- (4) (5): Event, Oneself state
- (1) (5) (3): Message, Oneself aim, Public

The document categorization process was accomplished in two steps: during the training step, a general inductive process automatically built a classifier by learning from a set of labelled documents. And during the test step, the performance of the classifier was measured. Due to the small size of our manually categorized corpus, we used the k-fold cross-validation method, with a fold value of k=10.

[3]http://bdb.bertsozale.com/en/web/haitzondo/view/-Mikel-Aizpurua

[4]http://bdb.bertsozale.com/en/web/haitzondo/view/-Karlos-Aizpurua

Agur ta erdi bertsozaleak
lehendabiziko ***sarreran,***
behin da berriro jarri gerade
kantatutzeko ***aukeran,***
ordu ilunak izanagaitik
*txapelketan gora-****beheran,***
saia nahi degu ta ia zuen
gogoko izaten ***geran.***

As a first introduction,
greetings to all improvisation fans. (1) (3)
Many times we were ready
to sing like now! (5)
Even though there are hard times
in our championship contest, (4) (5)
We will try to make our best
and we hope you find it to your liking! (1) (5) (3)

Figure 3: A welcome verse composed by Anjel Larrañaga

4.3 Pre-processing the Data

In order to reduce the dimensionality of the corpus, two pre-processing filters were applied. On the one hand, a stopword list was used to eliminate non-relevant words. On the other hand, a stemmer was used to reduce the number of attributes.

The number of different features in the unprocessed set of documents was 851, from which were extracted 614 different stems and 582 terms after eliminating the stopwords. So finally, we obtained a bag-of-lemmas with 582 different terms.

5 Experimental Results

In this section we show the results obtained in the experiments. There are various methods to determine algorithms' effectiveness, but precision and recall are the most frequently used ones.

It must be said that a number of studies on feature selection focused on performance. But in many cases, as happened to us, the are few in-

Category	ML method	Attribute selection	Performance	F-measure
Message	1-nn	None	64.62%	0.62
Location	SMO	InfoGain	89.62%	0.86
Public	SMO	ChiSquare	83.01%	0.81
Event	5-nn	None	78.30%	0.76
Oneself	SMO	InfoGain	62.26%	0.60
Miscellaneous	1-nn	GainRatio	87.74%	0.83

Table 1: Best results for each category

stances of positive classes in the testing database. This can mask the classifiers performance evaluation. For instance, in our testing database only 22 out of 212 instances correspond to class 2 ("Location"), giving an performance of 90.045 % to the algorithm that always classifies instances as 0, and thereby compressing the range of interesting values to the remaining 9.954 %. Therefore, in text categorization tasks is preferred the F-measure, the harmonic average between precision and recall.

Table1 shows the configurations that have achieved the best results for each category.

Based on the results of the table, we can state that they were good in three out of six categories (Location, Public and Miscellaneous); quite acceptable in one of them (Event); and finally, in the remaining two categories (Message and Oneself) the results were not very satisfactory.

Regarding to the learning algorithms, it should be pointed out that SMO and k-nn have shown the best results. We can state also that in most cases best accuracy rates have been obtained using dimensionality reduction techniques. Which in other words means that the selection of attributes is preferable to the raw data.

6 Conclusions and Future Work

In this paper we shown the foundations of the automated analysis of Basque impromptu greeting verses. The study proposes novel features of greeting-verses and analyses the suitability of those features in the task of automated feature classification. It is important to note that our primary goals were to establish the characteristics for the correct classification of the verses, and so to analyse their narrative structure. And, secondly, to validate different methods for categorizing Basque greeting verses.

Towards this end, we introduced different features related to improvised greeting verses and categorized them into six groups of Message, Location, Public, Event, Oneself and Miscellaneous. Then, we implemented six different approaches combining dimensionality reduction techniques and ML algorithms. One for each considered categories.

In our opinion, the most relevant conclusion is that k-nn and SMO have shown to be the most suitable algorithms for our classification task, and also, that in most cases attribute selection techniques help to improve their performance.

As a future work, we would like to assess the problem as a multi-labelling task (Zelaia et al., 2011), and see if that improves the results.

Finally, we must say that there is still much work to do in order to properly extract discourse-patterns from Basque greeting verses. To this end, we intend to use our classifiers to label larger corpora and find regular discourse patterns in them.

7 Acknowledgements

The authors gratefully acknowledge *Bertsozale Elkartea*[5] (Association of the Friends of Bertsolaritza), whose verse corpora has been used to test and develop the *Bertsobot* project.

This work has been partially conducted under the SAIOTEK projects XIMUR and POETAUTO, the Basque Government Research Team grant and the University of the Basque Country UPV/EHU, under grant UFI11/45 (BAILab).

References

Iñaki Alegria, Xabier Artola, Kepa Sarasola, and Miriam Urkia. 1996. Automatic morphological analysis of Basque. *Literary and Linguistic Computing*, 11(4):193–203.

John Langshaw Austin. 1975. *How to do things with words*, volume 88. Harvard University Press.

Ana Cardoso-Cachopo and Arlindo Oliveira. 2003. An empirical comparison of text categorization methods. In

[5]http://www.bertsozale.com/en

String Processing and Information Retrieval, pages 183–196. Springer.

Belur V Dasarathy. 1991. Nearest neighbor ({NN}) norms:{NN} pattern classification techniques.

Scott Deerwester, Susan T. Dumais, George W Furnas, Thomas K Landauer, and Richard Harshman. 1990. Indexing by latent semantic analysis. *Journal of the American society for information science*, 41(6):391–407.

Alexis Diaz Pimienta. 2001. *Teoría de la improvisación: primeras páginas para el estudio del repentismo*. Ediciones Unión.

Andoni Egaña, Alfonso Sastre, Arantza Mariskal, Alexis Diaz Pimienta, and Guillermo Velazquez. 2004. *Ahozko inprobisazioa munduan topaketak: Encuentro sobre la improvisación oral en el mundo : (Donostia, 2003-11-3/8)*. Euskal Herriko Bertsozale Elkartea.

Nerea Ezeiza, Iñaki Alegria, José María Arriola, Rubén Urizar, and Itziar Aduriz. 1998. Combining stochastic and rule-based methods for disambiguation in agglutinative languages. In *Proceedings of the 17th international conference on Computational linguistics-Volume 1*, pages 380–384. Association for Computational Linguistics.

George Forman. 2003. An extensive empirical study of feature selection metrics for text classification. *The Journal of Machine Learning Research*, 3:1289–1305.

John J Gumperz. 1982. Discourse strategies: Studies in interactional sociolinguistics. *Cambridge University, Cambridge*.

Mark Hall, Eibe Frank, Geoffrey Holmes, Bernhard Pfahringer, Peter Reutemann, and Ian H Witten. 2009. The weka data mining software: an update. *ACM SIGKDD Explorations Newsletter*, 11(1):10–18.

Thomas Hofmann. 2001. Unsupervised learning by probabilistic latent semantic analysis. *Machine Learning*, 42(1):177–196.

Thorsten Joachims. 1998. Text categorization with support vector machines: Learning with many relevant features. *Machine learning: ECML-98*, pages 137–142.

Sang-Bum Kim, Hae-Chang Rim, Dongsuk Yook, and Heui-Seok Lim. 2002. Effective methods for improving naive bayes text classifiers. *PRICAI 2002: Trends in Artificial Intelligence*, pages 479–484.

Edda Leopold and Jörg Kindermann. 2002. Text categorization with support vector machines. how to represent texts in input space? *Machine Learning*, 46(1):423–444.

Marvin Minsky. 1961. Steps toward artificial intelligence. *Proceedings of the IRE*, 49(1):8–30.

W Rhys Roberts and WD Ross. 2010. *Rhetoric*. Cosimo Classics.

John R Searle. 1969. *Speech acts: An essay in the philosophy of language*. Cambridge university press.

Fabrizio Sebastiani. 2002. Machine learning in automated text categorization. *ACM Comput. Surv.*, 34(1):1–47, March.

María Victoria Escandell Vidal. 2004. Aportaciones de la pragmática. *Vademécum para la formación de profesores. Enseñar español como segunda lengua (12) 1 lengua extranjera (LE)*, pages 179–197.

Svante Wold, Kim Esbensen, and Paul Geladi. 1987. Principal component analysis. *Chemometrics and intelligent laboratory systems*, 2(1):37–52.

Ana Zelaia, Iñaki Alegria, Olatz Arregi, and Basilio Sierra. 2005. Analyzing the effect of dimensionality reduction in document categorization for basque. *Archives of Control Sciences*, 600:202.

Ana Zelaia, Iñaki Alegria, Olatz Arregi, and Basilio Sierra. 2011. A multiclass/multilabel document categorization system: Combining multiple classifiers in a reduced dimension. *Applied Soft Computing*, 11(8):4981–4990.

Iraide Zipitria, Basilio Sierra, Ana Arruarte, and Jon A Elorriaga. 2012. Cohesion grading decisions in a summary evaluation environment: A machine learning approach.

GF Modern Greek Resource Grammar

Ioanna Papadopoulou
University of Gothenburg
ioannapapa78@hotmail.com

Abstract

The paper describes the Modern Greek (MG) Grammar, implemented in Grammatical Framework (GF) as part of the Grammatical Framework Resource Grammar Library (RGL). GF is a special-purpose language for multilingual grammar applications. The RGL is a reusable library for dealing with the morphology and syntax of a growing number of natural languages. It is based on the use of an abstract syntax, which is common for all languages, and different concrete syntaxes implemented in GF. Both GF itself and the RGL are open-source. RGL currently covers more than 30 languages. MG is the 35th language that is available in the RGL. For the purpose of the implementation, a morphology-driven approach was used, meaning a bottom-up method, starting from the formation of words before moving to larger units (sentences). We discuss briefly the main characteristics and grammatical features of MG, and present some of the major difficulties we encountered during the process of implementation and how these are handled in the MG grammar.

1 Introduction

Greek is a member of the Indo-European family of languages and constitutes by itself a separate branch of that family. Modern Greek (MG) can be easily traced back to Ancient Greek in the form of letters, word roots and structures, despite the fact that the language has undergone a series of transformations through the ages and has been a subject of considerable simplification. MG makes use of the Greek alphabet since the 8th century B.C. Today the language is spoken by approximately 13.1 million people worldwide. Some of the general characteristics of MG refer to the diversity of the morphology and the use of an extremely large number of morphological features in order to express grammatical notations. Words are in their majority declinable, whilst each of the syntactic parts of the sentence (subject, object, predicate) is a carrier of a certain case, a fact that allows various word order structures. In addition, the language presents a dynamic syllable stress, whereas its position depends and alternates according to the morphological variations. Moreover, MG is one of the two Indo-European languages[1] that retain a productive synthetic passive formation. In order to realize passivization, verbs use a second set of morphological features for each tense.

2 Grammatical Framework

GF (Ranta, 2011) is a special purpose programming language for developing multilingual applications. It can be used for building translation systems, multilingual web gadgets, natural language interfaces, dialogue systems and natural language resources. GF is capable of parsing and generating texts, while working from a language-independent representation of meaning. The GF Grammar is based on two different modules. An abstract module provides category and function declarations, thus it constitutes a representation of a set of possible trees that reflect the semantically relevant structure of a language, and one or more concrete modules that contain linearization type definitions and rules, therefore managing to relate the tree structures with linear tree representations. The RGL contains the set of grammars of natural languages that are implemented in GF. The parallelism of the grammars is inevitable, given that their development is based on the same rules and functions that are defined in a common abstract syntax. At the moment RGL covers 34 languages[2] that originate not only from the European continent, but from all over the world. The common API defines around 60 hierarchical

[1] The other one being Albanian

[2] http://www.grammaticalframework.org/lib/doc/status.html

grammatical categories, and a large number of syntactic functions. MG constitutes the newest addition to the RGL and its implementation consists of 28 concrete modules.

3 Morphology

Morphology constitutes the most important aspect of the Greek Language. The words are in their majority declinable, produced via a combination of meta-linguistic elements, such as a stem and an ending. The endings are assigned proportionally with the part of speech and the type, and act as carriers of grammatical notations, indicating the gender, the number, the case or the person, or in the case of verbs the tense, the mood, the voice and the aspect as well. Appendix A presents the parameter types and operations that are defined in the grammar. The implementation of the GF MG morphology started from scratch. All declinable words needed to undergo a first simplistic categorization in order to create basic declension tables, before moving to sub-categorizations that allowed us to treat the various irregularities that govern the morphological structure of MG. One of the main aspects of MG is the presence of a dynamic syllable stress, a phenomenon that created additional difficulties in the implementation of the morphology. A stress can move from a stem to an ending but in many cases the movement is realized inside the stem. Such issues are handled in GF with the introduction of pattern matching functions and pattern macros. The MG grammar includes 25 pattern matching functions and macros that indentify stressed vowels, while at the same time they perform over a string, checking the matches, transforming the stressed vowels into their unstressed form, and assigning the stress to the correct character. They also serve to assigning the appropriate case ending or handle irregularities, such as the addition of extra consonants and reduplication cases.

3.1 Declinable Parts of Speech

All nouns, proper nouns, adjectives, determiners, quantifiers, pronouns, participles, articles and verbs in MG are declinable and each category presents its own characteristics and irregularities. The implementation of the above categories follows a similar pattern: we first divide them into the main conjugations that grammars propose and then we make an exhaustive list of all the rules that specify their creation, as well as all the specific features which may affect their formation. The creation of nouns includes 17 distinct functions that are categorized depending on the noun ending, the stress movement, whether the noun is parisyllabic or imparisyllabic, or whether the noun augments its syllables when inflected. These functions also handle specific phenomena of the MG language, such as the change of gender of a noun in the plural form, or nouns that originate from Ancient Greek, and are still used nowadays, retaining intact their form and endings. Similarly 6 functions create adjectives, where we also introduce the degree parameter that creates additional forms for all three adjective genders. The formation of the pronouns is of special interest, as MG makes use of two distinct types, the emphatic and the weak. The weak form[3] occurs more often, whilst the use is always in close connection with verbs, nouns or adverbs. Our grammar introduces both forms of the pronoun, but it also alternates between them when the syntactic structure requires the use of a particular form. Greek proper nouns follow all the declension patterns and irregularities of common nouns morphology, meaning that they are primarily inflected for gender, case and number. Moreover, they present a major differentiation comparing to other languages, which refers to the introduction of the proper noun with a definite article that takes its form according to the grammatical features of the modified proper noun. The morphology of the verb in MG consists of a complex inflection system, as shown in Appendix B. Whilst in many languages, the grammatical notations are expressed with the use primarily of syntax, MG uses the combination of a stem and an inflectional ending to express grammatical categories such as person, number, tense, voice, aspect and mood. The fact that MG retains a productive synthetic passive formation increases drastically the number of possible forms of the verb, as most verbs have a second set of morphological forms for each tense in order to express passivization. Whilst Greek verbs are divided in two main categories, the second one subdivided into two smaller ones, (Holton et al ,1999; Iordanidou, 1999), the creation of the verb morphology in our grammar imposed the consideration of a number of specific parameters, among them the stress movement, the number of syllables which affects on the creation of the

[3] Clitic pronoun

imperative forms, the active stem forms upon which we create the passive stems, the formation of the passive perfective participle, reduplication patterns, internal augmentation phenomena. In addition to the above, we needed to handle various irregularities, which referred mainly to the formation of the imperative or dependent forms, the passivization or not of the verb, the occurrence of a participle, the formation of the active or passive simple past with the use of ending forms borrowed from Ancient Greek. All the above parameters resulted in the creation of 26 main functions that handle the changes in the inflected endings of the verbs, and 39 smaller functions that are connected to the main functions and help us handle the modifications that the stem is subjected to, when conjugated. Moreover, we must emphasize on the necessity to create a series of pattern matching functions that form and alter stems, for the production of the passive perfective according to the active perfective or imperfective, the passive imperative and the participles. A separate concrete module was created in order to deal exclusively with the complex MG verb morphology. Finally, as in the case of personal pronouns, another alternation appears in the formation of the possessive pronouns. Weak and emphatic forms of the possessive pronoun are both used in order to express possession. The first one being the enclitic genitive form of the personal pronoun, while the latter one, expressed via a combination of the definite article, the adjective *δικός* dikós "own" and the enclitic genitive form of the personal pronoun. Both forms are assigned via two different functions, defined in the abstract syntax:

```
PossPron : Pron -> Quant ;
PossNP   : CN -> NP -> CN ;
```

Table 1 presents an example of the main procedure, based on which we created the noun morphology and it is also representative of the process that was followed in order to handle the morphology of the main declinable parts of speech. The example concerns the creation of nouns of neuter gender, ending in –ι, such as the noun *αγόρι* agóri "boy".

Common abstract grammar : categories

```
Cat N ;
```

MG Resource grammar : Resource module

```
Param
Number = Sg | Pl ;
Case = Nom | Gen | Acc | Vocative |CPrep Prepos;
Gender = Masc | Fem | Neut | Change;

oper
Noun : Type = {s : Number => Case => Str ; g : Gender} ;

mkNoun_agori : (s: Str) -> Gender -> Noun =
\agOri,  g ->
  let
    agori = mkStemNouns agOri;
  in {
   s = table { Sg => table {
    Nom | Acc | Vocative|CPrep P_se |CPrep PNul =>
agOri ;
    Gen |CPrep P_Dat=> mkGenSg agori} ;
   Pl => table {
   Nom | Acc | Vocative|CPrep P_se |CPrep PNul =>
mkNomPl agOri;
   Gen |CPrep P_Dat=> mkGen agOri}} ; g = g } ;

mkStemNouns : Str -> Str = \s -> case s of {
 c + v@(#stressedVowel) + x@(_ + _) =>c + unstress
v + x } ;

mkGenSg : Str -> Str = \s ->
  case s of
  {x + "ος"  => x + "ους";  ............
   x + ("ι" | "υ")  => x + "ιού"; };

mkGen : Str -> Str = \s -> case s of {
   c + "άι" => c + "αγιών" ; ............
   c + v@(#stressedVowel) + x@(_ + _) + ("ι" | "υ")
=>c + unstress v +  x + "ιών" ; ............ } ;

stressedVowel : pattern Str = #("ά" | "ό" | "ί"| "έ" |
"ή" | "ύ"| "ώ" | "εύ");

stress : Str -> Str = \x -> case x of {
      "α" => "ά" ;
      "ο" => "ό" ; ........ };
```

MG Paradigms : Paradigms module

```
mkN = overload {
   mkN : (dentro : Str) ->  N
      = \n -> lin N (regN n) ;
   mkN : (s : Str)  -> Gender -> N
      = \n,g -> lin N (mkN1 n g) ;..................};

mkN1 : Str -> Gender -> N = \x,g ->
     case x of {................
       c + ("ι"|"υ"|"όι"|"άι") => mkNoun_agori x  g ;
       ............... } ** {lock_N = <>} ;
```

Lexicon :abstract	**fun** boy_N : N ;
Lexicon MG	**lin** boy_N = mkN "αγόρι" Neut;
Lexicon English	**lin** boy_N = mkN masculine (regN "boy") ;

Parsing into the abstract categories

```
Lang> parse –cat=N –lang=Gre "αγοριών"
boy_N

Lang> parse –cat=N –lang=Eng "boys'"
```

boy_N
Generating the full inflectional paradigms
Lang> linearize -lang=Gre -table boy_N s Sg Nom : αγόρι s Sg Gen : αγοριού s Sg Acc : αγόρι s Sg Vocative : αγόρι s Sg (CPrep P_se) : αγόρι s Sg (CPrep PNul) : αγόρι s Sg (CPrep P_Dat) : αγοριού s Pl Nom : αγόρια s Pl Gen : αγοριών s Pl Acc : αγόρια s Pl Vocative : αγόρια s Pl (CPrep P_se) : αγόρια s Pl (CPrep PNul) : αγόρια s Pl (CPrep P_Dat) : αγοριών
Lang> linearize -lang=Eng -table boy_N s Sg Nom : boy s Sg Gen : boy's s Pl Nom : boys s Pl Gen : boys'

Table 1: The Noun Morphology

4 Syntax

The GF abstract syntax provides rules for all the common phrase structures: noun phrases (constructed of pronouns, proper nouns or common nouns and their modifiers), adjectival and verb phrases with their complements. The MG grammar covers all the above structures and successfully correlates the language with the various languages included in the RGL. Due to the fact that MG is a highly inflected language and given that the various morphological features express grammatical notations, the word order in a phrase is relatively free. Although all six logical permutations of the major clausal constituents are usually considered grammatically correct (Tzanidaki, 1995), SVO[4] remains the predominant word order. The implemented rules in our grammar cover mainly the most common word order, unless the syntactic mechanisms of the phrase itself require otherwise.

4.1 Clauses

The formation of the clause relies on a number of parameters, namely the order, the tense, the polarity and the mood. In main indicative clauses the tense defines the point of time of the verb in relation to the time of speaking. MG has 8 tenses that are divided in three major categories: those that refer to the Present, the Past and the Future and denoting whether the action expressed by the verb is viewed either as occurring repeatedly, as a completed event, or as an event completed in the past, whose completion is relevant to some other point in time. Noun phrases (NP) represent the subject of the sentence and thus, they appear in the nominative case, while agreement rules pass the grammatical features of the NP to the form of the verb. For the creation of the predication rule in our grammar, which forms a clause, we needed to take into consideration the presence of subject NPs that present a negative connotation (i.e. *κανένας* kanénas "nobody") and impose the use of a negative polarity in the clause. Accordingly, we are making a distinction between the different moods, in order to assign the relevant particles that introduce the clause and which also vary depending on the polarity. Interrogative sentences do not defer from declarative sentences, in the sense that they use the exact same rules applied in declarations, while they are simply characterized by the addition of the question mark (;). *Wh*–questions are introduced with an interrogative word which may be indeclinable *τι* ti "what" or declinable for gender, number and case: *ποιός-ποιά-ποιό* poiós-poiá-poió "who". The selection of the appropriate gender of the interrogative word in our grammar is a subject of interest. Whilst in most cases the masculine gender is used as an abstract gender when introducing *wh*-questions, in particular contexts, when the gender of the subject under question is known, the interrogative word should be labeled by the gender of the known subject, without that implying that the use of the masculine gender in such cases in considered semantically incorrect. Relative clauses on the other hand, present a more complex syntactic structure and a number of possible alternations, as they are introduced by two main types of relative markers: the indeclinable *που* pou "that, which" or the declinable relative pronoun *ο οποίος* o opoíos "which". The MG grammar provides both forms and utilizes the two different relative markers, as the form alternates when its syntactic function in the relative clause requires a genitive, or when it appears in a prepositional or adverbial phrase. The antecedent of a relative sentence might appear in the form not only of a noun phrase but also of a sentence, as in the phrase "She sleeps, which is good". When the antecedent is sentential, the relative clause can be introduced either with *που* pou "that" or with the relative pronoun *ο οποίος* o opoíos "which",

---

4 Subject-Verb-Object

which appears mandatory in the neuter gender form. As Chatsiou (2010) notes, the use of the neuter gender is explained by the fact that the relative clause does not actually take a sentence as an antecedent, but it rather modifies an omitted or implied noun, such as *πράγμα* prágma "thing" or *γεγονός* gegonós "fact".

4.2 Verb Phrases

Verb phrases are constructed from verbs by providing their complements, whilst GF provides one rule for each verb category. Appendix C presents examples of verb complementation. Appropriate agreement rules are specified for the complementation of verbs that take one or more arguments, namely the accusative case for direct objects and a prepositional phrase or a genitive for indirect objects. The lack of infinite in MG created additional difficulties in the construction of verb phrases. While in many languages the embedded clause is infinitival, the verbal complementation in MG is realized via the use of finite subjunctive forms, which implies that in all cases, the sentence should show a subject or object agreement. Phrases in English such as "*I want to buy an apple*", that use the infinitive form of the verb *buy*, without any marking for person or number, can only be attributed in MG after considering the properties of the subject of the main clause, which becomes the subject of the verb of the subordinate clause. On the other hand, in order to achieve object agreement, it was necessary to create an extra record type that handles the object control complement. The creation of phrases such as "*I beg her to go*" is a typical case. The verb *beg* takes an NP complement, the direct object (*her*), which in MG has the form of a weak clitic pronoun, placed before the verb. In the subordinate clause, the NP complement becomes the subject of the verb *go*, and passes its number and person in the form of the embedded verb.

I beg her to go.
Εγώ την παρακαλάω να πάει.
Egō tin parakaláō na páei
I her-clit,acc,P3,Sg beg to go-P3,Sg,subj
I beg *her* (that *she* goes)

The same rule applies in cases of adjectival complementation, where, similarly, the NP complement should agree in gender and number with the adjective.

I paint them black
Εγώ τους βάφω μαύρους
Egō tous váphō maúrous
I them-*clit,acc,Masc,Pl* paint black-*acc,Masc,Pl*

4.3 Noun and Adjectival Phrases, Participles

As in most inflectional languages, where the constituents of the phrase are carriers of grammatical notations, MG noun phrases present a consistency in the phrase terms that is realized via the use of agreement rules: the gender, the number and the case of the noun or adjective should reflect in all the terms that define it. Moreover, the use of the definite article presents an extended necessity. Nouns are usually accompanied by a definite article, whilst this applies even in the case of proper nouns. The modification of NPs with participles is of special interest. In GF these constructions are assigned via functions that connect an NP and a transitive verb in order to create the participial NP (*the man tied*). Although MG makes wider use of a relative clause to express such structures, in the presence of a participle, the syntactic rules would suggest that it must be placed before the noun it is attributed to. Thus, it would be necessary to split the NP in its constituents, in order to introduce the participle before the noun and after the determiner. To handle this construction, the MG grammar creates polydefinite structures (Lekakou and Szendroi, 2012), where both the noun and the participle are each accompanied by their own determiner.

4.4 Idiomatic Expressions

The GF grammar deals with idiomatic expressions in a special module and manages to handle constructions that are formed in fixed ways, such as generic and impersonal clauses. The copula verb *είμαι eímai "to be"* used in the third person of singular accompanied by an adverb in the comparative form or by a neuter adjective used adverbially, can form impersonal clauses:

```
ImpersCl vp=predVP [](Ag Neut Sg P3)vp ;
```

Although MG makes use of two main moods, the indicative and the subjunctive, the latter one introduced with the particle *να* na "to" in sentences with positive polarity and μήν min "not" in cases of negation, our grammar required the addition of an extra mood form, the Hortative, in order to form imperative sentences where the speaker makes a suggestion or a wish i.e. the English sentences "let's go" or "let John go", which in MG , according to Chondrogianni (2011) are introduced with the hortative particle *ας* as "let".

5 Evaluation

The purpose of the evaluation of the grammar was not only to assess the correctness of the grammar but also to provide a proof- reading and verify the coverage of the resource library. The evaluation was conducted with the use of a test set, which includes 440 automatically – generated test examples, utilized in the Synopsis of the RGL[5] as well as 27 test definitions used in Khegai (2006). The test set provides linearization of trees, as seen in Appendix D, both in English and in MG, in order to assess the correctness of the MG translations, and it is organized in such way that it includes all the rules in the grammar and all possible combinations of the categories. The evaluation revealed a number of interesting findings. Some examples were indicative of the way a term can have a different lexical linearization, depending on the context in which it appears. Such is the adjective old (παλιός/ paliós), which was, initially, translated in our concrete Lexicon bearing the sense of something that is not new. That resulted in sentences such as *αυτός ο παλιός άνδρας* autós o paliós ándras "this old man", that, although syntactically correct, they fail in a semantic level, as the term *παλιός* is attributed to inanimate objects, whilst the sense of something that has lived for a long time requires a different lexical approach. Another observation refers to the use of the definite article, mainly with the presence of the mass noun or in apposition constructions. Whilst mass nouns are marked by the absence of the article, certain constructions in MG require its use in order to render a phrase grammatically correct. In addition, the test showed that some constructions predetermined in the abstract syntax, although they do not generate ungrammatical instances, they fail to produce outcomes that would constitute the predominant syntactic structure. Such is the case of the use of a relative clause, instead of a participial construction, when the semantic function of the verb requires it. The above findings concerned 15 of the sample sentences, out of which 9 referred to the use of the adjective old (παλιός/ paliós). With the exception of cases that are associated mainly with semantic and pragmatic connotations, which nonetheless are not the focus of the resource grammar, not major obstacles were encountered in the application of the MG resource grammar.

[5]http://www.grammaticalframework.org/lib/doc/synopsis.html

6 Related Work

Not many available computational grammars are noted for MG. One of the available grammars refers to MG Resource Grammar (Poulis et al 2005), built upon the theoretical framework of Head Driven Phrase Structure Grammar (Pollard and Sag, 1994). The implementation of the grammar is realized in the LKB grammar development system (Copestake, 2002), whilst the writing and testing makes use of LinGo Grammar Matrix tool (Bender et al, 2002) in order to implement quickly as many phenomena of the language as possible. The grammar concentrates on the implementation of a number of phenomena, such as locative alternation, word order, cliticization, politeness constructions and clitic left dislocation and it comes with a test suite, whilst the system provides a syntactic analysis for the test items. Another attempt refers to the large-scale systemic functional grammar of MG, developed by Dimitromanolaki et al (2001), in the context of M-PIRO, a multilingual natural language generation project, and based on descriptions of museum exhibits, generated automatically in three languages from a single database source. The grammar follows the approach of systemic grammars that are primarily concerned with the functions of the language, and with the way that these functions are mapped into surface forms.

7 Conclusion and Future Work

The result of the current work is the development and implementation of MG in GF. The grammar manages to correlate MG with the various other languages in the RGL. The current work consists of 28 concrete modules, covering orthographical, morphological and syntactic variations of the language. The testing and evaluation of the MG grammar revealed a high percentage of accuracy in the translation of English sentences to MG. At the same time it verified the complexity of MG and the challenges in the implementation. Future work refers mainly to providing a number of possible alternations in some constructions, namely the various word order structures or the different structures related to participial NPs. In addition, the coverage of language specific features is desirable, namely phenomena of clitic doubling and left dislocation, as well as fronted/focal constructions.

References

Aarne Ranta. 2011. *Grammatical Framework: Programming with multilingual grammars*. CSLI Publications, Stanford.

Aggeliki Dimitromanolaki, Ion Androutsopoulos, Vangelis Karkaletsis .2001. *A large scale systemic functional grammar of Greek*, 5th International Conference of Greek Linguistics, Sorbonne.

Aikaterini Chatsiou.2010. *An LFG Approach to Modern Greek Relative Clauses*. Ph.D. thesis, Department of Language and Linguistics, University of Essex.

Alexandros Poulis,Valia Kordoni, Julia Neu. 2005. *Implementation of a Modern Greek Grammar Fragment, using the LKB System and the LinGO Grammar Matrix*, Documentation, Department of Computational Linguistics, University of Saarland.

Ann Copestake. 2002. *Implementing Typed Feature Structure Grammars*. CSLI Publications

Anna Iordanidou. 1999. *Ta Rimata Tis Neas Ellinikis. 4, 500 Rimata 235 Ypodeigmata Klisis - 4500 Modern Greek Verbs* [in Greek],Patakis Publishers,Athens.

Carl Pollard and Ivan A. Sag. 1994. *Head-Driven Phrase Structure Grammar*. Chicago: University of Chicago Press.

David Holton, Peter Mackridge, Irene Philippaki-Warburton. 1999. *Greek: a Comprehensive grammar of the Modern language* [in Greek], Patakis Publishers, Athens.

Dimitra I. Tzanidaki. 1995. *Greek word order: towards a new approach*, UCL Working Papers in Linguistics.

Emily M. Bender, Dan Flickinger,Stephan Oepen. 2002. *The Grammar Matrix : An open source starter-kit for the rapid development of cross-linguistically consistent broad-coverage precision grammars.*In Proceedings of of COLING 2002 Workshop on Grammar Engineering and Evaluation,Taipei, Taiwan

Janna Khegai. 2006. *Language engineering in Grammatical Framework(GF)*. Phd thesis, Computer Science, Chalmers University of Technology.

Maria Chondrogianni. 2011. *The Pragmatics of Prohibitive and Hortative in MG*, in Kitis E., Lavidas N., Topintzi N. & Tsangalidis T. (eds.) Selected papers from the 19th International Symposium on Theoretical and Applied Linguistics (19 ISTAL, April 2009)pp. 135-142, Thessaloniki: Monochromia.

Marina Lekakou and Kriszta Szendroi. 2012. *Polydefinites in Greek: Ellipsis, close apposition and expletive determiners*, Journal of Linguistics , Volume 48, Issue 01, March 2012, pp 107-149.

Appendix A. Parameter Types and Operation Definitions

```
param

Case = Nom| Gen| Acc| Vocative| CPrep
    Prepos;
Gender = Masc | Fem | Neut | Change;
Agr    = Ag Gender Number Person ;
Mood   = Ind | Con | Hortative;
TTense =TPres | TPast| TFut | TCond |TImperf;
CardOrd = NCard Gender Case| NCardX |NOrd
  Gender Number Case ;
DForm = unit  |  teen | ten | hundr isVowel ;
isVowel = Is | isNot ;
Aspect = Perf | Imperf ;
Order = Main | Inv ;
Form = Weak |Emphatic ;
VForm =
     VPres Mood Number Person Voice Aspect|
     VPast Mood Number Person Voice Aspect|
     VNonFinite Voice|
     VImperative Aspect Number Voice|
     Gerund  |
     Participle Degree Gender Number Case;
Voice = Active | Passive;
Prepos =  P_se | PNul | P_Dat;

oper

  AAgr : Type = {g : Gender ; n : Number} ;
  VP = { v : Verb ;  clit,clit2 : Str ; comp
   : Agr => Str ; isNeg : Bool ; voice :
   Voice ; aspect :Aspect};
  NounPhrase = { s : Case  =>  {c1,c2,comp :
   Str ; isClit : Bool } ; a : Agr;
   isNeg:Bool};
  Noun : Type = {s : Number => Case => Str ;
    g : Gender} ;
  Adj  : Type = {s : Degree => Gender =>
    Number => Case => Str ; adv : Degree =>
    Str } ;
  Adv  : Type = {s :  Str } ;
  Verb : Type = {s : VForm => Str } ;
  Det  : Type = {s : Gender => Case => Str ;
     n : Number};
  PName : Type = {s : Number => Case => Str ;
     g : Gender} ;
  Pronoun : Type = { s : Case => {c1,c2,comp:
     Str ; isClit : Bool } ; a : Agr; poss :
     Str } ;
  Preposition = {s : Str ; c : Case} ;
  Quantifier  = {s : Bool => Gender => Number
     => Case => Str ; sp : Gender => Number
     => Case  => Str ; isNeg:Bool } ;
  Compl : Type ={s : Str ; c : Case ; isDir :
     Bool} ;
```

Appendix B. Verbs of First Conjugation

```
mkVerb1 :
(x1,x2,x3,x4,x5,x6,x7,x8,x9,x10,x11,x12,x13,x
14,x15 : Str) -> Verb = \paIzw, paIksw,
Epeksa, Epeza, paIz,paIks, Epeks, Epez, De,
p, p1, Imp, Imp2, Imp3 ,part->
  {
s = table {
 VPres Ind Sg P1 Active _ => paIzw ;
 VPres Ind Sg P2 Active _ => paIz + "εις" ;
 VPres Ind Sg P3 Active _=> paIz + "ει" ;
```

```
VPres Ind Pl P1 Active _ => paIz+ "ουμε" ;
VPres Ind Pl P2 Active _ => paIz + "ετε" ;
VPres Ind Pl P3 Active _ => paIz + "ουν" ;
VPres Ind Sg P1 Passive _ => paIz + "ομαι" ;
VPres Ind Sg P2 Passive _ => paIz + "εσαι" ;
VPres Ind Sg P3 Passive _=> paIz + "εται" ;
VPres Ind Pl P1 Passive _=> p + "όμαστε" ;
VPres Ind Pl P2 Passive _ => paIz + "εστε" ;
VPres Ind Pl P3 Passive _ => paIz +"ονται" ;
VPres _ Sg P1 Active _ => paIksw ;
VPres _ Sg P2 Active _ => paIks + "εις" ;
VPres _ Sg P3 Active _ => paIks + "ει" ;
VPres _ Pl P1 Active _=> paIks + "ουμε" ;
VPres _ Pl P2 Active _ => paIks + "ετε" ;
VPres _ Pl P3 Active _ => paIks + "ουν" ;
VPres _ Sg P1 Passive _ => pl + "ώ" ;
VPres _ Sg P2 Passive _ => pl + "είς" ;
VPres _ Sg P3 Passive _ => pl + "εί" ;
VPres _ Pl P1 Passive _ => pl + "ούμε" ;
VPres _ Pl P2 Passive _ => pl + "είτε" ;
VPres _ Pl P3 Passive _ => pl + "ούν" ;
VPast _ Sg P1 Active Perf => Epeksa ;
VPast _ Sg P2 Active Perf=> Epeks +"ες" ;
VPast _ Sg P3 Active Perf => Epeks +"ε" ;
VPast _ Pl P1 Active Perf =>paIks+"αμε" ;
VPast _ Pl P2 Active Perf =>paIks+"ατε" ;
VPast _ Pl P3 Active Perf => Epeks+"αν" ;
VPast _ Sg P1 Passive Perf => De +"ηκα" ;
VPast _ Sg P2 Passive Perf => De+"ηκες" ;
VPast _ Sg P3 Passive Perf => De +"ηκε" ;
VPast _ Pl P1 Passive Perf =>pl+"ήκαμε" ;
VPast _ Pl P2 Passive Perf=> pl+"ήκατε" ;
VPast _ Pl P3 Passive Perf => De+"ηκαν" ;
VPast _ Sg P1 Active Imperf => Epeza ;
VPast _ Sg P2 Active Imperf =>Epez+ "ες";
VPast _ Sg P3 Active Imperf => Epez +"ε";
VPast _ Pl P1 Active Imperf =>paIz+"αμε";
VPast _ Pl P2 Active Imperf =>paIz+"ατε";
VPast _ Pl P3 Active Imperf => Epez+"αν";
VPast _ Sg P1 Passive Imperf=>p+"όμουν";
VPast _ Sg P2 Passive Imperf=>p+"όσουν";
VPast _ Sg P3 Passive Imperf =>p+"όταν";
VPast _ Pl P1 Passive Imperf=>p+"όμασταν";
VPast _ Pl P2 Passive Imperf=>p+"όσασταν";
VPast _Pl P3 Passive Imperf=>p+"όντουσαν";
VNonFinite Active  => paIks + "ει";
VNonFinite Passive  => pl + "εί";
VImperative Perf Sg Active=> Imp2 ;
VImperative Perf Pl Active => Imp ;
VImperative Imperf Sg  Active => Imp3  ;
VImperative Imperf Pl Active =>paIz+"ετε";
VImperative _  Sg Passive = mkImperPassive
                              paIks + "ου";
VImperative _ Pl Passive => pl + "είτε" ;
Gerund => paIz + "οντας" ;
Participle d  g n c => (regAdj part).s !d!
      g !n !c}};
```

Appendix C. Verb Complementation Examples

```
  ComplVV v vp =
    insertComplement (\\a => case a of {
    Ag _ n p  => let
       vo= vp.voice ;
       as = vp.aspect  in
 "να" ++ vp.clit  ++ vp.clit2 ++ vp.v.s !
 VPres Con n p vo as ++ vp.comp ! a})
 (predV v) ;

 SlashV2V v vp = mkVPSlash v.c2 (predV v)
  ** {  n3 = \\a =>
        let agr = clitAgr a ;
        vo = vp.voice ;
           as = vp.aspect
       in
        v.c3.s  ++ "να" ++ vp.clit ++ vp.clit2
        ++ vp.v.s ! VPres Con agr.n agr.p vo
        as ++ vp.comp! a  ;
        c2 = v.c2
       } ;

    ComplSlash vp np = insertObject vp.c2 np
     (insertComplement (\\a => vp.c2.s  ++
      vp.n3 ! np.a ) vp )  ;
```

Appendix D. Example of the Test Set

```
mkUtt (mkNP (mkNP john_PN) (mkRS (mkRCl
which_RP (mkVP walk_V))))
John , who walks
ο Γιάννης , που περπατά

mkUtt (mkNP or_Conj (mkNP this_Det woman_N)
(mkNP john_PN))
this woman or John
αυτή η γυναίκα ή ο Γιάννης

mkUtt (mkNP or_Conj (mkListNP (mkNP this_Det
woman_N) (mkListNP (mkNP john_PN) i_NP)))
this woman , John or I
αυτή η γυναίκα , ο Γιάννης ή εγώ

mkUtt (mkCN big_A house_N  )
big house
μεγάλο σπίτι

mkUtt (mkCN big_A (mkCN blue_A house_N))
big blue house
μεγάλο μπλέ σπίτι

mkUtt (mkCN (mkAP very_AdA big_A) house_N  )
very big house
πολύ μεγάλο σπίτι

mkUtt (mkCN (mkAP very_AdA big_A) (mkCN
blue_A house_N)  )
very big blue house
πολύ μεγάλο μπλέ σπίτι
```

Collection, Annotation and Analysis of Gold Standard Corpora for Knowledge-Rich Context Extraction in Russian and German

Anne-Kathrin Schumann
Saarland University/University of Vienna
anne.schumann@mx.uni-saaarland.de

Abstract

This paper describes the collection, annotation and linguistic analysis of a gold standard for knowledge-rich context extraction on the basis of Russian and German web corpora as part of ongoing PhD thesis work. In the following sections, the concept of knowledge-rich contexts is refined and gold standard creation is described. Linguistic analyses of the gold standard data and their results are explained.

1 Introduction

Defining statements have long been recognised as a fundamental means of knowledge transfer. Corpus-based research on the description and automated extraction of such statements has produced results for a variety of languages, e.g. English (Pearson, 1998; Meyer, 2001; Muresan and Klavans 2002; Marshman; 2008), French (Malaisé et al., 2005), Spanish (Sierra et al., 2008), German (Storrer and Wellinghoff, 2006; Walter, 2010; Cramer, 2011), Slovenian (Fišer et al., 2010), "Slavic" (Przepiórkowski et al., 2007), Portuguese (Del Gaudio and Branco, 2007) and Dutch (Fahmi and Bouma, 2006; Westerhout, 2009). These studies describe linguistic properties of defining statements, lexico-syntactic patterns or extraction grammars. Not all of them report results of extraction experiments, but many of the papers that do so combine linguistically informed extraction methods with machine learning or heuristic filtering methods.

Only few studies, however, provide a systematic description of the gold standard annotation process (with Walter, 2010, and Cramer, 2011, being notable exceptions), although the identification of defining statements is a non-trivial issue and reliable data is needed for the comparison of experimental results. Moreover, descriptions of the linguistic properties of defining statements, including statistical studies, seem to be largely missing, while results of small-scale studies suggest that the amount of variation in empirical data is not appropriately depicted by the literature (Walter, 2010).

In this paper, we focus on the description of the gold standard annotation process for two languages, namely Russian and German. For Russian, research in the field is still restricted to isolated efforts, whereas for German different kinds of definitions (Walter, 2010, studies legal definitions whereas Cramer, 2011, focuses on lay definitions from web corpora) have been studied. We also provide information concerning the linguistic annotation of the gold standard data and linguistic analyses aimed at revealing typical linguistic properties of knowledge-rich contexts.

2 Knowledge-Rich Contexts and Definitions

Knowledge-rich contexts (KRCs) can be described as pieces of text that may be helpful in a conceptual analysis task. Such tasks are usually performed in the context of terminology work and translation which constitute the main application area of the present work. Examples 1 and 2 present KRCs found in our data.

For a more formal definition of KRCs, it is important to consider that KRC extraction is related to the development of terminological knowledge bases (Meyer et al., 1992) and concept systems. These systems stress the relevance of semantic relations holding between concepts. Consequently, KRC extraction aims at identifying contexts for specialised terms that provide semantic information about the underlying concepts, including information about semantic relations between concepts (see ISO 1087-1: 2000). Moreover, KRCs are related to a set of minimal validity criteria that, however, are less strict than the criteria applied to definitions.

In practice, the boundary between definitions and KRCs is not always clear. Several of the

1) Альтернативный источник энергии — способ, устройство или сооружение, позволяющее получать электрическую энергию (или другой требуемый вид энергии) и заменяющий собой традиционные источники энергии, функционирующие на нефти, добываемом природном газе и угле.
[An alternative source of energy is a method, a machine or a construction that enables the production of electrical (or of another, necessary kind of) energy, thus substituting traditional sources of energy based on oil, natural gas or coal.]

2) Das Verhältnis Energieertrag („Output") zu Input wird Leistungszahl genannt.
[The relation between energy output and input is called coefficient of performance.]

above-mentioned studies employ the term "definition", whereas the types of "definitions" subsumed under this term vary considerably. For our own work, we assume that definitions are subtypes of KRCs which echo the categories of "proper definition", "redundant definition", "complete definition" and "partial definition" as introduced by Bierwisch and Kiefer (1969) while covering a larger set of semantic relations, e.g. those relations that are relevant to terminological tasks, and satisfying less strict formal criteria.

3 Gold Standard Creation

The gold standard was created in three steps:

- In a *first step*, corpora were collected and KRC candidates were manually selected for annotation. Subcorpora were created to contain annotated KRCs.
- In a *second step*, more KRC candidates were selected from the subcorpora and annotated.
- In a *third step*, the gold standard was consolidated by applying qualitative criteria to the output of the previous two annotation steps.

3.1 Corpus Collection

Russian and German web corpora were crawled using the Babouk corpus crawling engine (de Groc, 2011). The web was chosen as our source of data since for many languages and specialised topics it offers a yet fairly unassessed wealth of data that can hardly be provided by traditional offline resources. Moreover, language workers use online resources extensively while the internet itself, given its known properties such as redundancy and noisiness (Fletcher 2004), has not yet been evaluated with respect to its usefulness for conceptual analysis tasks. Table 1 gives an overview over the Babouk corpora. The german_dev corpus was created within the TTC project[1].

Corpus	Domains	Tokens
russian_dev	cars	~350,000
russian_test	nuclear energy, cars, physics, …	~1,010,000
german_dev	wind energy	~990,000
german_test	IT, alternative energy sources, energy supply	~7,270,000

Table 1: Web corpora crawled with Babouk

From these corpora, KRC candidates (full sentences) were selected by the author, a trained translator, by manually inspecting a part of the texts in each corpus. The selection criteria were:

- the candidate must contain potentially relevant information for a conceptual analysis task,
- it must embody at least one of the following semantic relations: hyperonymy/hyponymy, meronymy, process, position, causality, origin, function, reference,
- at least one target term (a definiendum) can be identified as argument of one of the above-mentioned semantic relations,
- the information provided by the candidate must be currently valid (use of present tense) or temporal restrictions must be clearly marked,
- the candidate must at least be roughly attributable to one domain of interest,
- the information provided by the candidate must be generalisable or shed light on one interesting aspect of the definiendum.

[1] www.ttc-project.eu. The word counts were obtained from the linux wc function on the raw corpora.

Each candidate KRC together with at least one previously annotated definiendum candidate was then presented to two independent annotators, namely Master students of translation. Each annotator was a native speaker of the respective language and had been acquainted with the established validity criteria during an introductory seminar. Annotators were asked to give a simple binary assessment of the KRC status of each KRC candidate given the above validity criteria. For positive judgements, annotators were also asked to give a simple binary assessment of their annotation confidence (1 = "not very confident", 2 = "confident", hence the interval of average confidence for each annotator ranges between 1 and 2). Table 2 summarizes the results of this step by giving acceptance rates and average confidence for each annotator and corpus. Under "agreement", the table also summarises absolute and relative values for agreement on KRC validity judgements and confidence agreement (agreement on "high" and "low" confidence for a given candidate) for those KRCs in the gold standard that were marked "valid" by both annotators. Based on the results of this step, small sub-corpora were extracted from the web corpora to contain the KRC candidates agreed upon by all annotators.

3.2 Annotation Refinement

To achieve maximum coverage of the KRC annotation in the sub-corpora, we manually went through all four sub-corpora again to identify KRC candidates that may have been missed in the first candidate selection step. These new candidates were passed to four new annotators – two native speakers and experienced translators for each language – along with the same annotation criteria. This step resulted in the data summarised in table 3.

3.3 Discussion and Final Gold Standard Creation

Bierwisch and Kiefer (1969) are among the first to point out that linguistic criteria do not fully explain whether a statement can be considered defining or not. Cramer (2011) conducts extensive definition annotation experiments, concluding that the annotators' individual stance towards a candidate statement and the corresponding text, knowledge of the domain and other criteria influence whether a statement is considered defining. For a terminological setting, this is problematic, since these characteristics can be controlled only if the target users are known (e.g. in a small company setting, but not in the case of an online termbase).

The results of our own (small) annotation experiment seem to support Cramer's (2011) claim that individual criteria of the annotators influence the annotation process, resulting in different rates of acceptance/rejection and varying levels of confidence as summarised in tables 2 and 3: Although all annotators marked the vast majority of the KRC candidates presented to them as "valid", average confidence varies considerably between annotators, but also between corpora and annotation cycles. The different confidence levels and acceptance rates of the individual annotators indeed suggest that annotators develop individual annotation strategies while sudden confidence jumps (or drops) with, however, stable acceptance rates may be the result of changes in these strategies that, however, cannot be linked directly to linguistic criteria. Agreement seems to be generally higher in the first annotation cycle for both Russian and German which may be an effect of a more admissive pre-selection of candidates for the second cycle resulting in a potentially lower quality of candidates. The slightly, but consistently higher values achieved for russian_test in comparison to russian_dev may be an effect of the less 'technical' material in this corpus, since russian_dev contains a considerable amount of instructional texts which may not suit the annotators' expectations.

κ scores, if computed on the data, are low, however, it seems questionable whether they are applicable to this voting task in which no clearly negative examples were presented to the annotators. Moreover, it is unclear which κ level would be acceptable for a task as complex and fuzzy as this one. Finally, the small number of annotators (1 for the complete sub-corpora, 2 more for each pre-selected KRC candidate) does not allow for statistical generalisations concerning the KRC status of the annotated candidates. Given these reasons, we decided to apply qualitative criteria in order to improve the consistency of the data, e.g. by spotting false negatives (KRC candidates wrongly marked as "invalid" by at least one annotator) and false positives (KRC candidates wrongly marked as "valid" by the annotators). For example, we removed KRC candidates from the gold standard that had been annotated more than once, that turned out to be not compliant with the validity criteria, were longer than one sentence or that

Corpora	Annotators				Agreement	
	De1		*De2*			
	proportion of KRC candidates marked as "valid"	average confidence	proportion of KRC candidates marked as "valid"	average confidence	agreement on positive and negative judgements	agreement on high and low confidence
german_dev	347 (93%)	1.66	341 (92%)	1.84	326 (88%)	185 (68%)
german_test	290 (97%)	1.70	263 (88%)	1.83	262 (88%)	162 (70%)
	Ru1		*Ru2*			
russian_dev	289 (97%)	1.98	294 (98%)	1.83	290 (97%)	198 (83%)
russian_test	229 (100%)	1.99	225 (98%)	1.85	225 (98%)	159 (90%)

Table 2: Results of the first annotation cycle

Corpora	Annotators				Agreement	
	De3		*De4*			
	proportion of KRC candidates marked as "valid"	average confidence	proportion of KRC candidates marked as "valid"	average confidence	agreement on positive and negative judgements	agreement on high and low confidence
german_dev	63 (79%)	1.71	66 (83%)	1.50	51 (64%)	21 (46%)
german_test	45 (82%)	1.53	45 (82%)	1.51	41 (75%)	18 (50%)
	Ru3		*Ru4*			
russian_dev	64 (88%)	1.80	64 (88%)	1.59	65 (89%)	27 (63%)
russian_test	99 (94%)	1.86	102 (97%)	1.75	98 (93%)	67 (80%)

Table 3: Results of the second annotation cycle.

exhibited strongly erroneous language. With respect to boundary cases or linguistic defects of the KRCs, the resulting gold standard seems to be rather inclusive. Table 4 summarises the finalised gold standard.

Corpus	Tokens	KRCs
sub_german_dev	~ 160,000	337
sub_german_test	~ 170,000	295
sub_russian_dev	~ 99,000	292
sub_russian_test	~ 75,000	268

Table 4: Overview over finalised gold standard[2].

3.4 Coverage of the Annotation

Since one of the aims of the annotation was to achieve maximum coverage of identified KRCs in the gold corpora, we estimated the percentage of inadvertently missed KRCs in each sub-corpus, that is, we estimated an error rate based on KRC candidate misses. To this end, we randomly selected 500 sentences from each sub-corpus and assessed them with respect to their KRC status (given the validity criteria): Identified KRCs were counted as wanted hits, non-KRCs as wanted misses. Potential KRCs that had not been included in any of the annotation cycles were counted as unwanted misses. Based on these analyses, we calculated the proportion of unwanted misses along with 95% confidence intervals on each sub-corpus (see Sachs and Hedderich, 2009). The maximum proportion resulted to be of 0.02 (10 sentences on sub_german_test), resulting in a confidence interval of [0.0096, 0.0365]. We conclude that the proportion of unidentified (and thus unannotated) KRC candidates in our data is unlikely to be above 4% and therefore lies within still acceptable limits.

4 Corpus Annotation

The corpora crawled by Babouk come as plain text files along with separate XML headers containing metadata such as the online source of the text, seed terms used for crawling and the date when the text was extracted from the web. We performed preprocessing and linguistic annotation of the gold standard corpora and then formatted the data in XML. In a first step, we

[2] Word counts were obtained again with the linux wc function after sentence splitting.

used the Perl Lingua::Sentence module[3] for splitting the Russian and German corpora into single sentences. Exact duplicate sentences were removed with a simple Perl script. On all subcorpora, we performed POS tagging, lemmatisation and dependency parsing. Tagging and lemmatisation was performed for Russian using TreeTagger (Schmid, 1994) along with the tagset developed by Sharoff et al. (2008)[4]. For parsing Russian we used the model and pipeline for MaltParser (Nivre et al., 2007) provided by Sharoff and Nivre (2011). For the linguistic annotation of the German corpora we used the Mate toolsuite (Bohnet, 2010).

A simple XML format was developed for all Russian and German corpora. In this format, each token is annotated with the linguistic information outputted by the analysis tools. Moreover, a boolean attribute "isterm" is used to indicate whether a token matches one of the definienda identified as target terms during the gold standard annotation process for each corpus. KRCs identified during the annotation process are kept in tab-separated files together with their respective definienda and the annotators' confidence votes.

5 Linguistic Analyses

5.1 Method

Linguistic analyses of the gold standard KRCs were performed in order to arrive at a description of the specific linguistic properties of the KRCs. More specifically, we studied frequencies of different phenomena comparing the KRC data with an equal amount of randomly selected non-KRCs from the gold standard corpora as well as with frequencies from two non-specialised web corpus samples, a 2011 news crawl from the Leipzig corpus portal for German (NCL, Quasthoff et al., 2006) and an older version of the Russian internet corpus (RIC, Sharoff, 2006). We believe that with this double comparison we can distinguish between differences that occur between texts with a different level of specialisation (gold vs. RIC and gold vs. NCL) and differences that mark a stable feature of our gold data as compared to non-KRCs (KRCs vs. non-KRCs from the gold corpora). The Chi-Square and Fisher Tests were used to test for differences between the datasets. We used 95% confidence intervals for estimating the size of the differences between observed proportions, as suggested by Baroni and Evert (2008).

5.2 Results

Since results can be presented here only summarily due to space restrictions, we focus on observations on the levels of lexis and morphology. On the lexical level, we studied *POS* and *lemma frequencies.* Table 5 summarises the POS tags for which distributional differences were found between the Russian KRCs and both the RIC sample and the random non-KRCs from the Russian gold standard corpora while the numbers given are those for the comparison between gold standard and RIC. The tagset used is "Russian small"[5].

Tag	Prop. KRCs	Prop. RIC	χ^2	p	CI
S	0.439	0.365	112.20	< 0.01	[0.06, 0.09]
A	0.196	0.109	283.21	< 0.01	[0.08, 0.10]
ADV	0.013	0.032	76.75	< 0.01	[-0.02, -0,01]
PART	0.006	0.029	156.02	< 0.01	[-0.03, -0,02]
ADV-PRO	0.003	0.013	61.47	< 0.01	[-0.01, -0.01]
PRAE-DIC	0.001	0.006	38.74	< 0.01	[-0.01, 0]

Table 5: Results for comparison of POS frequencies Russian gold standard vs. RIC.

The table summarises proportions on the two corpora, chi-square and p-values as well as the 95%-confidence interval for the difference between proportions as outputted by the R[6] function prop.test().

On the level of *lemmata,* the same analysis showed that certain general nouns such as *вид* ("type", "kind") and *совокупность* ("the whole") for Russian or *Begriff* ("concept"), for German, were found significantly more often in the gold standard, whereas qualifying adjectives (*новый*, "new", *gut*, "good") and sentential adverbs (*даже*, "even", *nur*, "only") appear with a significantly lower frequency in the gold data.

[3] http://search.cpan.org/~achimru/Lingua-Sentence-1.00/lib/Lingua/Sentence.pm.

[4] The tagging model is available from: http://corpus.leeds.ac.uk/mocky/russian.par.gz.

[5] http://corpus.leeds.ac.uk/mocky/.

[6] http://www.r-project.org/.

Category	Prop. KRCs	Prop. RIC	χ^2	p	CI
perfective aspect	0.2168	0.6298	408.0662	< 0.0001	[-0.4498, -0.3762]
imperfective aspect	0.7814	0.3679	408.6745	< 0.0001	[0.3767, 0.4503]
imperative	0.0091	0.0195	3.7124	0.0540	[-0.0206, -0.0001]
passive	0.2168	0.0990	62.3199	< 0.0001	[0.0876, 0.1480]
infinitive	0.0747	0.1902	65.8157	< 0.0001	[-0.1429, -0.0881]
participle	0.0719	0.1504	35.2414	< 0.0001	[-0.1041, -0.0528]
first person	0.0009	0.0694	74.3668	< 0.0001	[-0.0833, -0.0536]
second person	0.0109	0.0366	15.1299	0.0001	[-0.0385, -0.0129]
third person	0.5383	0.3157	119.5548	< 0.0001	[0.1828, 0.2624]
present tense	0.7058	0.4170	198.2847	< 0.0001	[0.2499, 0.3278]
past tense	0.1949	0.3110	41.1045	< 0.0001	[-0.1514, -0.0807]
future tense	0.0118	0.0624	38.8885	< 0.0001	[-0.0661, -0.0350]
singular	0.5501	0.5090	3.8523	0.0497	[0.0001, 0.0821]

Table 6: Distributional differences of morphological markers between verbs in Russian KRCs and RIC.

Russian also shows fewer occurrences of modals (e.g.*должен,* "he must" and *мочь*, "may, can").

In another step, we studied *morphological properties* of verbs in the KRC samples in comparison, again, to similarly-sized samples from the reference web corpora (NCL for German, RIC for Russian) and samples of non-KRCs from the gold corpora. To this end, we analysed the morphological tags outputted by TreeTagger (for Russian) and mate (for German). The categories for which both comparisons gave significant results on Russian are summarised in table 6. The analysis shows that verbs in Russian KRCs are more often in imperfective aspect, passive voice and third person present tense. Less frequently in the gold standard we find imperative forms, verbal infinitives (maybe due to a lack of modals that need to be followed by an infinitive, see above) and participles. As previously, the German data echoes these results. A manual analysis of the *syntactic realisation* of the predicates in the KRCs gave evidence that Russian "unpersonal-definite" constructions (subjectless sentences with a verb in third person plural serving as predicate) and German presentatives may be light indicators for KRCs.

5.3 Discussion

Our results on the *lexical* level amount to a tendency towards an unpersonal style exhibited by KRCs in both languages. On the other hand, typical elements of defining statements (e.g. generalising adverbs or mentions of specific disciplines) that are described in the literature could not be found in high quantity. Obviously, larger datasets are necessary for an in-depth study of the lexical properties of KRCs. The *morphological properties* of verbs in the KRCs seem to support our hypothesis of an unpersonal, fact-oriented style, while imperfective aspect, present tense, presentatives and subjectless sentences can be understood as generalisation signals.

6 Conclusions and Future Work

In this paper, we proposed a methodology for the task of annotating a gold standard for KRC extraction. Our analysis suggests that decisions concerning the KRC-status of candidate statements are influenced by a range of factors that are not related to the linguistic surface of the KRC candidates themselves. Clearly, more empirical research on text-based knowledge acquisition is needed to arrive at more adequate models. The annotations carried out in the course of this study are transparent in that annotators' judgements can be used as hints for a more detailed study of boundary cases or external influencing factors. Nevertheless, further annotation work should use linguistic features of defining statements as optional signal. Our analysis of linguistic properties of KRCs supports hypotheses found in the literature, but also indicates that other, frequently described properties occur only rarely. Future work will deal with the question whether more linguistic information can improve KRC extraction.

Acknowledgement

The work described in this paper was partly funded by the CLARA project (EU/FP7), grant agreement n° 238405. I am also grateful to my anonymous reviewers for their helpful remarks. Last but not least, I am indebted to my colleagues José Martinez Martinez and Ekaterina Lapshinova-Koltunski for many interesting discussions and suggestions.

References

Baroni, M. and Evert, S. 2008. "Statistical methods for corpus exploitation". In Lüdeling, A. and Kytö, M. (eds), *Corpus Linguistics. An International Handbook* (Handbücher zur Sprach- und Kommunikationswissenschaft 29). Mouton de Gruyter, Berlin.

Bierwisch, M. and Kiefer, F. 1969. "Remarks on Definitions in Natural Language". In Kiefer, F. (ed), *Studies in Syntax and Semantics.* (Foundations of Language 10). Reidel, Dordrecht.

Bohnet, B. 2010. "Top Accuracy and Fast Dependency Parsing is not a Contradiction". COLING 2010, August 23-27, Beijing, China: 89-97. Available online at http://www.aclweb.org/anthology/C/C10/C10-1011.pdf.

Cramer, I. M. 2011. *Definitionen in Wörterbuch und Text: Zur manuellen Annotation, korpusgestützten Analyse und automatischen Extraktion definitorischer Textsegmente im Kontext der computergestützten Lexikographie.* Published PhD thesis. Technical University Dortmund. Available online at https://eldorado.tu-dortmund.de/bitstream/2003/27628/1/Dissertation.pdf.

de Groc, C. 2011. "Babouk: Focused web crawling for corpus compilation and automatic terminology extraction". IEEE/WIC/ACM: International Conference on Intelligent Agent Technology, August 22-27. Lyon, France: 497-498.

Del Gaudio, R. and Branco, A. 2007. "Automatic Extraction of Definitions in Portuguese: A Rule-Based Approach". In Neves, J., Santos, M.F. and Machado, J.M. (eds.) *Progress in Artificial Intelligence.* (Lecture Notes in Artificial Intelligence 4874). Springer, Berlin.

Fahmi, I. and Bouma, G. 2006. "Learning to Identify Definitions using Syntactic Features". Workshop on Learning Structured Information in Natural Language Applications at EACL 2006, April 3, Trento, Italy: 64-71. Available online at http://ai-nlp.info.uniroma2.it/eacl2006-ws10/WS10-eacl2006-proceedings.pdf.

Fišer, D., Pollak, S. and Vintar, Š. 2010. "Learning to Mine Definitions from Slovene Structured and Unstructured Knowledge-Rich Resources". LREC 2010, May 19-21, Valletta, Malta: 2932-2936. Available online at http://www.lrec-conf.org/proceedings/lrec2010/pdf/141_Paper.pdf.

Fletcher, W. H. 2004. "Making the Web More Useful as a Source for Linguistic Corpora". In Connor, U. and Upton, T. A. (eds), *Applied Corpus Linguistics. A Multidimensional Perspective.* Rodopi, Amsterdam/New York.

International Organization for Standardization. 2000. International Standard ISO 1087-1: 2000 – Terminology Work – Vocabulary – Part 1: Theory and application. ISO, Geneva.

Malaisé, V., Zweigenbaum, P. and Bachimont, B. 2005. "Mining defining contexts to help structuring differential ontologies". *Terminology 11 (1)*: 21-53.

Marshman, E. 2008. "Expressions of uncertainty in candidate knowledge-rich contexts: A comparison in English and French specialized texts". *Terminology 14 (1)*: 124-151.

Meyer, I. 2001. "Extracting knowledge-rich contexts for terminography: A conceptual and methodological framework". In Bourigault, D., Jacquemin, C. and L'Homme, M.-C. (eds), *Recent Advances in Computational Terminology.* (Natural Language Processing 2). John Benjamins. Amsterdam/Philadelphia.

Meyer, I., Skuce, D., Bowker, L. and Eck, K. 1992. "Towards a New Generation of Terminological Resources: An Experiment in Building a Terminological Knowledge Base". COLING 1992, August 23-28, Nantes, France: 956-960. Available online at http://acl.ldc.upenn.edu/C/C92/C92-3146.pdf.

Muresan, S. and Klavans, J. 2002. "A Method for Automatically Building and Evaluating Dictionary Resources". LREC 2002, May 29-31, Las Palmas, Spain: 231-234. Available online at http://www.lrec-conf.org/proceedings/lrec2002/.

Nivre, J., Hall, J., Nilsson, J., Chanev, A., Eryigit, G., Kübler, S., Marinov, S. and Marsi, E. 2007. "MaltParser: A language-independent system for data-driven dependency parsing". *Natural Language Engineering* 13(2): 95-135.

Pearson, J. 1998. *Terms in Context*. (Studies in Corpus Linguistics 1). John Benjamins, Amsterdam/Philadelphia.

Przepiórkowski, A., Degórski, Ł., Spousta, M., Simov, K., Osenova, P., Lemnitzer, L., Kuboň, V. and Wójtowicz, B. 2007. "Towards the automatic extraction of definitions in Slavic". BSNLP workshop at ACL 2007, June 29, Prague, Czech Republic: 43-50. Available online at http://langtech.jrc.it/BSNLP2007/m/BSNLP-2007-proceedings.pdf.

Quasthoff, U., Richter, M. and Biemann, C. 2006. "Corpus Portal for Search in Monolingual Corpora". LREC 2006, May 24-26, Genoa, Italy: 1799–1802. Available online at: http://www.lrec-conf.org/proceedings/lrec2006/.

Sachs, L. and Hedderich, J. 2009. *Angewandte Statistik. Methodensammlung mit R*. Springer, Berlin/Heidelberg.

Schmid, H. 1994. "Probabilistic Part-of-Speech Tagging Using Decision Trees". International Conference on New Methods in Language Processing, Manchester, England: 44–49. Available online at: ftp://ftp.ims.uni-stuttgart.de/pub/corpora/tree-tagger1.pdf.

Sharoff, S. 2006. "Creating general-purpose corpora using automated search engine queries". In M. Baroni and S. Bernardini (eds) *WaCky! Working papers on the Web as Corpus*. Gedit. Bologna. Available online at: http://www.comp.leeds.ac.uk/ssharoff/publications/wacky-paper.pdf.

Sharoff, S., Kopotev, M., Erjavec, T., Feldmann, A. and Divjak, D. 2008. "Designing and evaluating a Russian tagset". LREC 2008, May 28-30, Marrakech, Morocco: 279-285. Available online at http://www.lrec-conf.org/proceedings/lrec2008/.

Sharoff, S. and Nivre, J. 2011. "The proper place of men and machines in language technology. Processing Russian without any linguistic knowledge." Dialogue 2011, May 25-29, Bekasovo, Russia: 591-604. Available online at http://www.dialog-21.ru/digests/dialog2011/materials/ru/pdf/58.pdf.

Sierra, G., Alarcón, R., Aguilar, C. and C. Bach. 2008. "Definitional verbal patterns for semantic relation extraction". *Terminology 14 (1)*: 74-98.

Storrer, A. and Wellinghoff, S. 2006. "Automated detection and annotation of term definitions in German text corpora". LREC 2006, May 24-26, Genoa, Italy: 2373-2376. Available online at http://www.lrec-conf.org/proceedings/lrec2006/.

Walter, S. 2010. *Definitionsextraktion aus Urteilstexten*. Published PhD thesis. Saarland University. Available online at: http://www.coli.uni-saarland.de/~stwa/publications/DissertationStephanWalter.pdf.

Westerhout, E. 2009. "Definition Extraction Using Linguistic and Structural Features". First Workshop on Definition Extraction, Borovets, Bulgaria: 61-67. Available online at http://www.aclweb.org/anthology-new/W/W09/W09-4410.pdf.

Named Entity Recognition in Broadcast News Using Similar Written Texts

Niraj Shrestha
KU Leuven, Belgium
niraj.shrestha@cs.kuleuven.be

Ivan Vulić
KU Leuven, Belgium
ivan.vulic@cs.kuleuven.be

Abstract

We propose a new approach to improving named entity recognition (NER) in broadcast news speech data. The approach proceeds in two key steps: (1) we detect block alignments between highly similar blocks of the speech data and corresponding written news data that are easily obtainable from the Web, (2) we employ term expansion techniques commonly used in information retrieval to recover named entities that were initially missed by the speech transcriber. We show that our method is able to find the named entities missing in the transcribed speech data, but also to correct incorrectly assigned named entity tags. Consequently, our novel approach improves state-of-the-art results of NER from speech data both in terms of recall and precision.

1 Introduction

Named entity recognition (NER) is a task of extracting and classifying information units like *persons*, *locations*, *time*, *dates*, *organization names*, etc (e.g., Nadeau and Sekine (2007)). In general, the task involves labeling (proper) nouns with suitable *named entity tags*. NER is a very important pre-processing task in many applications in the fields of information retrieval (IR) and natural language processing (NLP). NER from speech data also displays its utility in various multimedia applications. For instance, it could be used in indexing video broadcast news using the associated speech data, that is, assigning names and their semantic classes recognized from the speech data as metadata to the video sequences (Basili et al., 2005).

NER from speech data is a difficult task and current state-of-the-art results are typically much lower than the results obtained from written text. For instance, the Stanford NER system in the CoNLL 2003 shared task on NER in written data report an F_1 value of 87.94% (Stanford, 2003). (Kubala et al., 1998; Miller et al., 1999) report a degrade of NER performance between 20-25% in F_1 value when applying a NER trained on written data to transcribed speech.

This lower performance has several causes. Firstly, speech transcribers often incorrectly transcribe phrases and even complete sentences, which might consequently result in many missing named entities. Secondly, many names were typically not observed in the training data on which the speech transcriber was trained (e.g., the problem is especially prominent when dealing with dynamic and ever-changing news data). The transcription then results in names and surrounding context words that are wrongly spelled, making the named entity recognition even more challenging. Finally, the named entity recognizer, especially when dealing with such unseen words, might incorrectly recognize and classify the named entities, and even tag non-names with named entity tags.

In this paper, we focus on the first two problems. We assume that similar written texts discussing the same news events provide additional knowledge about the named entities that are expected to occur in the spoken text. This external knowledge coming from written data then allows finding missing names and correcting incorrectly assigned named entity tags.

We utilize *term expansion and pseudo-relevance feedback techniques* often used in IR. The general idea there is to enrich queries with related terms. These terms are extracted from documents that were selected as being relevant for the query by the user or automatically by the IR system (Cao et al., 2008). Only certain terms are selected for expansion based on their importance in the relevant document and their semantic relation with the query. We apply a similar approach to expanding and correcting the set of named entities in a speech document by the named entities found in the related relevant written documents. Following this modeling intuition, we are able to improve the recall of NER from broadcast speech data by almost 8%, while precision scores increase for around 1% compared to the results of applying the same named entity recognizer on the speech data directly. The contributions of this article are:

- We show that NER from speech data benefits from aligning broadcast news data with similar written news data.
- We present several new methods to recover named entities from speech data by using the external knowledge from high-quality similar written texts.
- We improve the performance of the state-of-the-art Stanford NER system when applied to the transcribed speech data.

The following sections first review related research, describe the methodology of our approach and the experimental setup, and finally present our evaluation and discuss the results.

2 Related Work

Named entity recognition was initially defined in the framework of Message Understanding Conferences (MUC) (Sundheim, 1995a). Since then, many conferences and workshops such as the following MUC editions (Chinchor, 1997; Sundheim, 1995a), the 1999 DARPA broadcast news workshop (Przybocki et al., 1999) and CoNLL shared tasks (Sang, 2002; Sang and Meulder, 2003) focused on extending the state-of-the-art research on NER. One of the first NER systems was designed by Rau (1991). Her system extracts and identifies company names by using hand-crafted heuristic rules. Today, NER in written text still remains a popular task. State-of-the-art NER models typically rely on machine learning algorithms trained on documens with manually annotated named entities. Examples of publicly available NER tools are the Stanford NER, OpenNLP NameFinder[1], Illinois NER system[2], the lingpipe NER system[3].

[1]http://opennlp.sourceforge.net/models-1.5

[2]http://cogcomp.cs.illinois.edu/page/software_view/4

[3]http://alias-i.com/lingpipe/web/models.html

NER in speech data poses a more difficult problem. In speech data and its transcribed variants, proper names are not capitalized and there are no punctuation marks, while these serve as the key source of evidence for NER in written data. Additionally, speech data might contain incorrectly transcribed words, misspelled words and missing words or chunks of text which makes the NER task even more complex (Sundheim, 1995b; Kubala et al., 1998).

NER in speech data was initiated by Kubala (1998). He applied the NER on transcription of broadcast news and reported that the performance of NER systems degraded linearly with the word error rate of the speech recognition (e.g., missing data, misspelled data and spuriously tagged names). Named entity recognition of speech was further investigated, but the relevant research typically focuses on improved error rates of the speech transcriptions (Miller et al., 1999; Palmer and Ostendorf, 2001), on considering different transcription hypotheses of the speech recognition (Horlock and King, 2003; Béchet et al., 2004) and on the problem of a temporal mismatch of the training data for the NER and the test data (Favre et al., 2005). None of these articles consider exploiting external text sources to improve the NER nor the problem of recovering missing named entities in the speech transcripts. .

3 Methodology

The task is to label a sequence of words $[w_1, w_2, \ldots, w_N]$ with a sequence of tags $[t_1, t_2, \ldots, t_N]$, where each word $w_i, i = 1, \ldots, N$ is assigned its corresponding tag $t_i \in \{person, organization, location\}$ in the transcribed speech of broadcast news.

3.1 Basic Architecture

The straightforward approach to NER in speech data is to apply the NER tagger such as Stanford NER tagger (Stanford, 2012) directly to transcribed speech data. However, the tagger will miss or assign incorrect named entity tags to many named entities due to the inherent errors in the transcription process. In this paper, we use related written text to recover the incorrectly assigned tags and missing named entities in the transcribed speech data. We assume that highly similar blocks of written data give extra knowledge about the named entities that are incorrectly assigned to the speech data and about the named entities missed in the speech data. The basic modeling work flow is composed of the following steps:

1. Transcribe the speech document using a common ASR system (FBK, 2013) and recognize the named entities in the speech document by a state-of-the-art NER tagger such as (Stanford, 2012). We will call the obtained list of unique named entities the *SNERList*.
2. Find related written texts. For instance, news sites could store related written texts with the broadcast video; or broadcast services might store speech and written data covering the same event. If that is not the case, written news data related to the given speech data might be crawled from the Web using some of the text similarity metrics or information retrieval systems. In the experiments below we choose the most related written document.
3. Divide the speech and written documents into fixed-size blocks. Each block contains n consecutive words. In the experiments below n = 50.[4]
4. Compute the similarity between the transcribed speech blocks and blocks of written text using the cosine similarity between their term vectors and align highly similar blocks. We call this step the *block alignment between speech and written data.*
5. If the similarity between a speech block and a block of written text is higher than a certain threshold, build a list of all named entities with their corresponding tags in the written text block again using the same NER tagger.
6. Group the unique named entities and their tags obtained from the aligned blocks of written text into the *WNERList*. This list contains valuable knowledge to update the *SNERList*
7. Correct and expand the *SNERList* based on the *WNERList*. The intuition is that we should trust the recognized named entities and their tags in the written data more than the ones obtained in the transcribed speech.

[4]We opt for aligning smaller chunks of information, that is, blocks instead of the entire documents. Incorrectly transcribed speech data introduce noise which negatively affects the quality of document alignment and, consequently, the overall NER system. The idea of working with only highly similar small blocks aims to circumvent the problem of noisy document alignments.

3.2 Our NER Models

The models that we propose differ in the ways they build the complete *SNERList* for a given speech document (Step 7 in the previous section) based on the knowledge in the *WNERList*.

3.2.1 Baseline NER Model

We use the Stanford NER on the transcribed speech data without any additional knowledge from similar written data. We call this model **Baseline NER**.

3.2.2 Correction and Expansion of the SNERList: General Principles

The procedure proceeds as follows: Let $(x_i)_{t_j}$ be the occurrence of the word x_i tagged by named entity class t_j in the *SNERList* and $(x_i)_{t_k}$ be the occurrence of the same word x_i now tagged by the named entity class t_k in the *WNERList*. Here, we assume the *one-sense-per-discourse-principle*, that is, all occurrences of the word x_i in a document can only belong to one NE class. We have to update the recognized named entities in the speech transcripts, i.e., replace $(x_i)_{t_j}$ with $(x_i)_{t_k}$ if it holds:

$$Count\big((x_i)_{t_j}\big) < Count\big((x_i)_{t_k}\big) \qquad (1)$$

The counts are computed in the related written document. This step is the *correction* of the *SNERList*. Additionally, we can expand the *SNERList* with named entities from the *WNERList* that were not present in the original *SNERList*. This step regards the *expansion* of the *SNERlist*.

3.2.3 Correction and Expansion of the SNERList Solely Based on the Edit Distance

The model updates the *SNERList* as follows. First, it scans the speech document and searches for orthographically similar words that are tagged in the similar written blocks. Orthographic similarity is modeled by the *edit distance* (Navarro, 2001). We assume that two words are similar if their edit distance is less than 2. The model not only uses the tags of the *WNERList* to correct the tags in the *SNERList* (see previous subsection), - we call this model **NER+COR**-, we also use newly linked words in the speech data to named entities of the *WNERList* to expand the *SNERList*. The model is called **NER+COR+EXP-ED**.

These models assign named entity tags only to words in the speech document that have their orthographically similar counterparts in the related written data. Therefore, they are unable to recover information that is missing in the transcribed speech document. Hence we need to design methods that expand the *SNERList* with relevant named entities from the written data that are missing in the transcribed speech document.

3.2.4 Expanding the SNERList with Named Entities from Written News Lead Paragraphs

It is often the case that the most prominent and important information occurs in the first few lines of written news (so-called *headlines* or *lead paragraphs*). Named entities occurring in these lead paragraphs are clearly candidates for the expansion of the *SNERList*. Therefore, we select named entities that occur in first 100 or 200 words in the related written news story and enrich the *SNERlist* with these named entities. Following that, we integrate the correction and expansion of named entity tags as before, i.e., this model is similar to **NER+COR+EXP-ED**, where the only difference lies in the fact that we now consider the additional expansion of the *SNERlist* by the named entities appearing in lead paragraphs. This model is called **NER+COR+EXP-ED-LP**.

3.2.5 Expanding the SNERList with Frequent Named Entities from Written News

The raw frequency of a named entity is a clear indicator of its importance in a written news document. Therefore, named entities occurring in related written documents are selected for expansion of the *SNERList* only if they occur at least M times in the written document on which the *WNERList* is based. Again, the correction part is integrated according to Eq. (1). We build the *SNERList* in the same manner as with the previous **NER+COR+EXP-ED-LP**, the only difference is that we now consider frequent words for the expansion of the *SNERlist*. This model is called **NER+COR+EXP-ED-FQ**.

3.2.6 Expanding the SNERList with Frequently Co-Occurring Named Entities from Written News

If a word in the related written document co-occurs many times with named entities detected in the original speech document, it is very likely that the word from the written document is highly descriptive for the speech document and should be taken into account for expansion of the *SNERlist*. We have designed three models that exploit the co-occurrence following an IR term expansion approach (Cao et al., 2008):

(i) Each word pair (s_i, w_j) consists of one named entity from the *SNERList* and one named entity from the *WNERList* that is currently not present in the *SNERList*. The co-occurrence is then modeled by the following formula:

$$SimScore_1(w_j) = \sum_{i=1}^{m} \sum_{j=1}^{n} \frac{\sum_B C(s_i, w_j|B)}{\sum_B tf(s_i, B)} \quad (2)$$

where $C(s_i, w_j|B)$ is the co-occurrence count of named entity s_i from the *SNERlist* and named entity w_j from the *WNERlist* not present in the former. The written document is divided into blocks and the co-occurrence counts are computed over all blocks B defined in section 3.1. $tf(s_i, B)$ is the frequency count of speech named entity s_i in block B. We call this model **NER+COR+EXP-ED-M1**.

(ii) The next model tracks the occurrence of each tuple (s_i, s_k, w_j) comprising two named entities from the *SNERlist* and one named entity w_j not present in the list, but which appears in the *WNERlist*. The co-occurrence is modeled as follows:

$$SimScore_2(w_j) = \sum_{(s_i, s_k) \epsilon \Omega} \sum_{j=1}^{n} \frac{\sum_B C(s_i, s_k, w_j|B)}{\sum_B tf(s_i, s_k, B)} \quad (3)$$

Again, $C(s_i, s_k, w_j|B)$ is the co-occurrence count of speech named entities s_i and s_j with named entity w_j in the written block B. Ω refers to all possible combinations of two named entities taken from the *SNERlist*. We call this model **NER+COR+EXP-ED-M2**.

(iii) The co-occurrence count in this model is weighted with the minimum distance between named entity s_i from the SNERList and named entity w_j that is a candidate for expansion. It assumes that words whose relative positions in the written document are close to each other are more related. Therefore, each pair is weighted conditioned on the distance between the words in a pair. The distance is defined as the number of words between two words. The co-occurrence score is then computed as follows:

$$SimScore_3(w_j) = \frac{\sum_B \frac{C(s_i, w_j)}{minDist(s_i, w_j)}}{\sum_B C(s_i, w_j)} \quad (4)$$

where $minDist(s_i, w_j)$ denotes the minimum distance between words s_i and w_j. The model is **NER+COR+EXP-ED-M3**.

These 3 models are similar to the other models that perform the expansion of the *SNERlist*. The difference is that the expansion is performed only with candidates from the *WNERlist* that frequently co-occur with other named entities from the *SNERlist*.

4 Experimental Setup

4.1 Datasets and Ground Truth

For evaluation we have downloaded 11 short broadcast news from the Internet (the sources are `tv.msnbc.com` and `www.dailymail.co.uk`). The FBK ASR transcription system (FBK, 2013) is used to provide the speech transcriptions from the data. Since the system takes sound as input, we have extracted the audio files in the mp3 format using the ffmpeg tool (ffm, 2012). The transcribed speech data constitute our *speech dataset*. The following table shows an example of a manual transcription and the transcription outputed by the FBK ASR system. The speech documents need to be labeled with 143 unique named entities and their named entity tag.

Manual Transcription
hbo is debuting a documentary on thursday night about the very public american life of ethel kennedy. at 84, she's certainly a survivor having lost her husband and two of her 11 children. she has seldom spoken about her life about any of it. she's talked to us about the parts of her story she's chosen to reveal now.
i mean, how lucky could i really have been.
ethel kennedy makes a big distinction between counting her blessings and not looking back too much. while she does not enjoy being interviewed, she said yes to her daughter rory, a documentary filmmaker who wanted to tell her mom's extraordinary story............

ASR Transcription
HBO is debuting a documentary on Thursday night about the very public American wife of Ethel Kennedy any for she is certainly a survivor having lost her husband and two or for another job she has seldom spoken of our life about any other when she talked to us about the Passover story she's chosen to reveal now in highlighting Ethel Kennedy makes a big distinction between counting their blessings and not looking back to March washing does not enjoy being interviewed she said yesterday over borrowing a documentary film maker who wanted to calls...............

Figure 1: An example of the actual transcription done manually and the transcription done by the FBK ASR system.

Fig. 1 shows that the ASR transcription contains many words that are incorrectly transcribed. It is also visible that the ASR system does not recognize and misspells many words from the actual speech.

The related written news stories of the 11 broadcast news are collected from different news sources available on the Web such as `http://www.guardian.co.uk`, `http://www.independent.co.uk`, `www.cnn.com`, etc. The collected written news stories constitute our *written text dataset*.

In order to build the ground truth for our experiments, all 11 stories were manually transcribed. Stanford NER was then applied on the manually transcribed data. Following that, the annotator checked and revised the NER-tagged lists. The ground truth was finally created by retaining the revised lists of named entities with their corresponding tags. We work with the following 3 common named entity tags: *person*, *location* and *organization*.

4.2 Evaluation Metrics

Let FL be the final list of named entities with their corresponding tags retrieved by our system for all speech documents, and GL the complete ground truth list. We use standard precision ($Prec$), recall (Rec) and F-1 scores for evaluation:

$$Prec = \frac{|FL \cap GL|}{|FL|} \qquad Rec = \frac{|FL \cap GL|}{|GL|}$$

$$F_1 = 2 \cdot \frac{Prec \cdot Rec}{Prec + Rec}$$

We perform *evaluation at the document level*, that is, we disregard multiple occurrences of the same named entity in it. In cases when the same named entity is assigned different tags in the same document (e.g., *Kerry* could be tagged as *person* and as *organization* in the same document), we penalize the system by always treating it as an incorrect entry in the final list FL.

This evaluation is useful when one wants to index a speech document as a whole and considers the recognized named entities and their tags as document metadata. Within this evaluation setting it is also possible to observe the models' ability to recover missed named entities in speech data.

4.3 Parameters

The notion of "frequent co-occurrence" is specified by a threshold parameter. Only words that score above the threshold are used for expansion. Based on a small validation set of two speech documents and their corresponding written document, we set the threshold value for **NER+COR+EXP-ED-M1** and **NER+COR+EXP-ED-M2** to 0.01, while it is 0.002 for **NER+COR+EXP-ED-M3**. All results reported in the next section are obtained using these parameter settings, but by fluctuating

NER Model	Precision	Recall	F-1
Baseline NER	**0.407**	**0.567**	**0.474**
NER+COR	0.427	0.594	0.497
NER+COR+EXP-ED	0.411	0.601	0.489
NER+COR+EXP-ED-LP ($\|LP\| = 100$)	0.359	0.678	0.470
NER+COR+EXP-ED-LP ($\|LP\| = 200$)	0.322	0.678	0.437
NER+COR+EXP-ED-FQ ($M = 2$)	0.387	0.657	0.487
NER+COR+EXP-ED-FQ ($M = 3$)	0.411	0.650	0.504
NER+COR+EXP-ED-M1	**0.415**	**0.650**	**0.507**
NER+COR+EXP-ED-M2	0.414	0.622	0.497
NER+COR+EXP-ED-M3	0.384	0.664	0.487

Table 1: Results of different NE recovering models on the evaluation dataset.

them precision increases while recall decreases, or vice versa.

5 Results and Discussion

Table 1 shows all the results of our experiments, where we compare our models to the baseline model that uses the named entity recognizer for tagging the speech data, i.e., Baseline NER. We may observe that our system is able to correct the tag of some named entities in the transcribed speech data by the **NER+COR** model and expand some missed named entities by the **NER+COR+EXP-ED** model. All models are able to recover a subset of missing named entities, and that fact is reflected in increased recall scores for all models. The **NER+COR+EXP-ED-M1** model outperforms the other models and improves the F1 by 3% with an increase in 8% in recall and almost 1% in precision.

In our dataset there are 27 unique named entities that are in the ground truth transcription of the speech data, but are missing completely in the transcribed speech data. Out of these 27 named entities, 8 named entities do not occur in the written related documents, so we cannot learn these from the written data. Out of 19 named entities recoverable from written data our system is able to correctly identify 6 named entities and their tags with the **NER+COR+EXP-ED-M1** model. We can lower the threshold for the similarity score computed in Eq. (3). For instance, when we substantially lower the threshold to 0.001 we correctly find 12 missing named entities, but the increased recall is at the expense of a much lower precision ($P = 0.290, R = 0.699, F1 = 0.411$), because many irrelevant named entities are added to the final *SNERList*. We have also investigated why the remaining 7 named entities seen in the written data are not recovered even with such a low threshold. We noticed that those named entities do not co-occur with the named entities found in the speech transcripts in the considered blocks of the written texts. Hence, our methods can still be improved by finding better correlations between named entities found in the speech and related written documents. The named entity recognition in the related written texts is not perfect either and can entail errors in the corrections and expansions of the named entities found in the speech data.

6 Conclusions and Future Work

In this paper we have shown that NER from speech data benefits from aligning broadcast news data with related written news data. We can both correct the identified named entity tags found in the speech data and expand the named entities and their tags based on knowledge of named entities from related written news. The best improvements in terms of precision and recall of the NER are obtained with word expansion techniques used in information retrieval. As future work we will refine the named entity expansion techniques so to further improve recall and to better capture missing named entities without sacrificing precision, we will consider several speech transcription hypotheses, and we will try to improve the named entity recognition itself by making the models better portable to texts that are different from the ones they are trained on.

7 Acknowledgements

This research was supported by the EXPERTS Erasmus Mundus Action 2 scholarship of the first author and by the EU FP7 project TOSCA-MP No. 287532.

References

Roberto Basili, Marco Cammisa, and Emanuale Donati. 2005. RitroveRAI: A Web application for semantic indexing and hyperlinking of multimedia news. In *Proceedings of International Semantic Web Conference*, pages 97–111.

Frédéric Béchet, Allen L Gorin, Jeremy H Wright, and Dilek Hakkani Tur. 2004. Detecting and extracting named entities from spontaneous speech in a mixed-initiative spoken dialogue context: How may i help you? *Speech Communication*, 42(2):207 – 225.

Guihong Cao, Jian-Yun Nie, Jianfeng Gao, and Stephen Robertson. 2008. Selecting good expansion terms for pseudo-relevance feedback. In *Proceedings of the 31st Annual International ACM SIGIR Conference on Research and Development in Information Retrieval*, pages 243–250.

Nancy A. Chinchor. 1997. MUC-7 named entity task definition (version 3.5). In *Proceedings of the 7th Message Understanding Conference*.

Benoît Favre, Frédéric Béchet, and Pascal Nocera. 2005. Robust named entity extraction from large spoken archives. In *Proceedings of the Conference on Empirical Methods in Natural Language Processing*, pages 491–498.

FBK. 2013. FBK ASR transcription.

2012. ffmpeg audio/video tool @ONLINE.

James Horlock and Simon King. 2003. Discriminative methods for improving named entity extraction on speech data. In *Proceedings of the 8th European Conference on Speech Communication and Technology*, pages 2765–2768.

Francis Kubala, Richard Schwartz, Rebecca Stone, and Ralph Weischedel. 1998. Named entity extraction from speech. In *Proceedings of the DARPA Broadcast News Transcription and Understanding Workshop*, pages 287–292.

David Miller, Richard Schwartz, Ralph Weischedel, and Rebecca Stone. 1999. Named entity extraction from broadcast news. In *Proceedings of the DARPA Broadcast News Workshop*, pages 37–40.

David Nadeau and Satoshi Sekine. 2007. A survey of named entity recognition and classification. *Lingvisticae Investigationes*, 30(1):3–26.

Gonzalo Navarro. 2001. A guided tour to approximate string matching. *ACM Computing Surveys*, 33(1):31–88.

David D. Palmer and Mari Ostendorf. 2001. Improving information extraction by modeling errors in speech recognizer output. In *Proceedings of the 1st International Conference on Human Language Technology Research*, pages 1–5.

Mark A. Przybocki, Jonathan G. Fiscus, John S. Garofolo, and David S. Pallett. 1999. HUB-4 information extraction evaluation. In *Proceedings of the DARPA Broadcast News Workshop*, pages 13–18.

Lisa F. Rau. 1991. Extracting company names from text. In *Proceedings of the 7th IEEE Conference on Artificial Intelligence Applications*, pages 29–32.

Erik F. Tjong Kim Sang and Fien De Meulder. 2003. Introduction to the CoNLL-2003 shared task: Language-Independent named entity recognition. In *Proceedings of the 7th Conference on Natural Language Learning*, pages 142–147.

Erik F. Tjong Kim Sang. 2002. Introduction to the CoNLL-2002 shared task: Language-independent named entity recognition. In *Proceedings of the 6th Conference on Natural Language Learning*, pages 1–4.

Stanford. 2003. Stanford NER in CoNLL 2003.

Stanford. 2012. Stanford NER.

Beth Sundheim. 1995a. Named entity task definition. In *Proceedings of the 6th Message Understanding Conference*, pages 317–332.

Beth Sundheim. 1995b. Overview of results of the MUC-6 evaluation. In *Proceedings of the 6th Message Understanding Conference*, pages 13–31.

Reporting Preliminary Automatic Comparable Corpora Compilation Results

Ekaterina Stambolieva
University of Wolverhampton
West Midlands WV1 1LY
United Kingdom
ekaterina.stambolieva@euroscript.lu

Abstract

Translation and translation studies rely heavily on distinctive text resources, such as comparable corpora. Comparable corpora gather greater diversity of language-dependent phrases in comparison to multilingual electronic dictionaries or parallel corpora; and present a robust language resource. Therefore, we see comparable corpora compilation as impending in this technological era and suggest an automatic approach to their gathering. The originality of the research lies within the newly-proposed methodology that is guiding the compilation process. We aim to contribute to translation and translation studies professionals' work by suggesting an approach to obtaining comparable corpora without intermediate human evaluation. This contribution reduces time and presents such professionals with non-static text resources. In our experiment we compare the automatic compilation results to the labels, which two human evaluators have given to the relevant documents.

1 Introduction

In translation and translation studies large collections of texts serve as invaluable resources, which help translators interpret better and faster previously unseen text, extract terms, and look for context-dependent translation equivalents. These big sets of texts are referred to as corpora within professional literature. According to Aarts (1991) "a corpus is understood to be a collection of samples of running texts. The texts may be spoken, written or intermediate forms, and the samples may be of any length". Furthermore, the corpus content is collected by following unambiguous linguistic criterion (EAGLES, 1996). A widely used translator's working tool are electronic multilingual dictionaries, which store words and their equivalents in different languages. Nevertheless, the electronic dictionaries lack some translation equivalents and as they are static, this gap is not filled in.

The constant enrichment of the languages themselves results in the birth of new words, terms and translation equivalents on a regular basis. The static electronic dictionaries are difficult to update frequently, hence they are not described as a highly-robust resource for mining translation alternatives. A valuable alternative source of textual materials that aids translators is parallel corpus. The parallel corpus is compiled of snippets of text that are aligned on sentence level and are exact translations of each other in one or more languages. This kind of corpora is a perfect language resource for translators. When in doubt, the translators can explore the available parallel corpora, either with the use of specialised software or not, to analyse language structures, unknown phrases, register, and so on. Talvensaari et al. (2007) state the translation process with the use of comparable corpora as a similarity thesaurus improves the quality of the translations. However, collections of compiled parallel texts are scarce and their domain coverage is poor. Some topic specific parallel corpora exist, such as the EuroParl set (Koehn, 2005), grouping legislative documents written in one of the twenty-three official European Languages. Here comes the advantages of using comparable corpora over parallel ones or dictionaries - the comparable corpora are more robust than electronic dictionaries, and are more available than parallel corpora.

A good stimulus motivating the current research is that comparable corpora preserve the all language structures and ways of expressions, thereupon keeping all cultural aspects of the language. This is also suggested by Bekavac et al. (2004). They emphasise on the importance of comparable corpora with respect to the fact such collections preserve the cultural variations of the languages involved. Contrary to direct translation snippets, comparable texts can convey the most important information to the readers, following each specific language construction and structure. In this like of thought the parallel text corpora can suffer from lack of language-specific cultural marks because of the fact they require exact translations rather than preserving the language variety richness. Another idea that inspires research in the compilation of comparable corpora problem is that similar texts may be easier to find. Therefore, when a good methodology to the gathering of such collections is presented, the accessible similar texts can be collected to help researchers and professionals in translation. Likewise, Skadiņa et al. (2010 b) and Skadiņa et al. (2010a) argue that the advantages of comparable corpora in Machine Translation are considerable and more beneficial than those of parallel corpora. The researchers state that comparable corpora are a good substitute for parallel ones and they can compensate for the parallel corpora's lack.

2 Corpus. Parallel and Comparable.

Definition and explanation of the most important terms to be known is provided: a corpus and the different types of corpora that can be collected. In the work of Bowker and Pearson (2002) a detailed explanation on the importance of corpora is given. Depending on the purpose of the corpus, several different types of corpora can be categorised. Bowker and Pearson (2002) argue distinct corpora exist. Relying on the purpose they have been constructed for, the corpora can be general reference ones or specific purpose ones. Written and spoken corpora are classified depending on the electronic format data they consist of: either text or speech files accordingly. The variety of languages to be identified in the corpora group them into monolingual and multilingual. "A monolingual corpus is one that contains texts in a single language, while multilingual corpora contain texts in two or more languages." (Bowker and Pearson 2002) The corpora build from collections of documents in two languages are called bilingual, and in the cases with more than two present languages, the corpora are referred as multilingual.

2.1 A Parallel Corpus

The multilingual corpora are divided into subcategories that are parallel and comparable corpora. Bowker and Pearson (2002) restrict the monolingual corpora in the sense they do not dissemble them into parallel and comparable. In translation and translation studies a monolingual corpus can be built to be comparable but not parallel. The definition of parallel corpora according to Bowker and Pearson (2002) is "parallel corpora contain texts in language A alongside their translations into language B, C, etc." Thus a corpus build from documents in the same language cannot contain more than one ways of presenting the same exact information, meaning that the only translation a snippet of text can have in the same language is the initial snippet of text itself.
In other hand, the comparable corpora consist of texts in several languages that are not exact interpretations of one another, but having the same communicative function. Some comparable corpora indicators are listed as time-frame, topic, degree of technicality, and type of text.

2.2 A Comparable Corpus

The degree of similarity between comparable corpora documents has not yet been formalised strictly and leaves space for different interpretations of similarity, thus contributing to abundant text collections of similar or semi-similar documents. The current research endeavors to assemble a collection of comparable documents that are closely related to each other and can be used by professional translators in their everyday work. The adopted definition of comparable corpora for this work is provided by McEnery (2003) - "Comparable corpora are corpora where series of monolingual corpora are collected for a range of languages, preferably using the same sampling and frame and with similar balance and representativeness, to enable the study of those languages in contrast" (McEnery 2003).
Otero and López (2010) provide a simplified description of comparable corpora than McEnery (2003). Their definition is "a comparable corpus is one which selects similar texts in more than one language or variety".

In like manner, Talvensaari et al. (2007) interpret comparable corpora. In their views, "comparable corpora consist of document pairs that are not translations of each other but share similar topics." According to Tao and Zhao (2005) "Comparable text corpora are collections of text documents in different languages that are similar about topics; such text corpora are often naturally available (e.g., news articles in different languages published in the same time period)". In a like manner they argue that "comparable text corpora are collections of text documents in different languages that are about the same or similar topics." Fung and Cheung (2004) define comparable corpora as being noisy-parallel: "A noisy parallel corpus, sometimes also called a 'comparable' corpus, contains non-aligned sentences that are nevertheless mostly bilingual translations of the same document. Another type of corpus is one that contains non-sentence-aligned, non-translated bilingual documents that are topic-aligned. For example, newspaper articles from two sources in different languages, within the same windows of published dates, can constitute a comparable corpus." (Fung and Cheung 2004).

Skadiņa et al. (2010a) describe comparable corpora in a slightly different manner. They are referring to a comparable corpus as a "collection of similar documents that are collected according to a set of criteria, e.g. the same proportions of texts of the same genre in the same domain from the same period ... in more than one language or variety of languages ... that contain overlapping information." The comparability features they are using hence are genre, domain, size, and time span. The level of comparability of corpora can be distinct depending on the texts in the documents. An important is that Skadiņa et al. (2010a) define different levels of comparability between documents. They distinguish three different types of comparable corpora or three separate levels of similarity. The first one is called strongly comparable corpora. The strongly comparable texts are "closely related texts reporting the same event or describing the same subject. These texts could be heavily edited translations or independently created, such as texts coming from the same source with the same editorial control, but written in different languages... or independently written texts concerning the same object, e.g. news items concerning the same specific event from different news agencies". The second level of similarity is when the documents are marked as weakly comparable. The weakly comparable documents are "texts which include texts in the same narrow subject domain and genre, but varying in subdomains and specific genres". Hence the similarity features of the documents collected in a weakly comparable corpus are genre and domain. The reason these types of documents are classified as weakly similar is that in the different genres of distinct domains the texts are not restricted to be describing the same event as if they were strongly comparable. The last type of comparable texts Skadiņa et al. (2010a) propose is a non-comparable corpus. The non-comparable texts are described as "pairs of texts drawn at random from a pair of a very large collection of texts (e.g. the Web) in the two languages".

3 Relevant Literature

Relevantly to the current research, Gatto (2010) gives a perspective on how comparable corpora are built and explored from translators in LSP translation. She emphasises on the fact the manual acquisition of comparable corpora "for a specific translation task ... is deemed too time-consuming, and the results are more often than not disappointing." Gatto (2010) explores the benefits of a semi-automatic comparable corpora compilation tool in a class-based environment for translators. As most of the work on building comparable corpora, for example as in Tao and Zhai (2005), Gatto is focused on bilingual document sets instead of exploring multilingual texts. She indicates the scarcity of the parallel and comparable corpora resources available ad hoc to translators. In her study she investigates the problem of building a similar document collection that is fast to assemble and in the same time beneficial and appropriate to the translators' needs. She seeks for a tool that can support translation trainees in their activities that is "primarily conceived of as a tool helping language professionals build the corpus they need, whenever they need, and as quickly as possible" (Gatto 2010). The tool Gatto evaluates with her students has web access and performs seed word searches online. Therefore, using the Web as a corpus (Kilgarriff 2003) and information retrieval techniques, a comparable corpus is assembled. The aspect that Gatto ephrasises on in her work is that at each step the tool waits for human verification of results. She argues the latter is an important contribution to more accurate comparable document selection for the reason dubious texts is manually checked for relevance and comparability. In Gatto's research, the retrieved web pages are based on automatic criterion and human intelligence selection. An important remark stated by Gatto (2010) is that a web crawling tool for building comparable corpora performs "better than a student can manually do, while still allowing significant interaction with the machine".

The conclusion is that such a semi-automatic system outperforms translation students' efforts to compiling a comparable corpus. This assumption gives motivation further research in the manners of developing software to collect similar documents to ease translator's work to be undertaken.

Corpora, being parallel or comparable, can be extracted from the Web. The work of many researchers, as Gatto (2010), Ion et al. (2010), Otero and López (2010), Skadiņa et al. (2010b), Talvensaari et al. (2008), shows different techniques to their automatic and semi-automatic gathering. Kilgarriff (2003) argues that the entire Web can be recognised as one corpus. Skadiņa et al. (2010b) note that the comparable documents are mined without great difficulty since they are more available than the parallel texts.

Contrary to mining corpora from the Web, many research papers are dedicated to employing multiple similarity metrics. These evaluate the degree of comparability between documents in the collections. Examples of works that aim to find comparability features and scores between documents are those of Bekavac et al. (2004), Sharoff (2010), Steinberg et al. (2006), and Talvensaari (2007).

As in the work of Talvensaari et al. (2008), the web crawling of the potential similar texts is initiated by providing a set of seed words to be queried to a web search engine. The results are retrieved and post-processed, and new keywords to serve as seed words for a consecutive search are extracted. The technique to election of keywords is a simple frequency word count. In the current research we concentrate on using whole documents as seeds to mine similarity.

A good stimulus motivating the current research is that comparable corpora preserve the all language structures and ways of expressions, thereupon keeping all cultural aspects of the language. This is also suggested by Bekavac et al. (2004). They emphasise the importance of comparable corpora with respect to the fact they preserve the cultural variations of the languages involved.

Skadiņa et al. (2010b) and Skadiņa et al. (2010a) argue that the advantages of comparable corpora in Machine Translation are considerable and more beneficial than those of parallel corpora. The researchers suggest that comparable corpora are easier and more available to collect online than parallel ones as one of obvious benefits. Also, they suggest the texts in the comparable corpora gather greater diversity of language-dependent phrases, terms, and ways of expression. An interesting observation that Skadiņa et al. (2010a) make is that comparable corpora are a good substitute for parallel ones and they can compensate for the parallel corpora's lack.

Concentrating on comparability metrics is vital for the research of automatic compilation of comparable corpora. Skadiņa et al. (2010b) focus additionally on relevance evaluation metric design. The aim of Kilgarriff (2003) includes the comparability evaluation between two collections of documents and the advantages/disadvantages of known evaluation metrics. Saralegi et al. (2008), as Tao and Zhao (2005), compare documents based on time-frame topic distributions delineated metric. Similarity metrics on word level are discussed by Deerwester et al. (1990); Dagan, Lee and Pereira (1999); and Baeza-Yates and Ribeiro-Netto (1999). Lee (1999) and Dagan et al. (1999) rely on word-co-occurrence text comparison. The current research incorporates a Latent Semantic Analysis (LSA) technique as in Radinsky et al. (2001) and in Deerwester et al. (1990).

4 Approach

The proposed methodology incorporates Latent Semantic Analysis (LSA) and unsupervised machine learning (ML), the k-means algorithm, to automatically collect a comparable document corpus from a given set of texts (Stambolieva 2013). LSA is employed to identify word similarity and map this similarity to concepts. By identifying such concepts LSA reduces the space of the documents to be asserted to a two-dimensional one. In the current scenario, each concept consists of a normalized word form, a lemma, with its correspondent context-dependent part-of-speech tag. In order to for the concepts to be more context-aware, noun phrases in both languages are identified and included in the concept space with a NP part-of-speech tag.

Additionally, the ML algorithm learns from the similar concept space and predicts which documents are comparable to each other and which are not. Moreover, a possibility to identify more than one comparable corpus is presented to the learning algorithm.

To the best of our knowledge, an approach to the compilation of comparable corpora that relies on LSA with k-means has not been suggested yet. We invest into presenting a reasoned definition of the notion of comparable corpora. Accompanying to that, we perform language analysis tasks such as lemmatization and noun phrase identification to investigate whether these tasks help learn comparable corpora more accurately.

5 Data

The experimental corpus is manually collected following a procedure of document collection translators follow (Zanettin 2002), when compiling their own specific purpose comparable corpora. The corpus contains documents in the narrow topic of psychometrics, in particular psychometric properties and evaluation. Noise is included in the corpora as some texts that are not on psychometrics, but still on psychology, are added. Additionally, newswire texts than have no resemblance at all with the suggested similar psychometrics documents are provided as a supplementary noise. The domain of the collected documents is psychology since psychometrics is a sub-topic of psychology. The corpus is consistent of documents written either in English or Spanish. The total number of documents, which are manually collected, is 26. We try to mimic the process translators choose related linguistics resources during translation. As time is of importance they would not invest much of it in searching for comparable documents, therefore we decided 26 is a sufficient number for the current experiment.

The distribution of topics in the psychometrics corpus is 6 psychometrics texts in Spanish, 9 psychometrics texts in English, 3 psychology but not psychometrics texts, and 8 non-psychology texts in English. Two manual evaluators label the documents in the corpus as comparable or not according to a set of evaluation guidelines. Table 1. shows the how the evaluators label the collection of Spanish and English texts.

Evaluator	**Psychometrics + Psychology**	**Newswire**
Evaluator 1	15	11
Evaluator 2	18	8

Table 1: Evaluators' manual comparability labels

6 Evaluation Metrics

The evaluation metrics used to evaluate the performance of the suggested methodology are precision, recall, purity, mutual information (MI), entropy (H) and normalized mutual information (NMI). These metrics are all explained in details by Manning et al. (2008).

7 Experiment

The aim of this experiment is to assemble a comparable corpus from different documents, in which some are found comparable and others are withdrawn from the elected comparable set due to similarity disagreement. Thus, the experimental corpus accumulates roughly two types of texts, therefore can be separated into two subsets – psychometrics (and psychology), and newswire category. Therefore, we aim at compiling a weakly-comparable bilingual corpus (Skadiņa et al. 2010a), whose domain is psychology and which contains psychology and psychometrics texts. Experiments with different k, number of resulting clusters, are performed. When k equals the number of manually evaluated number of categories, namely two, the purity of the resulting corpus is calculated. The purity score is 0.6538, which is not close to 1. Purity translates the corpus quality trade-off dependently on the number of clusters The purity result indicates that documents from both the two different labels are collected together into a comparable cluster. The precision scores of the run experiments with 2, 3, 4 and 5 clusters to be identified are shown in Table 2. The recall scores of the run experiments with 2, 3, 4 and 5 clusters to be identified are shown in Table 3. *2cl*, *3cl*, *4cl*, and *5cl* respectively show learning text comparability results when 2, 3, 4 and 5 resulting clusters are compiled.

Topic	**2cl**	**3cl**	**4cl**	**5cl**
Psychometrics + Psychology	1	1	1	1
Newswire	0.42	1	1	1

Table 2: Clustering precision

Topic	**2cl**	**3cl**	**4cl**	**5cl**
Psychometrics + Psychology	0.35	0.65	0.83	0.65
Newswire	1	0.34	0.61	0.42

Table 3: Clustering recall

The precision of most of the resulting clusters equals 1, which means the documents from the same category, psychology, are appropriately grouped together. The recall shows another fashion that is occurring in the resulting clusters. The lower the score is, the closer to 0, the larger number of documents labeled in the other category, newswire, are also grouped together with the correctly identified psychology ones. The last observation means in the case of correctly grouped documents that are comparable to each other, texts that are not similar to them are also nominated and selected as part of the comparable corpus.

The corpus is very heterogeneous in the sense it consists of articles written in both Spanish and English in categories such as psychometric evaluation, psychometric properties, psychology, and press texts. Hence, the learning algorithm is not able to produce better results by learning from the identified concepts in the corpus. A cause for that fact, except the heterogeneity of the experimental corpus, can be the distribution of concepts over the documents. Moreover, when Spanish documents are preprocessed, a translation engine, Google Translate[1], is used as the main source of mining translation equivalents into English. Nevertheless it is constantly being enriched with new translation pairs and is a very robust source of interpretations; the translations it has provided are not to be considered perfect and can leave room for mistakes. Therefore, the translation output reflects directly on the distribution of concepts in the documents of the Spanish-English corpus.

To further explore the clustering quality of the comparable corpus selected, when two clusters are expected, *2cl*, NMI is calculated (see Table 5.). NMI requires MI, H(Ω) and H(C) calculations, which are respectfully the mutual information between the documents in the cluster, or the comparable corpus, the entropy of the documents with the same label, and the entropy between the document with the same class – comparable or non-comparable. Opposed to purity, the NMI metric is used to show the quality of clusters independently on the number of clusters. NMI is roughly 0.54, which indicates the normalized mutual information between the texts in the automatically compiled comparable collection is not high. In it, there are 11 psychology documents and 8 newswire ones, out of 18 psychology and 8 newswire texts. This results show the approach has difficulties disambiguating between the newswire and psychology texts and that text similarity is found between then when it should not. We hope further investigations will suggest improvements to the methodology in order for it to increase performance.

[1] http://translate.google.com

No. Clusters	MI	H(Ω)	H(C)	NMI
2	0.5025	0.8511	0.9842	0.5475

Table 5: Mutual Information, Entropy and Normalized Mutual Information over clustering results of two corpora

8 Future Work

A further improvement of the methodology is to involve human translators in judging the results of the comparable corpora compiled. The linguistic analysis tasks are prone to mistakes, which can reflect on the learning algorithm performance. Further improvement of their performance can only prove beneficial to our research. Furthermore, a new source of translation, which suggests better translation equivalents, is welcome. Recognition of diasystematic text markers, such as diachronic ones, can suggest new potential meta-information features to be considered when searching for comparability between documents.

Including all of the aforementioned, we aim at collecting a bigger initial document set on which we can evaluate our approach. Future works additionally include extending the methodology to cover other languages than English and Spanish.

9 Conclusions

This paper presents preliminary results on the automatic compilation of comparable corpora with respect to their usage in translator's work. We aim to develop a systematic methodology, which relies on LSA and a ML algorithm, to ease the comparable corpora collection by translation professional. We critically discuss our results obtained on a small experimental bilingual corpus and propose further development suggestions.

References

Jan Aarts. 1991. Intuition-based and Observation-based Grammars. In K. Aijmer and B. Altenberg, editors, *English Corpus Linguistics: Studies in Honour of Jan Svartik*, pages 44-65, Longman, London.

Ricardo Baeza-Yates and Betrhier Ribeiro-Neto. 1999. *Modern Infromation Retieval*, Addison Wesley.

Božo Bekavac, Petya Osenova, Kiril Simov and Marco Tadic. 2004. Making Monolingual Corpora Comparable: a Case Study of Bulgarian and Croatian. In *Proceedings of LREC2004*, pages 1187-1190, Lisbon.

Lynne Bowker and Jennifer Pearson. 2002. *Working with Specialized Language: A Practical Guide to Using Corpora*. London. New York: Routeledge.

Igo Dagan, Lillian Lee and Fernando Pereira. 1999. Similarity-based models of word co-occurrence probabilities. *Machine Learning*. 34(1-3):43-69.

Scott Deerwester, Susan Dumais and Richard Harshman. 1990. Indexing by latent semantic analysis. *Journal of the Americal Society for Information Science*. 41(6):391-407.

EAGLES, The European Advisory Group on Language Engineering Standards. 1996. Available at <http://www.ilc.cnr.it/EAGLES/home.html>.

Pascale Fung and Percy Cheung. 2004. Mining Very Non-Parallel Corpora: Parallel Sentence and lexicon Extraction via Bootstraping and EM. In *Proceedings of EMNLP*, pages 57-63, Barcelona, Spain.

Maraistella Gatto. 2010. From language to culture and beyond: building and exploring comparable web corpora. In R. Rapp, P. Zweigenbaum, and S. Sharoff, editors, *Proceedings of the Third Workshop on Building and Using Comparable Corpora: applications of Parallel and Comparable Corpora in Natural Language Engineering and the Humanities (BUCC 2010)*, pages 72-78, Paris, France.

Radu Ion, Dan Tufiş, Tiberiu Boroş, Alexandru Ceauşu and Dan Ştefănescu. 2010. On-line Compilation of Comparable Corpora and Their Evaluation. In *Proceedingds of the 7th International Conference of Formal Approaches to South Slavic and Balkan Languages (FASSBL7)*, pages 29-34, Dubrovnic, Croatia.

Phillip Koehn. 2005. Europarl: A Parallel Corpus for Statistical Machine Translation. In *Proceedings of Machine Translation Summit*, pages 79-86, Phuket, Thailand.

Adam Kilgarriff. 2001. Comparing corpora. *International Journal of Corpus Lingusitics*, 6(1):97-133.

Lillian Lee. 1999. Measures of distributional similarity. In *Proceedings of ACL 1999*, pages 25-32.

Christopher D. Manning, Prabhakan Raghavan and Hinrich Schűtze. 2008. *Introduction to Information Retrieval*, pages 356-358, Cambridge University Press.

Tony McEnery. 2003. Corpus Linguistics. In R. Mitkov, editor, *The Handbook of Computational Lingustics*. pages 448-464, Oxford University Press, Oxford.

Pablo Gamallo Otero and Isaac González López. 2010. Wikipedia as Multilingual Source of Comparable Corpora. In *Proceedings of the 3rd workshop on BUCC(LREC 2010)*, pages 21-25.

Kira Radinsky, Eugene Agichtein, Evgeniy Gabrilovich and Shaul Markovitch. 2011. A word at a time: Computing Word Relatedness using Temporal Semantic Analysis. In *WWW'11*, pages 337-346.

Xabier Sarageli, Inaki San Vincente and Antton Gurrutxaga. 2002. Automatic Extraction of bilingual terms from comparable corpora in a popular science domain. In *Proceedings of the workshop on Comparable Corpora, LREC'08.*

Serge Sharoff. 2010. Analysing similarities and differences between corpora. *In Proceedings of the 7th Conference of Language Technologies (Jezikovne Tehnologije)*, pages 5-11, Ljubljiana. Slovenia.

Inguna Skadiņa, Ahmet Aker, Voula Giouli, Dan Tufiş, Robert Gaizauskas, Madara Mieriņa and Nikos Mastropavlos. 2010a. A Collection of Comparable Corpora for Under-Resourced Languages. In I. Skadiņa and D. Tufiş, editors, In *Proceedings of the 4th International Conference Baltic HLT 2010*, pages 161-168.

Inguna Skadiņa, Andrejs Vasiljeiv, Raivis Skadiņš, Robert Gaizauskas, Dan Tufiş and Tatiana Gornostay. 2010b. Analysis and Evaluation of Compoarable Corpora for Under Resourced Areas of Machine Translation. In *Proceedings of the 3rd Workshop on Building and Using Comparable Corpora. Applications of Parallel and Comparable Corpora in Natural Language Engineering and the Humanities*, pages 6-14.

Ekaterina Stambolieva. 2013. Learning Comparable Corpora from Latent Semantic Analysis Simplified Document Space. In *Proceedings of the Sixth Workshop on Building and Using Comparable Corpora (BUCC 2013)*, pages 129-137, Sofia, Bulgaria.

Ralf Steinberger, Bruno Pouliquen, Anna Widiger, Camelia Ignat, Tomaž Erjavec, Dan Tufiş and Dániel Varga. 2006. The JRC-Acquis: A multilingual aligned parallel corpus with 20+ languages. In *Proceedings of the 5th International Conference on Language Resources and Evaluation (LREC'2006)*, pages 2142-2147, Genoa, Italy.

Tuomas Talvensaari, Jorma Laurikkala, Kalevro Järvelin, Martti Juhola, and Heikki Keakustalo. 2007. Creating and Exploiting a Comparable Corpus in

Cross-language Information Retrieval. *ACM Translations on Information Systems*, 25(1).

Tuomas Talvensaari, Ari Pirkola, Kalevro Järvelin, Martti Juhola and Jorma Laurikkala. 2008. Focused Web Crawling in the acquisition of comparable corpora. *Information Retrieval*, 11:427-445.

Tao Tao and Cheng Xiang Zhai. 2005. Mining Comparable Bilingual Text Corpora for Cross-Language Information Integration. In *Proceedings of the eleventh ACM SIGKDD international conference on Knowledge discovery in data mining*, pages 691-696.

Author Index

Agirrezabal, Manex, 119
Ai, Renlong, 1
Alabbas, Maytham, 7
Astigarraga, Aitzol, 119

Bhaskar, Pinaki, 14, 22, 30
Boudokhane, Manel, 100

Costetchi, Eugeniu, 38
Cruz Diaz, Noa P., 45

Danilova, Vera, 51
De Amaral, Aurore, 58

Espinosa Anke, Luis, 63

Glavaš, Goran, 71

Hromada, Daniel, 79

Jalalvand, Shahab, 86
Janicki, Maciej, 93

Khoufi, Nabil, 100
Kurtasov, Andrey, 107

Li, ChunGen, 113

Osinalde, Mikel, 119

Pakray, Partha, 30
Papadopoulou, Ioanna, 126

Rodriguez, Igor, 119

Schumann, Anne-Kathrin, 134
Shrestha, Niraj, 142
Štajner, Sanja, 71
Stambolieva, Ekaterina, 149

Vulić, Ivan, 142

Association for Computational Linguistics
209 N. Eighth Street
Stroudsburg, Pennsylvania 18360

CURRAN ASSOCIATES INC
proceedings
.com